THE DOCTRINE OF CHRISTIAN OR EVANGELICAL PERFECTION

The Doctrine of Christian or Evangelical Perfection

By
HAROLD WILLIAM PERKINS
B.A., D.D. (Lond.)

— THESIS APPROVED FOR THE —
DEGREE OF DOCTOR OF DIVINITY
IN THE UNIVERSITY OF LONDON

WIPF & STOCK · Eugene, Oregon

Wipf and Stock Publishers
199 W 8th Ave, Suite 3
Eugene, OR 97401

The Doctrine of Christian or Evangelical Perfection
By Perkins, Harold William
ISBN 13: 978-1-62032-679-4
Publication date 11/15/2012
Previously published by The Epworth Press, 1927

To
MY WIFE

WHOSE COMPANIONSHIP IN THE SERVICE
OF THE CHURCH
HAS ENABLED ME TO UNDERTAKE
THIS WORK

Was it not great? Did not he throw on God
   (He loves the burthen)—
God's task to make the heavenly period
   Perfect the earthen?

   —BROWNING : *A Grammarian's Funeral.*

PREFACE

THE subject of this essay is one which has been on my mind throughout my ministry. It possesses, in common with other doctrines of the Christian Faith, the property of alternately attracting and repelling the minds of men. The thought came to me that it would be a real gain to the Church, in its endeavour to express the Christian consciousness, if some inquiry were made into the sources from which the idea of Evangelical Perfection has sprung, together with some survey of the historical developments which it has undergone. This ought to enable us to perceive what is essential and permanent in the doctrine, and thus to present it in a form which would appeal to the modern mind. The research work undertaken as a consequence has profoundly modified and enlarged my views. It has covered a wide area, including a fresh study of biblical teaching, of influences outside Christianity which have affected the doctrine, of developments in the Early Church, and of resultant divergences, especially in Roman Catholic, Methodist, and Quaker teaching. In order to avoid cursoriness, I have in most cases, where any passage has seemed to bear on the subject, read carefully the whole of the context in the original.

I desire to express my indebtedness for many of the thoughts which have ripened in my mind to my former tutors in Handsworth College, Drs. W. T. Davison and J. G. Tasker. In preparing the material for this work I have been assisted by the advice of Professor H. T. Andrews, and of the tutors at Handsworth at the time when I commenced the actual research, Professors F. Platt and W. F. Lofthouse. At a later stage I have profited by the counsel of my colleague, Dr. Vincent Taylor, in shaping the final form of the book. The encouragement given by my father, the Rev. William Perkins, when informed of the task to which I had set myself, meant a great deal; and his death before it was completed took away for the moment much of the desire for achievement.

With all this it is fair to say that, not only the initial conception, but the whole method of investigation, has been my own. Historical sketches are to be found in Baron von Hügel's book on Eternal Life, and in some of the works on Mysticism. Nevertheless, the niche for which this work is designed is one which has not yet been filled. For, while the mystical element in religion becomes prominent in any teaching of full attainment, yet there is a clear distinction between Mysticism and Evangelical Perfection; the latter denotes a state which need not be consciously mystical at all. The fullest summary that I have seen of the forms which the doctrine has assumed is in the article on Christian Perfection in the *Encyclopædia of Religion and Ethics*; and its author, Dr. Platt, wrote to me thus; 'The subject, strange to say, is a by-path in Christian theological systems, and one has to wander in search in many ways. But with time and patience much may be gathered; and a good modern treatise on the subject is needed, and would be valuable.'

Besides claiming originality in the choice and in the general treatment of the subject, I venture to think that my examination of it has brought some definite additions to our theological knowledge. If I make such a claim, it is not without a sincere sense of the imperfection and unworthiness of those additions; but I am anxious not to shirk responsibility for the conclusions to which I have been led. In the Fifth Part a summary of these conclusions is given; and an attempt is made to formulate a statement of the doctrine which shall have as its foundation the Historic Revelation, and yet be in touch with the thought of our day.

Complete impartiality I do not pretend to have achieved. There are preconceptions which have entered into one's spiritual constitution. To me it seems that I find Christ and learn to know Him in the Scriptures as in no other way, neither through the Church, nor through the Inward Witness. Because of this deep preconception, which my father taught me, and which my mature judgement has confirmed, I have all the more striven to do justice to those who in the Quest have been swayed by other considerations. And there has emerged, as a direct result of research, and not in any way as a preconceived notion, the idea that for that union, towards which all the Churches are moving, those who are definitely and consciously aiming at perfection may provide valuable guidance through the unification of their methods of attainment. If this treatise should shed any light on that path to union, it will far more than fulfil the expectation of its author. It has sometimes seemed to me that such a union will form in part what we think of as the Beatific Vision. That which we see and are able now to apprehend by faith may fairly and rightly be represented as a State of Perfection; but it is seen and apprehended as one may perceive in a dimly-lighted room the face of a friend. 'For indeed it is a foretaste (so little as it is), and an earnest or handsel of the sight or contemplation of heavenly joy, not clearly, but half in darkness, which shall be perceived, and made a clear light or sight in the bliss of heaven.'[1]

HAROLD W. PERKINS.

[1] Walter Hilton, *The Scale of Perfection*, Bk. I., chap. ix.

GENERAL CONTENTS

	PAGE
PREFACE	vii

PART I—PROLEGOMENA

CHAP.
I. THE NEED FOR A DOCTRINAL STATEMENT . . 3
II. THE SOURCES OF THE DOCTRINE 18

PART II—BIBLICAL

III. THE IDEA OF PERFECTION IN THE OLD TESTAMENT AND IN JUDAISM 31
IV. NEW TESTAMENT WAYS OF EXPRESSING PERFECTION 54
V. THE NEW TESTAMENT DOCTRINE OF THE PERFECTION OF CHRIST 62
VI. THE NEW TESTAMENT DOCTRINE OF THE PERFECTING OF BELIEVERS 76
VII. THE NEW TESTAMENT DOCTRINE OF THE PERFECTING OF THE CHURCH 89

PART III—HISTORICAL

VIII. INFLUENCES OUTSIDE CHRISTIANITY WHICH HAVE AFFECTED THE CONCEPTION OF EVANGELICAL PERFECTION 97
IX. THE IDEA OF PERFECTION IN THE EARLY CHURCH . 128
X. CLEMENT OF ALEXANDRIA AND ORIGEN . . 142
XI. AMBROSE, AUGUSTINE, AND DIONYSIUS THE AREOPAGITE 155

PART IV—THE RESULTANT DIVERGENCES

		PAGE
XII.	THE IDEA OF ATTAINMENT UNDER THE SANCTION OF THE CHURCH	181
XIII.	THE IDEA OF ATTAINMENT THROUGH OBEDIENCE TO THE WORD	204
XIV.	THE IDEA OF ATTAINMENT THROUGH THE WITNESS OF THE SPIRIT	230

PART V—CONSTRUCTIVE

XV.	A SUMMARY OF CONCLUSIONS	251
	APPENDIX: WESTERN MYSTICISM	287
	BIBLIOGRAPHY	291
	INDEX	295

PART I
PROLEGOMENA

CONTENTS OF PART I

I. THE NEED FOR A DOCTRINAL STATEMENT

		PAGE
1. Objections to a Doctrinal Statement Answered	. . . . . .	3
2. Value of an Intellectual Presentation of the Ideal	. . . . .	4
3. A Definition of the State of Perfection	. . . . . .	6
4. Implications Involved in the Definition	. . . . .	8
(1) *Metaphysical*	. . . .	8
(2) *Ethical*	. . . .	11
(3) *Evangelical*	. . . .	14

II. THE SOURCES OF THE DOCTRINE

Introductory: The Seat of Authority in Religion	. . . . .	18
1. The Written Word	. . . .	19
2. The Visible Church	. . . .	22
3. The Witness of the Spirit in Man	. . . .	24

Chapter I

THE NEED FOR A DOCTRINAL STATEMENT

1. Objections to a Doctrinal Statement Answered

It would be hard to over-estimate the rich store of devotional literature on the subject of Christian Perfection. But few and slight have been the attempts to weigh and sum up the results of faith, both in the history of the Church and in the experience of individuals, in anything that might be called a doctrinal statement. Hence there is justification for making an attempt which is urgently demanded by the intellectual and spiritual needs of our age. In this book a survey will be made of the history of the doctrine, i.e. of the forms which it has assumed in the minds of doctors and saints, in ecclesiastical symbolics, and in the movements which from time to time have revived the Church.

Some have regarded the history of doctrine as the story of a Fall; as though the truth had been displayed once for all in revelation, and anything in the nature of intellectual definition marked a lapse. The objections urged against dogma in general apply with peculiar force to the doctrine of Perfection. They are such as these: Sanctification is in effect advance in love; but love is an emotion; therefore the higher stage must mean more intense emotion; and reason has, and can have, nothing to do with it. Again, one of the surest marks of progress is humility; but knowledge puffs up. Jesus rejoiced because the process by which the Father reveals Himself in the Son is hidden from the wise and prudent, and can be understood by babes. Moreover, there is a risk of becoming word-spinners. We may be confused as to the doctrine of Perfection, and yet have a right apprehension of the state. Why should we not give up any endeavour to define it exactly?

These are valid objections. The spiritual history of mankind provides abundant instances of failure through coldness, pride, and the confusing of words with reality. Yet we must bear in mind that these objections are of the nature of caveats, and must not be considered as final. In the determination of doctrine something is lost which we cannot recapture.

> Nothing can bring back the hour
> Of splendour in the grass and glory in the flower.

But the endeavour to understand, and to express, and to evaluate spiritual experience is so inevitable that we must trust it is leading to a greater gain. We must beware of what Plato called misologia : as there are misanthropists who distrust and dislike mankind, so there are misologists who distrust dialectic and the exercise of the reason. It was the mark of the great pessimists to proclaim that the only value of the reason was in enabling the soul to escape at last from the self-consciousness which it had itself invoked.[1] To deny the right of the reason leads finally to the pessimistic conclusion that reason has no other issue but despair.

2. Value of an Intellectual Presentation of the Ideal

Intellectual representation must not, of course, be confounded with spiritual energy. 'It is impossible to enjoy at one and the same moment the blessedness of devotion and the colder satisfaction of reflex thought. We cannot have at once that which belongs to the thought of God, and that which belongs to thinking about our thought of Him.'[2] Yet the conscious reason, at once discursive and regulative, may be of the highest service in the progress of the soul. It furnishes that equanimity by which the soul steadies itself in its career. Progress is made by a movement of the soul which involves pleasure and pain, and which necessitates an exertion that cannot be long sustained. Hence there must be alternating periods of rest and restraint. These are not to be thought of as times of coldness : the fire of Divine Love still burns ; but it is regulated by the equally Divine Reason. We may compare the phrase in which the poet sings of the ideal relations between man and woman, ' Then come the world's great bridals, chaste and calm.' Such adjectives imply, not the

[1] *E. R. E.* ix., 809b. [2] J. Caird, *Introduction to Philosophy of Religion*, p. 42.

absence of passion, but the controlling influence of a calm chastity. We should aim at portraying Christian Love as at once ardent and ethical, and therefore incapable of being chilled by philosophical thought.

This equanimity may be compared, to use a simile of Bergson's, with the action of a strong swimmer steadying himself in the current in order to look round. It is characteristic of the soul's eternal life, as is shown in a saying which has proved of supreme value for religious experience, 'In My Father's House are many resting-places.' These resting-places, like the eagle's nest, are needed for the blessedness, and indeed for the very life of the soul. Speaking in the same passage of the Indwelling of the Father and the Son, Christ said : ' We will make Our Abode with him.' Such a word tells of a Divine Presence, not as a visitant from another sphere, disturbing and overwhelming, but as one bringing perpetual and serene comfort. The higher stages of the spiritual life are marked by the peace which comes when there is no wavering in the upward aim.

The action of the reason, moreover, discriminates between the motives which urge the soul forward, and purifies them. In his book on *The Philosophy of Religion* Dr. Galloway devotes much attention to what he calls the spiritualization of feeling. This is a valuable phrase. The spiritual includes the ethical as well as the emotional ; and that Agape which is an adequate predicate for God is ethical in itself. No better illustration of this can be given than Plato's myth in the Phaedrus. Socrates had been praising the non-lover, who is so sane and strong ; but his daimon bade him recant his depreciation of love. Then he unfolded his myth. There is a place even above heaven, which no poet can worthily sing, wherein is the true knowledge of That-Which-Is. The chariots of gods and men drive past, and catch some vision of the true, the beautiful, the good, a vision which is clear in proportion as the fiery horses are firmly controlled by reason, the charioteer. One of the horses by which the soul of man is carried along is of good stock, but the other is evil. ' Wherefore hard and irksome must be the driving of the chariot be for such as we are.'[1] It is the part of the charioteer to break in the unruly horse, so that when the time of vision comes he may have him well in

[1] Phaedrus, 246b.

hand. Reason in itself has no motive power; its purpose is to bring into subjection the carnal mind that it may gaze on the Beloved with reverence and purity. Love in one form or another is the motive power always; but for the soul's ascent it is necessary to discriminate between the forms of love; and that can only be by reason reflecting on the whole revelation of God. Where reason is dethroned the gates are always opened for a flood of antinomian excess.

A further benefit conferred by intellectual representation is that it assists in conserving the progress made in hours of insight. After Pascal's death there was found stitched in the lining of his doublet what is known as his memorial: undoubtedly he used it to recover a definite experience of passion and fire, which gave him absolute certitude, 'in the year of grace 1654.' I have recorded a somewhat similar instance in the case of a Methodist local preacher in 1822.[1] These are examples of what every earnest seeker discovers, namely that the attempt to make some statement to oneself of a spiritual experience, while it can never be satisfactory, is of value both for expressing one's thoughts to others, and for conserving the knowledge gained for oneself. Similarly the doctrinal statements of the Church enable it to express and thus to conserve the results of Faith in God as shown in the conscious experiences of its members.

On two subjects especially, which are attracting much attention to-day, it is hoped that some light will be shed. The subjects to which I refer are: the Reunion of Christendom; and the ethicizing of our conception of the future life, so as to bring it into closer relation with the life of the Church in this world. While these may be discussed under many aspects, there is a method of approach from the standpoint of Christian Perfection which is distinctly helpful.

3. A DEFINITION OF THE STATE OF PERFECTION

It is advisable at this stage to define our subject. BY THE PHRASE CHRISTIAN OR EVANGELICAL PERFECTION WE DENOTE A SPIRITUAL STATE, MEDIATED BY THE HOLY SPIRIT, IN WHICH THE BELIEVER IN CHRIST HAS A FULL ASSURANCE OF HIS REDEMPTION THROUGH THE BLOOD OF CHRIST, AND ENJOYS

[1] p. 214.

UNBROKEN COMMUNION WITH THE LOVE OF GOD. This definition is necessarily subjective, and may be corrected or enlarged by further study. Some comment, however, may be called for on certain points.

(1) It is a spiritual state, that is to say, it is the highest reality of which we are aware. Here we trench on psychology, which has much to say on the succession of psychoses, and on the differentiation of them. For religious purposes what is needed is to insist that we are able to discriminate between the states through which we pass as higher and lower, nearer or farther from God; that we are able to choose; and that our choice steadily tends to become fixed and final. When we say that such a state is mediated by the Holy Spirit, we are uttering our conviction that it is not detached and isolated. It is incredible that this moment, whose glory we recognize, should not have come from God. That which would be evanescent obtains permanence in Him. The fugitive moment receives the seal of eternity.

(2) A query may be raised as to the word Assurance. Is it not possible to have the condition without the conscious assurance of it? Are there not differences in temperament, and varieties of experience? Have not many difficulty in uttering their deepest thoughts? We must all admit the force of these questions. This is surely the last subject on which one would wish to be dogmatic or exclusive. Nevertheless, a spiritual condition must tend to become conscious; and such self-consciousness, while partly no doubt intellectual, is in a still deeper sense spiritual. So far as it is intellectual, it will vary with intellectual capacity, and even with intellectual idiosyncrasy; so far as it is spiritual it will tend to become universal, although its intellectual expression may continue to vary.

(3) Some may demur to the expression, Blood of Christ, a phrase which may easily be misunderstood. But even when 1 Peter was written it had already become a recognized Church formula. The root idea is in Lev. xvii. 11, 14 : ' The life of the flesh is in the blood . . . it is the blood that maketh atonement by reason of the life.' The idea of the Blood of Christ includes the fact of His Death; but it dwells still more on the Life, given up indeed, but according to Christian belief continued and efficient still. The central idea is the entire

dependence of the believer on Christ's redemption, a dependence which does not grow less with his own spiritual progress.

(4) The definition further declares that it is a state of happiness and of unbroken communion. If there be a breach of the communion, there is so far forth a loss of the state. But it is not implied that the communion is always consciously apprehended on our side. Indeed it is not wise for us to spend more than comparatively a small part of our time in meditation and contemplation. There are obligations which arise as the direct result of communion with the love of God, which should exclude carelessness in regard to the moral law, or negligence in regard to social and political duties. Where the communion with eternal love is fully realized, it will issue in the bringing forth of much fruit.

4. IMPLICATIONS INVOLVED IN THE DEFINITION

(1) *Metaphysical*

In the definition suggested there are certain assumptions, metaphysical, ethical, and evangelical, which will be examined and tested throughout this investigation. Some preliminary observations, however, may be made. It is implied that there is One, in whom is all Perfection. But some evil and loss, metaphysical and ethical, is involved in any creation, as Leibniz clearly showed. These evils must be transcended if man is to attain a state which may be described as perfect. It might be imagined that the best way by which man could achieve his end would be by ruling out all thought of God. Thus Protagoras said: 'Man is the measure of all things, of being how it is; of non-being how it is not.' Again: 'Of the Gods I have nothing to say; neither that they are, nor that they are not; for there is much that hinders me—the obscurity of the matter, and the shortness of human life.' Zeller praises in these words the statuesque style and the classic calmness with which they are uttered. But man has never been able to content himself with that agnostic tranquillity. It is a necessary postulate for our subject that human perfection demands union with the One who transcends all incompleteness. The ideal set forth is not so much that of being a perfect man, as of union with the perfections of God.

THE NEED FOR A DOCTRINAL STATEMENT 9

It is this deep conviction which has given force and persistence to the ontological argument. Thus Lotze, while agreeing that the proof as enunciated by Anselm and Descartes lacks cogency, is not prepared to dismiss it. 'This is obviously a case where an altogether immediate conviction breaks through into consciousness; to wit, the conviction that the totality of all that has value—all that is perfect, fair, and good—cannot possibly be homeless in the world or in the realm of actuality, but has the very best claim to be regarded as imperishable reality.'[1] John Caird discusses it more fully. Writing from the Hegelian standpoint, he propounds the view that the individual consciousness can only realize itself through a thought or a self-consciousness which is beyond all individual selves, and forms the unity at once of all thinkers and all objects of thought. This is the way in which Hegel reconciles pluralism with unity. The kingdom of the Father passes through the kingdom of the Son, with its infinite variety and personal pathos, into the kingdom of the Spirit where God is all in all, subsisting as a community.

In all that is visible we see unrest, disorder, and manifold evils; yet we are conscious of an invisible universe where all is order and beauty and peace. The relation between that invisible perfection and the manifest imperfection around us baffles our thought. It is the supreme drama, on which the curtain never falls, the drama of creation. Yet it fills us with boundless optimism, because of the wisdom and love which it unfolds. In this drama we have a necessary place; we only discover its presence through the action developing within our own nature. It is revealed to us that a similar drama is progressing in those around us. That discovery leads to a fuller knowledge of ourselves. From this interaction with other spirits we learn of the Over-Spirit, in whom we have our being.

It is further assumed in the definition that the union with God in which Perfection consists must not be conceived Pantheistically. It might be suggested that all that is needed is acquiescence in things as they are. The typical Pantheism of Spinoza teaches that all things are produced by the consummate perfection of God, since they followed necessarily from a given most perfect nature; but that we must not

[1] *Introduction to the Philosophy of Religion*, chap. i.

attribute this to any goodwill, but rather say that all things are predetermined by His nature. *Reality and Perfection are one and the same thing.*[1] According to Spinoza, if we fail to perceive perfection everywhere, that must be due to the inadequacy of our understanding of the divine mind. We expect a purpose and a principle which in truth are due to our limitations. 'That eternal and infinite Being which we call God or Nature acts by the same necessity as that by which It exists, for we showed that It acts from the same necessity of Its nature as that by which It exists. Therefore the reason or cause why God or Nature acts or why They exist is one and the same; therefore as God exists with no end in view, He cannot act with an end in view, but has no principle or end either in existing or acting.'

This Pantheistic teaching appears in all forms of Mysticism; and we find that earnest seekers after perfection are invariably attracted towards Mysticism. Hence there is the utmost need that we should acknowledge and absorb the truths which Pantheism has laid hold of, and at the same time perceive wherein it fails and threatens to become soul-destructive. Two lines of thought will help us here. The first is to develop the idea of the love of God, till we recognize its creative activity. Spinoza regards human perfection as consisting in a willing submission to an eternal order. This constitutes man's true happiness, and enables him to gain such a firm hold on reality that those shadows which are usually called good (*divitiae, honor, libido*) do not tempt him. This state comes to a man because it is in the course of his nature. 'We do not enjoy beatitude because we master our passions; on the contrary we master our passions because we enjoy beatitude.' This conception of God and of Nature would make the one who has attained cease to expect or even desire any return or reward. He would love God or Nature, but without even wishing that God should love him in return. All the love that is in the universe is in the souls of men, or of such-like creatures, except that self-love which must exist in a Being of whom we predicate thought as well as extension. 'The love of the soul for God is the very love of God wherewith God loves Himself.' It is in protest against such teaching as this that we need to develop the idea of the love of God in accordance

[1] *Realitas est Perfectio* (*The Ethics*), Prop. xx.

with our knowledge of His eternal Fatherhood. In direct opposition to Pantheistic teaching we say that we have learnt to love, 'because He first loved us.' While we assimilate all that is noble in the teaching of Spinoza, we contend that it is the prevenient love of the eternal Father which is the source of all the love that is in creation.

The second line of thought is in regard to personality, human and divine. On this great and difficult subject all that need be said here is that the human personality, which is the starting-point of all our thought, must depend on the perfect Personality of God. This sublime truth is apprehended by us through His self-manifestation; but He could not reveal Himself as personal unless He were essentially a Person. ' The thought of God as perfect Person is the thought of a spiritual Self which is fully self-determined, and contains within itself the wealth of differences that are necessary to a spiritual identity.'[1] *The union which we seek with the Divine Love must not be thought of primarily as the fusion of two substances, but as the fellowship of two personalities.* Moreover, the fellowship possible in the Church of Christ for many persons, united in love, and seeking a worthy end, affords us the best mirror of the Divine Love. Thus we may say that Christian Perfection will mean, not the losing of individuality, but the full development of it in communion with the source of all personality; and that such development will always be within the precincts of a society.

(2) *Ethical*

From the metaphysical assumptions involved in our definition we pass on to the ethical. It is a metaphysical assumption to say that God delights in persons and in their development: He is the God of Abraham and Isaac and Jacob. But it is an ethical assumption to say that He delights in their holiness, and that the love which we attribute to God is holy love. The Christian conscience is convinced that the Divine Love can find no pleasure where there is sin; until that obstacle is removed it is impossible to enter into the joy of the Lord.

Many of the older writers on Perfection begin by stating

[1] Galloway, *The Philosophy of Religion*, p. 502.

that it is not Adamic, i.e. it is not simply a return to the innocent happiness associated with Eden. But modern thought is quite certain that man has not fallen from an original state of intellectual and moral perfection. This is indeed an idea which has only the slightest support in Scripture. Moreover, ' genetic psychology has established that man is (necessarily and normally) an impulsive before he is a volitional animal, and a volitional before he is a moral agent; and so furnishes knowledge which makes superfluous all conjectures as to a root of sin at birth, or an innate sinfulness which, when moral consciousness awakes, steps forth.'[1] Nevertheless, the fact of a universal tendency to sin in the human race constitutes the chief problem of to-day, as of all the ages of man. The attempt of F. R. Tennant and J. Royce to reconstruct the doctrine of original sin is of the utmost value to theology, and not least to the subject before us. The evil bias lies in the deep-rooted desires of our animal nature, which Aquinas and the other Schoolmen call the *fomes peccati*, the fuel, or, rather, the tinder of sin. The development of social life and civilization leads to a sense of mutual service and of sacrifice; but it also intensifies the meaning of life, its beauty and glory; hence the conflict. The thought which St. Paul uttered in Rom. vii. 7-25 can be readily translated into the terms of modern psychology. The law of the community, the social law, whose highest expression is in the Word of God, came to him; but its coming awoke him also to a sense of grandeur in life, and provoked a desire for self-satisfaction, for property, for his own comfort and happiness. The awakening, therefore, brought a tragic sense of conflict, as though he were being torn asunder. In his higher self, the thinking and reasoning part, he responded joyfully to the law of God. But the lower self continued to demand satisfaction, with special urgency, since the civilised community in its progress provided so many forms of self-gratification. We see from this survey, from the modern no less than the older outlook, how difficult, we might almost say how impossible, it is to break from this bondage. Yet, if we can only look forward to deliverance after we have been freed from the lower nature, that cannot be described as a victory over sin. Sin remains master so far as this life is concerned.

[1] F. R. Tennant, *E. R. E.* ix. 564b.

The Doctrine of Christian Perfection, therefore, rests on the hypothesis that the Divine Love is continually striving to overcome the sinfulness of human nature. The Spirit of God is seeking the alienated spirit of man. The Christian conscience, under the convicting power of that Holy Spirit, is assured of the reality of sin, of righteousness, and of judgement. The overcoming of the antagonism issues in a flood of penitence, as the sinful soul realizes that the Spirit which has been seeking it is the Spirit of Love, and that in all the punishment which has befallen it there is a purpose whose end is everlasting joy. Barclay thus describes some of the scenes from which the name Quaker arose : ' Sometimes the power of God will break forth into a whole meeting, and there will be such an inward travail, while each is seeking to overcome the evil in themselves, that by the contrary working of these opposite powers, like the going of two contrary tides, every individual will be strongly exercised as in a day of battle, and thereby trembling and a motion of the body will be upon most, if not upon all, which, as the power for truth prevails, will from pangs and groans end with a sweet sound of thanksgiving and praise.'[1] The bodily trembling will vary with temperament, culture, and power of restraint ; but the essential experience has the mark of universality upon it.

Stress must also be laid, from the ethical as well as from the metaphysical standpoint, on the fact that the relationship is between persons. All the terms lose their meaning, unless so interpreted. Thus R. C. Moberly shows that no explanation of Atonement can be adequate which is not at every point in terms of Personality : he then proceeds to the more difficult task of proving that no explanation of Personality is adequate, which is not, in point of fact, in terms of Atonement.[2] The human personality, which is demanded for any ethical conception, finds itself in reconciliation with the Divine. Hence the Divine Love appropriates a new, and significantly personal, name, the name of Grace. The idea in the word Grace is pre-eminently ethical. It implies a full recognition of the fact of sin ; but even that is subordinate to its recognition of the victorious Love of God, breaking through, overcoming, and bringing full reconciliation. The note of joy, which is inherent in the word, and which is marked in the classical

---

[1] *Apology*, Prop. xi. 8.   [2] Pref. to *Atonement and Personality*, p. xiii.

use of it, is brought out even more clearly in the New Testament, with its assurance of eternal salvation. 'By Grace have ye been saved.'

Under the conditions of this present life, even in its highest stages, this can only be realized by Faith. It is the contention of the present writer that that applies also to the life beyond. Faith, Hope, and Love *abide*, i.e. they belong to the eternal order. Love is the greater attribute; but the others have their place, even in eternity. It follows that, whatever meaning we give to Perfection, we must make it applicable to the present as well as to the future. We can never concede that the hindrance is purely that of flesh and blood. Our aim must be to give an ethical content to Faith and Hope, and to make it plain that the full assurance of Faith and of Hope tends to fill the whole nature with the Divine Love. The apostolic terminology may be altered by modern psychology, which is opposed to any dividing of the personality. But its significance is not affected. The idea of Faith in particular cannot be dissociated from an exercise of the will, and therefore involves a present appropriation. The conscious assurance of reconciliation with God must be attained by Faith in some present moment, a present moment which tends to become an eternal Now. The state of Grace implies an ever-present forgiveness, and an ever-present assurance.

(3) *Evangelical*

In discussing the metaphysical, and still more the ethical, implications of the definition of this doctrine, no attempt was made to ignore the evangelical assumptions. The Christian conscience is an entity to which we may appeal, to which, as a matter of fact, we always are appealing, for light and direction. It might have been possible to investigate the problem of human perfection apart from the Gospel of Jesus Christ, or at any rate without assigning any pre-eminence to that Gospel. Certain implications would have been involved in such an investigation. But our subject is definitely evangelical. The groundwork of the whole is the Person and Work of Christ. It is necessary to take note of the impact made on Christian thought by such teaching as that of Gautama,

Plato, and Plotinus; but this will be treated as quite subordinate to the message of the Gospel.

The title of this book presupposes that the Divine Perfection has been communicated to man through Christ. This gift may be called Christian Perfection, seeing that it is to be received by one who follows and believes in Jesus the Christ. Or it may be spoken of as Evangelical Perfection inasmuch as it is set before us as a part, and the crowning part, of the Evangel. In other words we assume first that God is able and willing to communicate His own perfection to man, and then that He has actually done so in an historic person.

We shall not be inclined to look harshly on any one who is staggered by such a claim. Yet it is the foundation of the edifice. It distinguishes the definitely Christian idea from the world-wide conception of union with God. Thus, for example, Plotinus gives an account of the soul's awakening, and of the manner of its purification and illumination, until it is ready for the vision. This vision he rightly conceives as given. The soul has been straining upward so far by its own unaided effort out of its desire for the Good. Now, when it has reached the highest which it can, it finds a Helper; it becomes simply passive, and waits for a revelation which it can neither hasten nor delay. Even such an emphasis on revelation was something new in Greek philosophy. But the Christian Way goes far beyond: our movement towards the Divine from beginning to end is a response to an antecedent movement of the Divine towards us.

The perfection of Christ, both in His Person and in His Work, will be discussed in chapter V; but we may say at once that it means much more than mere sinlessness. There are many declarations in Christian classics of the Lord's unique freedom from sin, such as that of Tertullian: 'Solus enim Deus sine peccato, et solus homo sine peccato Christus, quia et Deus Christus.'[1] Or that of Origen: 'Solus Jesus Dominus meus in hanc generationem mundus ingressus est.'[2] But we must look further for some dynamic which shall make that sinlessness available for the uplift of humanity into communion with God. Moreover, in some way, only dimly seen as yet, if He is the true Light, coming into the world, He must enlighten everyone. In the New Testament salvation

[1] *De Anima*, chap. 41. [2] Hom. xii. in Lev.

is proclaimed through Christ, and through Him alone; He fills the whole spiritual universe. But His gracious, saving influence has been felt in ages before His earthly advent, and in lands which He never traversed. Faith turns towards Him, but not towards any action of His; special attention, however, is directed towards His death as the crowning act of obedience.

The classical passage is Rom. v. 1–11, which is thus summarized by Sanday and Headlam : 'The state which lies before the Christian should have consequences both near and remote. *The nearer consequences, peace with God and hope which gives courage under persecution : the remoter consequence, an assurance, derived from the proof of God's love, of our final salvation and glory.* The first step (our present acceptance with God) is difficult ; the second step (our ultimate salvation) follows naturally from the first.' The distinction here made between near and remote is a distinction not in time but in logic, although, in the experience of each believer, the remoter consequence will naturally become apparent later, sometimes much later, in time. What we can assert with confidence is that in the New Testament the whole process, present, future, and eternal, is dependent on Christ. It is His obedience which in some way validates the whole. ' He is made unto us *wisdom from God, and righteousness, and sanctification, and redemption.'* [1]

The whole idea of Christian Perfection rests on the hypothesis that it is possible to enter into communion so deep that our life shall be hid with Christ in God. But this implies communion with the sacrificial energy of redeeming love. St. Paul speaks of filling up, through the discipline which came to him in the flesh, something which was lacking in the afflictions of Christ.[2] The call is a present one, in the days of our flesh. Let us press on, or rather let us be borne along to perfection. We gladly recognize the presence of a Power, not ourselves, making for righteousness. But we also feel that a definite demand is made upon us. ' Further evidence of man's free appropriation of the Spiritual Life, and his inner at-one-ment with it is conspicuously present in the fact that its development in our midst is conditional on his own work. Nothing links him more closely with that life, leading him to find his

---

[1] 1 Cor. i. 30.   [2] Col. i. 24.

THE NEED FOR A DOCTRINAL STATEMENT 17

very self in it, than the trouble and care, the pain and sacrifice, which this labour requires of him.'[1] Our definition must associate the state of perfection with the Divine yearning for universal salvation. Origen has a singularly beautiful comment on 1 Cor. xv. 28 : 'When the Son shall have finished His office and brought all His creatures to the top of perfection, then He Himself shall be called subject in those whom He hath put under the Father, and in whom He has perfected the work that the Father gave Him to do, that God may be all in all. Then, and not till then, shall Christ's joy be full.'[2] The problem set before us is to define the state of perfection in such a way as to leave open the vista of such a consummation in eternity, while at the same time using terms which are applicable to the possibilities of this present life.

[1] Eucken, *The Meaning and Value of Life*, p. 99.
[2] Hom. in Lev. vii. 2, cit. C. Bigg, *The Christian Platonists of Alex.*, p. 212n.

Chapter II

THE SOURCES OF THE DOCTRINE

Introductory: The Seat of Authority in Religion

THE need for a doctrinal statement has been examined in the first chapter; but the precise form must be determined by a review of the sources from which the evangelical conception has been drawn. These sources are, the Written Word, the Visible Church, and the Witness of the Spirit within the soul. In each source we find a divine and a human element. The confusion of these constituents has been behind most of the controversies which have swept through ecclesiastical history. The research work undertaken by the writer has led to the conclusion *that the divergences which have arisen in regard to the doctrine have been due to the stress laid on one or other of these sources. This conclusion not only affords an historical explanation of the divergences, but indicates lines of reunion; for it suggests that the divergences are not in regard to the fundamental conceptions of perfection, but in regard to the methods sanctioned by the various authorities.*

A famous discussion of this subject is that by James Martineau in *The Seat of Authority in Religion*. Some authority is implied in religion, an authority to which our assent is asked, and to which we render an elective obedience. This authority, says Martineau, has been misplaced: by the Catholics the Church has been invested with it, by the Protestants the Bible. But the authority is within us. He is careful indeed to declare that this authority is not purely subjective. ' Here then in the sphere of ends which, absent from human intention, yet obviously lie within the embrace of an intellectual system of the world, we have a further test, no longer intuitive, but susceptible of outward application, *for discriminating the divine and human agencies in history.* Instances of its use will not be wanting as the story of Christendom unfolds. But the inner test must be our chief dependence in tracing our way along the fragments of a path to the fountain head of that marvellous and fertilizing power.'[1] This is in line with his whole treatment of the teleological argument. He develops it in agreement with modern thought, laying stress, not on 'partial samples,' which seem to show design, but on the general trend of nature, which can only be explained through the controlling presence of a Reason and Will, transcendent and divine. Both the cosmological and the teleological arguments stand : we must think of God at once as Cause and as Perfection or End. But, in spite of this Rationalism, there are tendencies in Martineau to Mysticism and Intuitivism, as is clearly seen in the above extract.

In the study of the Doctrine of Christian Perfection one has, like Martineau, ' to trace one's way along the fragments of a path to the fountain head.' The theistic convictions which underlie the present work have not been formed without an earnest endeavour to do justice to the Rational and Mystical elements in religion. But far more value is attached to the Historical Revelation as recorded in the Scripture, and to the Development in the Church, than would have been allowed by Martineau. A brief survey of the sources may serve to indicate the value attached to each. It may be said at once, however, that, in the writer's judgement, it is fatal to attempt anything in the nature of a comparative scale. The aim is rather to discern the divine element in each, which must lead to those central and eternal principles which make for unity ; and at the same time to recognize that it is the human element which gives variety and interest to the whole ; and so, if it be possible, to seek for a synthesis which shall do justice to the human imperfections which add salt to life, and to the divine perfections which give stability to it.

1. THE WRITTEN WORD

No one can read Church History without being impressed by the solidity of the testimony to the value of the Bible. The dissentients only evince the general consensus. Marcion, for instance, and some of the Gnostics repudiated the Old

[1] *The Seat of Authority in Religion*, III. i. 299.

Testament, and declared that there was no continuity in the revelation. With Marcion, said Tertullian, everything happened suddenly (*subito*). But the Church, in spite of the irreparable breach with Judaism, held fast to the sacred books. There can be no question as to the steadying influence of this amid the inrush of Hellenism. The books of the New Testament, when their position became assured, helped to preserve the authority of the Old: it became the main argument for the ancient scriptures that they witnessed to Christ. Through all the ages the Written Word has meant much in the life of Christians.

And yet it is not infallible! There is no denying that this has been a great blow to believers, especially in the Protestant Churches. To press on to perfection seems a mockery when the very scripture which commands it is itself imperfect. That is the logic, the very natural logic, by which the infallibility of Scripture has been maintained: it has been conceived that any criticism was equivalent to an attack. Protestantism has wished to retain the infallibility of the Scripture, while rejecting that of the Church. But no distinction can be made. Augustine avowed in controversy with the Manichees: 'Evangelio non crederem nisi me ecclesiae catholicae commoveret auctoritas.'[1] The Church decided the canon of Scripture, and they stand or fall together.

Is the loss as great as we have feared? One is tempted to wonder whether our fathers did really hold that rigid view of plenary inspiration. This is not to question the honesty of their statements, but to suggest that those strong declarations as to every yod and tittle simply proclaimed intense convictions as to spiritual values. The statements certainly were strong enough, and that among Catholics as well as Protestants. The Council of Trent declared that all truth and discipline are contained in the written books and in the unwritten traditions which were received by the apostles from the mouth of Christ Himself, or came from the apostles themselves under the dictation of the Holy Spirit (*Spiritu Sancto dictante*), and have so come to us as though actually handed down.[2] Yet it will be noted that the Council puts the unwritten traditions on a level with the written, and by so doing in effect takes away much of the authority of Scripture. In the end the decision

[1] *Adv. Man.* v. [2] Sess. IV. *De Canon. Scrip.*

lies with the holy mother Church which alone is able to judge of the true meaning and interpretation.

The Protestant Churches have never been satisfied either with the claim that the Church should be the arbiter of Scripture, or with the allegorism of Origen or Swedenborg. Calvin gave his whole strength to the discussion.[1] He refused to allow that Scripture depends on the Church, for that would be insulting to the Holy Spirit; but he regarded it as having evidence in itself, which is apparent to those elect to salvation. This circular reasoning, in one of such logical powers as Calvin, shows how hard he was pressed between the Roman Church on the one side, and the Libertines on the other.

In view of these facts we may say that the gains of modern criticism far outweigh its losses, *even for those who have been accustomed to make every step towards full attainment dependent on receiving the sanction of Holy Writ.* The victory in regard to the right to criticize is by now so assured that it is rather laid upon us to declare steadfastly the abiding worth and authority of the sacred writings. They stand on a basis not less secure than before. Frank, unrestricted criticism is helpful, and in the end constructive. To many who have not much time for study, the firmness of the building which is being reared may come as a surprise. ' History is the record of God's dealing with men, and in the history of Jesus Christ we recognize the supreme appeal of God to men. All that lights up that record, all that brings out its meaning and value may become a means of grace. In the experience of many the newer lines of study have opened the avenues that led them to faith in Christ ; and for many more, so far from impoverishing their inheritance in the Bible, the intenser modern study has profoundly enriched it.'[2]

The authority of the Word is closely bound up with the doctrine which we are investigating. Our first religious activity takes the form of the Institution in which we find ourselves, and on which we depend. We accept the authority of its sacred word. Thus we use the evangelical terminology in regard to perfection, often startling and even repugnant, just because we find it embedded in the New Testament. With the growth of our mental strength comes a normal

[1] *The Institutes*, I. vi.–ix.
[2] Statement on the Evangelical Faith and the Modern View of Scripture issued by the Free Church Council.

healthy tendency to criticize. But we cannot rest there; it is equally normal that we should turn towards some definite, positive faith, in which we can go forward to accomplish our term of service.

> The morning drum-call on my eager ear
> Thrills unforgotten yet: the morning dew
> Lies yet undried along my field of noon.
> But now I pause at whiles in what I do,
> And count the bell, and tremble lest I hear
> (My work untrimmed) the sunset gun too soon.

It is in the full attainment of spiritual life that we obtain confidence and strength to take advantage of each spiritual opportunity, unhurried and unafraid. It is there also that we learn the worth of that Written Word, in which we are told of the preparation for, and of the actual, historical incarnation of the Word of God. The Bible retains its supremacy precisely because it deals with the perfect revelation of Divine Love.

2. THE VISIBLE CHURCH

Not less vital than the question of the authority of the Bible is that of the authority of the Church. It has been said that the idea of the Kingdom is fundamental and final; and that the Church is merely a temporary expedient to aid in realizing it. But that statement is quite inadequate. Nor is the problem solved by the distinction made by the Reformers between the Visible and the Invisible Church, important though that distinction may be. The idea of the Invisible Church ' lifts us at once into the region where all the realities are transcendental and all are spiritual, where God is all in all to man, and man lives in conscious fellowship with God and loving obedience to Him.'[1] But a visible organization is implied in the gathering together of disciples by Christ, and in the facts which lie behind the Pauline metaphor of a Body; and the developments recorded later were needed to enable the Body to exercise its functions in obedience to the Head.

Of the Church glorious things are spoken. Even when we pass from the time of the apostles there is still a glow as men tell of the spiritual home which they have found. The

[1] *Christ in Modern Theology*, p. 545.

anonymous writer to Diognetus about the middle of the second century was filled with awe as he reflected that the invisible God, the All-Ruler, the All-Maker, had sent down no subordinate officer, no angel or ruler, whether of those entrusted with the government of things in earth or things in heaven, but the very architect and creator of the whole. He had come to win men by gentleness and persuasion through His Church; hence we may say in a word, ' What the soul is in the body, Christians are in the world.'[1] It seemed incredible that any who held Christ as Head should not be united with His visible Body.[2] From the beginning the Church has been conscious that it has been chosen of God in Christ Jesus before the foundation of the world. Harnack says, in agreement with Weizsäcker, that the necessity of distinguishing itself from Judaism was the main, preliminary condition for revealing the full self-consciousness of the Church. The leading part in opening the eyes of the Church to its distinctive mission was played by St. Paul; but the thought was there, and would have found utterance in any case. The Shepherd of Hermas, at one time very influential, although it has now no living value, which moved in a sphere of thought quite distinct from St. Paul's, has the idea of an elder, premundane Church, of which the earthly is a type. In the account of the Eucharist in the Didache, which is also entirely free from Pauline influences, there occurs this interesting local note in the prayer: ' As this broken bread was scattered upon the mountains and being gathered together became one, so may Thy Church be gathered together into Thy Kingdom from the ends of the earth. . . . Remember, Lord, Thy Church to deliver it from all evil, and *to make it perfect in Thy Love;* and bring it together from the four winds, when it has been sanctified, into Thy kingdom which Thou hast prepared for it; for Thine is the power and the glory for ever and ever.'[3]

This Church-consciousness is of the utmost importance for the right understanding of Christian Perfection. ' The mere fact that from the beginning of Christendom there were reflections and speculations, not only about God and Christ, but also about the Church, teaches us how profoundly the Christian

---

[1] *Ad Diog.* 5.
[2] Habere caput Christum nemo poterit, nisi qui in ejus corpore fuerit, quod est ecclesia. Augustine, *De Unit. Eccl.*, chap. 49.
[3] Didache, 9-10.

consciousness was impressed with being a new people, viz., the people of God. These speculations of the earliest Gentile Christian time about Christ and the Church, as inseparable correlative ideas, are of the greatest importance, for they have absolutely nothing Hellenic in them, but rather have their origin in the apostolic tradition.'[1] If we accept this statement, we must qualify it with the acknowledgement that Hellenism, when it did act on Christian thought, found nothing more congenial than this conception of an ideal Church eternal in the heavens, the home of the spiritual. Our aim is to attain evangelical perfection in fellowship with others within the Society, whose mission it is to share in the priestly, mediatorial work of the eternal Son of God. The historical survey in Part III. will be an examination of the question whether the experience of men justifies so lofty an aim.

3. THE WITNESS OF THE SPIRIT IN MAN

The promise that, when the Spirit of Truth is come, He will guide into all the truth,[2] cannot be confined to the circle of disciples to whom it was first addressed; the comfort of the Paraclete is for all Christians in all ages. Moreover, it is necessary to be quite clear as to the continuity of the Spirit's influence, whether manifested in the historic revelation in the Word, or in the historic organisation of the Church, or in a movement in the souls of individual believers. In the orientation of the soul towards God, in which it receives a lucid assurance of its fellowship with the Divine, the work of the Spirit is knit with that of Christ. The sin of blasphemy against the Holy Ghost, which is called an eternal or aeonian sin, is the sin of ascribing to Jesus an unclean spirit.[3] It is the function of the Paraclete to glorify Christ. No distinction was made in the Church at first between the Son and the Spirit. Thus Justin, thinking of the Logos Spermatikos on which Stoicism laid so much stress, ascribes to the Logos the Spirit's sanctifying work.[4] Clearer definition came to the Church; but we may see in the primary indifference to distinction a proof of how

[1] Harnack, *Hist. of Dogma*, I. iii. 153. [3] Mark iii. 28–30.
[2] John xvi. 13. [4] *Apol.* i. 33.

perfect was the sequence from what Jesus began to do and to teach, to what He continues to do and to teach, after He had given commandment through the Holy Ghost unto the apostles whom He had chosen, in the historic organization of the Church, and in continuous revelation in the souls of believers.

The continuity of the Spirit's work may be seen from Origen's résumé of the Regula Fidei, the Rule of Faith accepted in his day.[1] The Spirit is the sanctifier of all saints, both under the old and the new dispensation. The Scriptures were written by His agency; and it is He who makes plain their hidden meaning. It was from this last statement that Origen was able to move out into the field of speculation which he loved, without abandoning his allegiance to the historic faith. The realm of the Spirit was in one sense less than that of the Father or of the Son, since it was confined to that part of the rational creation which was in process of being sanctified. But if it was more restricted, it was in another sense the highest of all. Origen's strong expressions of subordination need to be supplemented by his appreciation of the unity of the Divine Nature and Energy.

When we examine the witness of the Spirit in any Christian community, with its human alloy, we are struck by two marks, which stand in curious opposition to each other. It may have the mark of an intense emotionalism; it may be enthusiastic, ecstatic, mystic. Or it may have the mark of a pure Rationalism. These two have unexpected affinities. A noble example is seen in Martineau, whose seat of authority appears at first purely rational, but who also gives intimations of the value attached to the emotional and the intuitive. On the other hand, the Society of Friends lays stress on an immediate revelation of the Spirit to the soul; yet there are tendencies among them towards an advanced form of Rationalism. Barclay, for instance, in the second proposition of his *Theses Theologicae* lays this down: 'Seeing no man knoweth the Father but the Son, and he to whom the Son revealeth Him; and seeing the revelation of the Son is in and by the Spirit; therefore the testimony of the Spirit is that alone by which the true knowledge of God hath been, is, and can be only revealed.' But this testimony or witness of the

[1] *De Prin. Pref.* 4–8.

Spirit, he goes on to say, can never contradict the outward testimony of the Scriptures, or right or sound reason. Here we may note the nature of the argument, from which it is obvious that Barclay relies, not merely on an intuitive, immediate revelation, but also on the force of logic. The reference to the Scriptures suggests that he is swayed more than he realizes by the historic witness of the Church. The way in which the argument is presented is not due purely to either intuition or reason. The reference to the Trinity shows that its form is conditioned by the Written Word, and by that Word as its doctrine has undergone development within the Church. *This is a valuable indication of a possible unification of the three sources, especially in relation to the attainment of evangelical perfection.*

Our voyage over the waters of life must be in perpetual jeopardy, though guided by the best counsels of men, unless there be some Divine Word, which may enable us to make the journey in security.[1] The quest for perfection depends on the possibility of finding such a Word. Neither in the Written Word, nor in the Visible Church, nor in the witness of the Spirit in our own souls have we an infallible guide. Yet it appears to us that there is some union, in which the three meet, whereby there is given absolute security of the love of God in Christ, both in the present moment and in eternity. To obtain full assurance of this is what is meant by entering on the way of perfection. This way may be designated as scriptural, catholic, and spiritual, if we include in the attribute spiritual, the mystical and the rational. Almost all earnest Christian seekers, to whom our attention is confined, have, as a matter of fact, availed themselves of all three guides. The proof of this will depend on an investigation of the Biblical teaching (in Part II.), of the historical development within the Church (in Part III.), and then of the divergences which have arisen as the result of various bodies of Christians laying special emphasis on one or other of the sanctions (in Part IV.). To seek, as the Lutherans did, for some Formula Concordiae, which should set forth the fundamental points of agreement, and which should indicate lines of possible unification, ought not to be altogether futile. One is encouraged in this by modern movements towards union, and by the progress of

[1] See the pathetic yearning expressed by Simmias in the Phaedo, 85a.

theological and psychological knowledge. In Part V. some attempt will be made to vindicate the Evangelical Doctrine of Perfection in the light of modern thought, and to show in what way it may be regarded as the decisive factor for the reunion of Christendom.

PART II
BIBLICAL

CONTENTS OF PART II

III. THE IDEA OF PERFECTION IN THE OLD TESTAMENT AND IN JUDAISM
                                                                                     PAGE
1. Hebrew Terms to Express the Idea of Perfection 32
2. The Development of Old Testament Teaching Regarding God 35
3. Old Testament Teaching Regarding Man and his Religious Needs . . . 42
4. The Idea of a Perfect Mediator 47
    (1) *The Perfect Prophet* 48
    (2) *The Perfect Priest* 49
    (3) *The Ideal King* 49
    (4) *The Ideal Environment* 51
5. Summary 52

IV. NEW TESTAMENT WAYS OF EXPRESSING PERFECTION
1. Words that Convey the Idea of Preparedness 54
2. Words that Convey the Idea of Wholeness or Completeness 56
3. Words that Convey the Idea of Fullness 56
4. Words that Convey the Idea of Attaining an End 59

V. THE NEW TESTAMENT DOCTRINE OF THE PERFECTION OF CHRIST
1. Christ as the Perfect Revelation of God 62
2. The Perfect Obedience of Christ 66
3. The Perfect Priesthood of Christ 69
4. The Perfect Dynamic in Christ 72
5. Summary 75

VI. THE NEW TESTAMENT DOCTRINE OF THE PERFECTING OF BELIEVERS
1. Obstacles to the Perfection of the Individual 76
2. Ways of Overcoming 80
    (1) *The Way of Obedience to the Law* 80
    (2) *The Way of Self-surrender* 81
    (3) *The Way of Faith* 82
    (4) *The Way of Mystical Union* 84
    (5) *The Way of Knowledge* 85
    (6) *The Way of Love* 86
3. Questions which have to be Faced. 88

VII. THE NEW TESTAMENT DOCTRINE OF THE PERFECTING OF THE CHURCH
1. The Attitude of the Church towards the Individual and towards the World . 89
2. The Ideal of the Church's Life and Witness on Earth 90
3. The Missionary Ideal of the Kingdom 93
4. The Eternal Life of the Church in Heaven 93

CHAPTER III

THE IDEA OF PERFECTION IN THE OLD TESTAMENT
AND IN JUDAISM

AT first sight there seems little in the Old Testament of special application to our subject. The idea of perfection appears to have arisen to satisfy the aesthetic and speculative sides of our nature; and it is in these that the religion of the Hebrews was lacking. In the end this was no loss. The peril of being led away from ethical considerations by the allurements of art and philosophy is so great that we are thankful for the fact that the atmosphere in which the idea of evangelical perfection arose was on the whole free from both. A people among whom poetry, music, and to some extent sculpture are found, cannot indeed be said to be destitute of art; and in later years we find a certain amount of speculation, mainly on the problem of suffering. Still it is evident that both the aesthetic and the speculative interests were quite subordinate. And this was of the last importance. When Hellenism came in like a flood, there was grave danger that ethical values should be lowered. The Maccabaean prophet, whose writings have been incorporated with those of Zechariah, and who raised the battle-cry: 'Thy sons, O Zion, against thy sons, O Greece!'[1] was only expressing with peculiar pungency a real moral need. For the conception of evangelical perfection we are debtors both to the Jew and to the Greek; but we have abundant cause for gratitude that the foundation had been well and truly laid before men turned to Plato and Plotinus to complete the structure.

Our study cannot be confined within the Canon. Other Jewish writings affected the atmosphere in which Christ found Himself. This is particularly manifest in the Messianic consciousness of Jesus and His eschatological utterances.

[1] Zech. ix. 13.

1. HEBREW TERMS TO EXPRESS THE IDEA OF PERFECTION

(1) There is a well-known construction in Hebrew in which the infinitive absolute is used either before or after a finite verb to give intensity by the repetition of the word to the action or state predicated ; before the verb it gives emphasis ; after, it usually denotes the prolonging of the action. Thus the tabu that prohibited the eating of the tree ran : Thou shalt surely die.[1] The idea of intensity passed into that of completeness, as in such a phrase as this : ' I will not utterly destroy the house of Jacob.'[2] The destruction which is negatived is one whose intensity would leave nothing undevoured. A fine example of another but similar way of declaring perfection is found in Isa. xxvi. 3 : ' Thou wilt keep him in perfect peace.' In the original the idea of perfection is obtained by doubling the word peace.

(2) The word כָּלָה denotes the accomplishment of a design, as in the illuminating phrase : ' I have seen an end of all perfection.'[3] The psalmist was thinking of the steady accomplishment of one design after another, and at the same time of a moral law, exceeding broad and outlasting all. This word was used of the achievement of the design of creation : ' The heaven and the earth were finished.'[4] When the plans of David and Solomon reached fruition in the completion of the Temple, a similar phrase was employed.[5] So also it is said of the word of Yahweh : ' It shall not return unto me void, but it shall accomplish that which I please.'[6] The fulfilment of prophecy is often expressed by this root. The anger of Yahweh is described as making a full end by its consuming power[7] : in several places the striking formula is found, ' a consummation, and that determined,'[8] a decisive decree of destruction. In all these forms there is the thought of a purpose, human or divine, finding its fulfilment.

(3) The root כלל is used in conjunction with יפִי or a similar word to denote perfection in beauty. Ezekiel employed it in depicting Jerusalem and Tyre.[9] The lamentation over Jerusalem takes an added bitterness from the memory of Ps. xlviii. : 'Is this the city that men called The perfection of

---
[1] Gen. ii. 17. [4] Gen. ii. 1. [7] Ps. xc. 7 ; Ezek. xi. 13.
[2] Amos ix. 8. [5] 1 Kings ix. 1. [8] Isa. x. 23, xxviii. 22 ; Dan. ix. 27.
[3] Ps. cxix. 96. [6] Isa. lv. 11. [9] Ezek. xvi. 14, xxvii. 3.

beauty, The joy of the whole earth?'[1] The same root is used in the form כָּלִיל as equivalent to עֹלָה, but bringing out more explicitly the fact that in the burnt offering the *whole* was offered to the Deity: in Ps. li. 19 both words are used. The blessing on Levi in Deut. xxxiii. 8–11 describes this offering of the whole as one of the privileges of the tribe.

(4) The next word to discuss is חֵרֶם, the ban or tabu. A nation or its leader going to battle might put the lives of the enemy or their property under a tabu, i.e. might declare them forfeited to God, the idea being that in so repudiating any personal profit they laid their God under peculiar obligation to come to their help. Thus, on the Moabite Stone, Mesha, king of Moab, wrote: ' Chemosh said to me, Take Nebo over against Israel; and I went by night, and fought against it from break of dawn till noon; and I took it, and put them all to death . . . for I had made it tabu to Ashtar Chemosh.' In the Old Testament the idea is most clearly discerned in such cases as those of Achan and Saul where the ban has been broken. Sometimes the tabu was thought of as the spontaneous offering of the people, sometimes as due to a divine command. ' Thou shalt devote their gain to Yahweh, and their substance to the Lord of the whole earth.'[2] The religious value of the tabu lay in inculcating fidelity with the Unseen. Its importance for our subject consists in the fact that it contains in germ the idea which developed into the evangelical counsels, the idea namely of the value of the renunciation of personal boons in order to obtain a spiritual victory.

(5) The root שׁלם, especially in the form שָׁלוֹם, speaks of a prosperity, a well-being, which tends to perfection. It goes back to the idea of being quit. No one has any claim against you. You are at peace with God, when even He cannot make any further demand upon you for what you have not done or paid. Then comes security, which finds expression in the שֶׁלֶם, the peace-offering. We have noted the emphatic duplication of peace in Isa. xxvi. 3. Peace is the crown of the priest's blessing; it is the benison with which one bids farewell. Immanuel is styled the Prince of Peace; and the psalmist can conceive no greater good than abundance of it.[3] The

---

[1] Lam. ii. 15.   [2] Mic. iv. 13.   [3] Ps. lxxii. 7.

34   THE IDEA OF PERFECTION

word also denotes full devotion to the worship of Yahweh, without any deviation after other gods. Thus it is said of Amaziah that he did that which was right in the eyes of Yahweh, but not with a perfect heart.¹ An enigmatic use occurs in Isa. xlii. 19 (' Who is blind as he that is at peace with me ? '), where the marginal translation is, ' He that is made perfect or recompensed.' The verse is probably a gloss ; but it is of importance as showing a use of the pu'al of the verb to express a complete reconciliation. The word in its highest sense stands for a state of serenity, due to a reconciliation with God, in which man finds his true prosperity.

(5) A most important root is תמם. One form of it, Thummim, denoted one of the sacred lots.² These fell into disuse with higher conceptions as to the method of communication with God. Moreover, an ethical connotation became fixed in the use of any form of this radical. It might be used either of God or man. Thus in Psalm xviii. it is declared of the God whose way is perfect, that He girdeth the king with strength, and maketh *his* way perfect.³ Very occasionally it is used disparagingly of the simplicity which, as most languages show, men have considered akin to righteousness.⁴ It often implies sincerity and integrity, and is then hardly to be distinguished from יָשָׁר.⁵ In Psalm xviii. 25-28 it is joined with mercy or piety and purity, as among the attributes which ensure Divine favour. But any human perfection is always and essentially derivative. Noah was righteous and perfect in his generations, because he walked with God.⁶ When God appeared to Abraham to make a covenant with him to endless generations, He said : ' I am El Shaddai ; walk before me, and be thou perfect.'⁷ This covenant marks an advance on that recorded in Gen. xv., which has very primitive elements. The reconciliation effected by the animal sacrifices is to be continued in a covenant of abiding union. In later writings the idea was further developed. The man whose heart was perfect before God had a light to guide him in his path. ' The righteousness of the perfect shall direct his way.'⁸ Or again : ' The path of

---

¹ 2 Chron. xxv. 2.
² Very interesting is the reading of 1 Sam. xiv. 41, as restored from the LXX. ' If the iniquity be in me or in Jonathan my son, give Urim ; but if it be in the people, give Thummim.'
³ Ps. xviii. 30 ; Deut. xxxii. 4.   ⁴ 2 Sam. xv. 11.   ⁵ Job i. 1.
⁶ Gen. vi. 9.   ⁷ Gen. xvii. 1.   ⁸ Prov. xi. 5.

IN THE OLD TESTAMENT AND IN JUDAISM   35

the righteous' (synonymous with perfect) ' is as the light of dawn, that shineth more and more unto the perfect day.'[1]

2 THE DEVELOPMENT OF OLD TESTAMENT TEACHING REGARDING GOD

It is of the last importance for our subject that we should understand the progress of the Old Testament ideas of God, for they exhibit the form in which Christ uttered His message. The evangelical conception of perfection looks back to the Old Testament idea of a covenant with Yahweh. We have here no speculative conception of the Absolute. The French translation, The Eternal, even less than ours, THE LORD, does justice to the intense personality of Yahweh. It has been suggested that the name came from the God of the Kenites, the tribe to which Moses' father-in-law belonged. What is certain is that at first He was regarded simply as the God of the tribes of Israel. The very early song of Deborah indicates that His abode is in Sinai, although Israel has come to Canaan.[2] But He will come to their help, and He expects them to stand by Him when He goes forth on what a lost book describes as the Wars of Yahweh. He was a War-God, and the virtues which His worship brought out were the military virtues. The Old Testament conception of Deity sprang, not from any personification of nature, nor from any speculations as to the Infinite, but from the idea of an Unseen Helper during the hardships of the sojourn in the wilderness.

As the Hebrews became settled, and eventually dominant, a gentler era began. But other dangers arose with prosperity. It was easy to confuse Yahweh with the Baalim whom the Canaanites worshipped at so many shrines and with so many licentious rites. Was He not also called Baal or Lord? Amos and Hosea show how the problem was dealt with by the best minds.[3] The sterner virtues of fidelity to one's word, and of justice between man and man, must be preserved. Yet Hosea showed that a new gentleness may be learnt from the bountiful provision which Yahweh's love had made for his people. Yahweh, God of Hosts, was the old name, meaning the Unseen Inspirer and Leader of the tribes in their battle array; but

[1] Prov. iv. 18.   [2] Judges v.   [3] Hos. ii. 16-17.

Amos unfolded a larger thought, when he bade men seek ' Him that maketh the Pleiades and Orion (i.e. the hosts of heaven) . . . Yahweh is His Name.'[1] Even more important than this enlarged view of the extent of His domain is the growing conviction that His Name must be associated with righteousness and holiness. So in two passages Amos says: ' The Lord God hath sworn by His holiness,' and again 'hath sworn by Himself.'[2] To swear by His holiness is to swear by Himself. This view of the essential righteousness and holiness of the Deity is of such value for the spiritual progress of humanity that it demands special attention.

In all stages of society judgements have to be given between men. The one in whose favour judgement is given, whether by a court of law or by the facts of life, is in the right. Hence *righteousness* is often practically equivalent to success or prosperity. In the Song of Deborah, when it is said that in the time of desolation they rehearsed the righteous acts of Yahweh towards the villages of Israel, that refers to the deliverances which He had wrought, and the times of prosperity which He had given. This view is prominent in Deuteronomy and in the Deuteronomic redactor of the history of the Judges and the Kings. Prosperity depends on the dominance of the pitying salvation of God, and adversity on that of the sins of men.[3] In the account of Cyrus he is described as the one whom righteousness meets wherever he goes, which is as much as to say, the man on whose steps victory attends.[4]

This conception is exposed to many rude shocks in life ; as, for instance, at the battle of Megiddo (608 B.C.), when the most pious of all the kings, whose memorial is like the composition of incense, sweet as honey in every mouth, and like music at a banquet of wine,[5] was defeated and slain. A scathing attack on the whole conception is the leit-motiv of the book of Job. Hence righteousness came to be defined, in more ethical terms, in relation to the Divine grace, especially towards the poor and the afflicted. It must not be confounded with the Glory of the LORD ; but it did come to equal a manifestation of His essential loving-kindness as the basis of the covenant which He had made with His people. No distinction is to be drawn

---

[1] Amos v. 8. [2] Amos iv. 2, vi. 8. [3] *De Civ. Dei*, xvi. 43.
[4] Isa. xli. 2. [5] Sir. xlix. 1.

between the justice and the mercy of God. Of His grace he has entered into a covenant relation. The sins of Israel disturb, but they do not end it. He will not give them up, just because He is God and not man, the Holy One in the midst of them. There is to be a renewal of the covenant, a new betrothal in righteousness, and in judgement, and in lovingkindness, and in mercies.[1] These attributes are similarly grouped by Jeremiah: ' Let him that glorieth glory in this, that he understandeth, and knoweth me, that I am the LORD which exercise lovingkindness, judgement, and righteousness, in the earth: for in these things I delight, saith the LORD.'[2] On this passage Calvin makes a characteristic comment: the lovingkindness of God is shown in the salvation of the elect, His judgement in the damnation of the wicked; His righteousness is that attribute which gives assurance that His decrees will stand for ever.[3] But this distinction marks a deterioration from the nobler view of the Old Testament prophet. Righteousness is shown equally in the judgement which is needed for discipline, and in the lovingkindness which refuses to give up.

This righteousness is active: it is a force, a thought, a word, which cannot return void[4]; and it is a saving force, for goodness is behind it. To believe that is to enter into union with God. The classic statement is this: ' Abram believed in the Lord; and He counted it to him for righteousness.'[5] Negatively this imputed righteousness is equivalent to a pardon for offences.[6] The sacrificial system, it is worth noting, while intended to keep alive the sense of sin, provided no remedy for serious sin. There is plenty of forgiveness in the Old Testament, but it is due to the intrinsic graciousness of the Divine nature. On man's side is needed penitence and amendment. Punishment there may be, even after penitence, but it will be disciplinary and purgatorial. The prophet of the exile commenced his message with a word of comfort to the heart of Jerusalem, because the term of her purgatorial service was ended.[7] Divine righteousness would henceforth be manifested purely in delivering grace. The activity of the righteousness of Yahweh may for a time bring suffering and exile, but its final issue must be prosperity and blessing. An eschatological writing, which has been incorporated with Isaiah, though it is probably later

---

[1] Hos. ii. 19.   [2] Jer. ix. 24.   [3] *Inst.* I. x.   [4] Isa. lv. 11.
[5] Gen. xv. 6.   [6] Ps. xxxii. 1, 2.   [7] Isa. xl. 2.

D

even than the exile, has this beautiful word: ' The work of righteousness shall be peace ; and the effect of righteousness quietness and confidence for ever.'[1]

The idea of *holiness* is closely associated with that of righteousness, but must not be confused with it. It is always significant of the presence of the Deity, and is never applied to things or people except in some definite religious connexion. Certain people or places or days were hallowed, i.e. specifically associated with the Deity. Scrupulous care had to be taken lest the Divine wrath should break out in a flame of jealousy. The unwary hand of Uzzah caused the Holiness of Yahweh to break out to his destruction.[2] We have learnt from Otto to use the word ' numinous ' to describe the psychosis into which a man passes when he becomes conscious of the Divine Presence. ' The noble religion of Moses marks the beginning of a process, which from that point onward proceeds with ever-increasing momentum, by which the " numinous " is throughout rationalized and moralized, i.e. charged with ethical import, until it becomes " the holy " in the fullest sense of the word. The culmination of the process is found in the Prophets and in the Gospels. And it is in this that the special nobility of the religion revealed to us by the Bible is to be found, which, when the stage represented by the Deutero-Isaiah is reached, justifies its claim to be a universal world-religion. Here is to be found its manifest superiority over, e.g. Islam, in which Allah is mere " numen," and is in fact precisely Yahweh in his pre-Mosaic form and upon a larger scale. But this moralizing and rationalizing process does not mean that the numinous itself has been overcome, but merely that its preponderance has been overcome. The numinous is at once the basis upon which, and the setting within which, the ethical and rational meaning is consummated.'[3]

Ritschl suggested that the covering of the Atonement was not so much a hiding of sin, as a shade from the Glory of the Presence. Some such thought seems to have been behind the Rabbinic imagery of the Shekinah, the manifested Glory of God, not fully God, and therefore bearable by human sight, and conspicuous in the Cherubim of Glory overshadowing the mercy-seat.[4] It was not only the Splendour that was to be feared : there was a Divine Jealousy, a heat of righteous anger, the

---

[1] Isa. xxxii. 17. [2] 2 Sam. vi. 8. [3] *The Idea of the Holy*, p. 77. [4] Heb. ix. 5.

jealousy as of a husband, which was a consuming fire. The best theistic thought has sought to retain the ideas of splendour and of passion in regard to God, but refined and purified.

The personal distinction of the Holy Spirit, which became of such value for theology, is only faintly foreshadowed in the Old Testament and in Judaism. All spirit life is the expression of the energy of Yahweh ; but men may have some life, even some spirit life, and yet not enter into communion with the essential Deity. Hence the prayer of the Psalmist : ' Cast me not away from Thy presence ; and take not Thy Holy Spirit from me.'[1] Hence the prophet's contrition at the remembrance of that rebellious temper which had grieved the Holy Spirit.[2] More significant still are such phrases as that which declared that Yahweh's Spirit clothed itself with Gideon[3] ; and that higher one where Trito-Isaiah added another to the Servant Songs : ' The Spirit of my Lord Yahweh is upon me.'[4] In the apocryphal work known as the Psalms of Solomon, mention is made of the Messiah coming in the power of the Holy Spirit. The people in the days of Messiah will partake of the essential holiness of God. ' There shall be no iniquity in His days in their midst ; for all shall be holy, and their king is the Lord Messiah.'[5]

The development of the Divine Perfection which we have been discussing may be spoken of as intensive ; but it was accompanied by an extension of the sphere of His authority in three directions : (1) to take in the whole realm of nature ; (2) to take in all the nations of the earth ; (3) to include Sheol.

(1) Of the first little need be said. Whatever limitations there may have been in primitive thought, they were swept away by the prophets. The very name, God of Hosts, was taken to include the Hosts of Heaven. ' He bringeth out their host by number : He calleth them all by name.'[6] ' Do not I fill heaven and earth ? is the oracle of Yahweh.'[7] The creation epics of Gen. i. and Ps. civ. leave nothing outside His sway.

(2) From the religious standpoint more significance attaches to the extension of His rule among men. It was an extension

[1] Ps. li. 11.   [2] Isa. lxiii. 10.   [3] Judges vi. 34.   [4] Isa. lxi. 1.
[5] Ps. Sol. xvii. 36.   [6] Isa. xl. 26.   [7] Jer. xxiii. 24.

by no means welcomed. Many clung to the thought that He belonged to Israel, just as Israel was His peculiar possession. Even the prophets of the exile, Ezekiel and Deutero-Isaiah, when they speak of the Holy One of Israel, seem implicitly to be making a claim on behalf of Israel on One whom they yet recognize as absolutely the Holy One. Even so advanced a work as the Wisdom of Solomon, which perceives that 'Thou hast mercy on all men, because Thou hast power to do all things,' nevertheless speaks of the land which 'in Thy sight is most precious of all lands.'[1] This persistent particularism was intensified in many minds by the trials of Israel: it was never stronger than in the time of Jesus. But the effort to proclaim the LORD's perfection won the victory. The growth of moral sensibility made all prophetic minds feel that the favour shown to Israel brought with it increased responsibility.[2] Contact with the nations produced the sense of a common humanity. Very impressive is the oracle which joins Israel with its two great oppressors: 'Blessed be Egypt my people, and Assyria the work of my hands, and Israel mine inheritance.'[3] It came to be felt that the mission of Israel was in fact a priestly mission.[4] The conviction that the gods of the heathen were nothing completed the victory. The dealings of the God of Israel could only be justified by concluding that in some way even the heathen were under His care, and somehow even their prayers reached Him. This height was attained in Jonah, and in the oracle in Mal. i. 11 : 'For from the rising of the sun even unto the going down of the same my name is great among the Gentiles ; and in every place incense is offered unto my name, and a pure offering : for my name is great among the Gentiles, saith Yahweh, God of Hosts.'

(3) The last domain to pass under the sway of Yahweh was Sheol. He was eminently the God of life. He was the inspirational force which men felt when they were urged to anything brave and generous. His was the breath which breathed into them their own soul life. Life consisted of flood and ebb according to the pulsation of His Spirit. That is the logic of Yahwism : to some great souls it seems to have been sufficient. The grass withereth, the flower fadeth ; but it is enough to know that the word of our God stands for ever.

[1] Wisdom xi. 23 and xii. 7. [2] Amos iii. 2. [3] Isa. xix. 24, 25.
[4] Isa. lxi. 6 and Zech. viii. 23.

But to many this brought little comfort. This bright world of sunshine and life belonged to Yahweh; but the soul of man in it seemed like a stranger and a sojourner with Him, as all our fathers have been.[1] There is an obvious danger of bitterness and pessimism, as we see exemplified in Hezekiah's psalm,[2] and in Ecclesiastes. This line of thought resulted in Sadduceeism, and found its noblest utterance in Ecclesiasticus.

But the conviction arose that something was lacking to the glory of Yahweh, if He were unable to save even in Sheol. It was agreed by all that He could save from Sheol, in the sense that He could bring back a soul from the verge of the Pit, as in the case of Hezekiah. He could bring back a few who had passed within its gates. Then at last the thought came that even Sheol might have a place in the normal exercise of His power. Might it be possible that Sheol was a kind of restchamber, within which the soul might wait in a dim, practically unconscious existence? This aspiration finds pathetic articulation in Job xiv. 13–15. When the breath of Yahweh blows in wrath, it is like the sirocco, and withers up all human life [3]; but Job dreams that there may be a place of safety, appointed by Yahweh Himself, in which the soul of the righteous may find a covert from the storm. When the fierceness of His anger is past, the soul may return again, to be remembered by Him in covenant mercy once more. A similar thought finds utterance in the Apocalypse, Isa. xxiv.–xxvii., especially xxiv. 22 and xxvi. 19–21. Daniel xii. 1 still more plainly advertises that this renewed remembrance will be for judgement. There was purification in Sheol, as is expressly stated in the Books of Adam and Eve, for Adam was delivered to Michael for that purpose[4]; and later writers conceived that the prayers and sacrifices offered on earth might avail.[5] Thus the clear conviction was reached that the authority of God extended even to Sheol. It was not possible to realize this with the imagination then, or to prove it by argument; nor is it now. *But it was this profound conviction which added the last touch to that conception of a perfectly righteous and holy God, to whose kingdom there was no frontier in any direction, which it was the mission of Israel to proclaim to the world.*

---

[1] Ps. xxxix. 12.   [2] Isa. xxxviii. 9–20.   [3] Isa. xl. 7.
[4] Leckie, *The World to Come*, p. 72   [5] 2 Macc. xii. 38–44.

3. OLD TESTAMENT TEACHING REGARDING MAN AND HIS RELIGIOUS NEEDS

When we turn from God to man, we may put the question before us in this form : How did the thought of Israel, through the long periods of the Old Testament and in later Judaism, conceive of the origin and destiny of man ? Was it such that the idea of man as sharing in the perfections of God would be congenial to it ? Both accounts in Genesis of the making of man bear witness to a fundamental conviction that he has been fashioned by Divine Hands. The words 'image' and 'likeness' have given rise to much controversy. 'What exactly is meant in the Priestly Code (Gen. i. 26, 27, v. 1, 3, ix. 6) by "the image of God" is uncertain; probably no more than writers such as Ben Sira or Pseudo-Solomon seem to have associated with the phrase. In Ecclus. xvii. 1 ff., the image of God would appear to be identical with supremacy over the beasts and with rationality; the Book of Wisdom asserts these properties of man, though not expressly in connexion with the divine image (ix. 2, 3 ; cf. Ps. viii. 6), which, in ii. 23, it associates with immortality of the soul. It is not until we come to the apocalyptic books and the rabbinic writings that the image of God is taken to include more remarkable endowments; and the identification of it with moral excellencies was due to Christian teachers.'[1] *A late development in Christian thought distinguished between the image and the likeness, and made evangelical perfection to consist in the recovery of the likeness,* the *donum super-additum,* which had been bestowed in addition to the *donum naturale,* which had not been lost even by the Fall. But all this belongs to a much later time. It is sufficient for our immediate purpose to note how deep-rooted was the belief that the bond which united man to God was genetic. Gen. v. 3 says : 'Adam begat in his own likeness after his image.' The use of the same phraseology indicates a similarity between the generation of man from God, and of one man from another. The dangers of such a conception have not prevented it from influencing later Jewish and Christian thought. Even Clement-Alex. considered that man's likeness to God lay in his generative power. 'Man becomes an image of God, inasmuch as man co-operates in the generation of man.'[2]

[1] F. R. Tennant, *The Doctrine of the Fall,* 104*n.*   [2] Paed. ii. 10 p. 220.

With this idea of man's divine origin Hebrew thought coupled an equally strong conviction of his weakness. The name ' Adam ' was connected with the ground ' Adamah.'[1] This derivation is wrong ; but it shows the working of Hebrew thought. Davidson suggests that there is significance in the connexion of Adam with the lightest and apparently least material part of the ground, namely, the dust. But the dust rather represents the frailty of man, and the slight hold which he has on reality. The Spirit of Yahweh gives him a fugitive soul-life ; but when that is withdrawn, he returns to the dust-land. If he is to rise again, it must be from the earth dust of Sheol.[2] The idea of strength and energy is associated with the words ' spirit,' and (in a less degree) ' soul,' which speak of man's union with God, while the idea of weakness is inherent in the words 'flesh ' and ' dust,' which denote that he is also earth-born. The phrase which most nearly expresses what we mean by humanity is All-flesh. Thus, when the Divine wrath was threatening to sweep away the whole congregation, Moses and Aaron cried out, ' O God, the God of the spirits of All-flesh.'[3] It must always and carefully be borne in mind that no separation is made between the spiritual and the material part of man. If the prophet says that All-flesh is grass, he also says that All-flesh shall see the Glory of Yahweh.[4] Jeremiah declares that Yahweh will plead with All-flesh.[5]

The idea of a fall of man from a state of original perfection became so fixed in the mind of Christendom that it is surprising to find how slight is the reference in the Old Testament. Hosea says of the falling away of Ephraim and Judah, that they, like Adam, have transgressed the covenant ; but that may simply mean ' in human fashion.'[6] We may note the gibe of Eliphaz : ' Art thou the first man that was born ? "[7] and the lamentation in Ezekiel, in which the king of Tyre, ' full of wisdom and perfect in beauty,' is compared with the first man ' in Eden the garden of God.'[8] In these instances pre-eminence is assigned to the first man ; and in Ezekiel there is some reference to the expulsion from Eden, including mythological elements of great antiquity. The Old Testament acknowledges in man a bias to sin, but with no special allusion to

---

[1] Gen. ii. 7.   [2] Dan. xii. 2.   [3] Num. xvi. 22.   [4] Isa. xl. 5, 6.
[5] Jer. xxv. 31 ; cf. Isa. xlix. 26, lxvi. 23 ; Ezek. xx. 48 ; Zech. ii. 13.
[6] Hos. vi. 7.   [7] Job xv. 7.   [8] Ezek. xxviii. 11-15.

Gen. iii.[1] Only in later Judaism is any causal relation traced ; and of the later writers quite as many ascribe the entrance of sin to the lust of the Watchers, the angelic sons of God, of Gen. vi. 1–6. In this later Judaism were unfolded those views of the natural disposition of man's heart which form the basis of the Doctrine of the Fall and of Original Sin. The root idea is in Gen. vi. 5 : ' Every imagination of the thoughts of his heart was only evil continually.' The word Yezer (imagination, device, purpose) as applied to man's heart acquired the technical meaning of a natural bias to evil. Afterwards a distinction was made between the natural bias to sin, and a redeeming tendency to good, which came through the law. The Alexandrian Jews, such as Pseudo-Solomon and Philo, were particularly anxious to avoid attributing the origin of sin to God. A disposition arose to conceive of a state, before the Fall, of idyllic bliss, and also to regard the disobedience of Adam as the cause of the evil which has come upon his race. Tennant thus sums up Philo's description of Adam : ' Physically he was perfect ; being superior to all his descendants as regards beauty, and endowed with gigantic stature. He had converse with incorporeal beings higher than himself, with whom he associated in a state of happiness. He was free from all disease and affliction ; possessed extraordinary powers of perception, so as to be able to perceive " the natures, essences and operations which exist in heaven " ; and was in enjoyment of the most perfect human bliss.'[2] The causal connexion between Adam's fall from this state, and the sinful and doomed condition of humanity, is most clearly shown in 4 Ezra vii. 48 : ' O thou Adam, what hast thou done ? for though it was thou that sinned, the evil is not fallen on thee alone, but on all of us that come of thee.' The Old Testament teaching on man turned in one direction towards Pantheism, such as we see in modern time in the Jew Spinoza ; and in another towards the Pessimism, which lies so heavy on Jewish apocalypse, especially 4 Ezra ; although the Old Testament itself is on the whole free from either Pantheism or gloom. But it became apparent that man's state is one of moral weakness, which is either the necessary result of his creaturehood, or which is the effect of an actual falling away ; but which in any case implies a state of loss tending to hopelessness.

---

[1] Hughes, *Eth. of Jewish Apoc. Lit.*, pp. 149 ff.   [2] *Doctrine of the Fall*, p. 134.

The characters delineated in the Old Testament are usually frankly admitted to be imperfect. There are a few, however, to whom no definite fault is attributed. Thus of Enoch it was said that he walked with God, and that he was not, for God took him. That vague phrase greatly impressed later Judaism. It was understood to mean that he was given the privilege of traversing unknown realms, and learning the secrets of futurity. The references in the New Testament[1] show conclusively that the ideal of Enoch was in the air, and must have influenced the inception of the evangelical ideal.

The stories of Joseph and Samuel possess a perennial fascination : they are depicted as those who from youth ordered their lives in accordance with the Lord's will. Among the kings Josiah's name was most fragrant. He came to the throne in a time of revival, the value of which we can discern from Jeremiah and Deuteronomy. To this revival he gave his whole-hearted support ; and to the Jew his life seemed flawless.

Two other names may be mentioned, Job and Daniel. In these cases we are invited to view, not merely their actions, but their inner thoughts. The character of Job has for us a reality much superior to that of Enoch or Josiah. Not only is he explicitly stated to be perfect and upright ; but Yahweh Himself declares that He can find no fault in him, and even the Satan can only say that he has not been fully tried. Moreover, chapter xxxi. consists of a wonderfully valuable exposition of the way of perfection. While it deals largely with relations with one's fellows, it also inculcates fidelity towards the Unseen: a man must not utter falsehood before God, or deny His name. The author does not consider that the outcries wrung from Job by mental and bodily anguish seriously affect his true perfection. Job himself expressly repudiates any claim to sinlessness before God. The perfection of Daniel is viewed from another side. There is a resemblance to the story of Joseph ; but the visions of Daniel are fraught with mighty eschatological conceptions, some of them of the utmost sublimity. They show how the idea of a perfect character, taken from a dim, traditional figure,[2] came to demand the idea of a perfect environment.

Scattered through the Old Testament are descriptions of a

[1] Heb. xi. 5 is based on the LXX translation of Gen. v. 24 : Jude 14 quotes from the apocryphal book of Enoch, which has come down to us in an Ethiopic translation.
[2] Ezek. xiv. 14, xxviii. 3.

perfect man or woman, not attached to any particular name. Such are Ps. xxiv. 3-6, Ezek. xviii. 5-9, Prov. xxxi. 10-31. In all the ideal is truly ethical. It is not considered that there can be any conflict between one's duty to one's neighbour and to God. There is a tendency to dwell on the prohibitions rather than the positive commands. In the case of the woman emphasis is laid on the exercise of those practical virtues, of which Martha has been taken as the typical exponent.

In the apocryphal writings the moral ideal received much attention. In those affected by Hellenic influences the superior worth of the contemplative life was generally recognized. 'The wisdom of the scribe cometh by opportunity of leisure.'[1] This distinction between the state possible to the artificer, and the higher state open only to one who had leisure for contemplation profoundly influenced Christian thought and practice. The natural Jewish tendency was rather to conceive that a man was perfect, when he had scrupulously fulfilled all the Divine Commandments. This became for many the carrying out of the ceremonial law. The moral law was not abrogated or overlooked; but the emphasis, in such writings as Jubilees, came to be on matters which are not ethical at all. Where stress was laid on the moral law it was often expounded with rigidity. There was a danger of setting forth righteousness as a transaction between God and man, in which man also may acquire a credit balance, or at least be able to wipe out a debit. 'It is better to give alms than to lay up gold; alms doth deliver from death, and it shall purge away all sin.'[2] But the higher view is found: in the same book is the negative side of the Golden Rule, 'What thou thyself hatest, do to no man.'[3] The highest point is reached in the Testaments of the Twelve Patriarchs, which appears to have exerted a greater influence on the mind of Jesus than any other book. It especially commends single-mindedness, denoting by that term a state in which the whole nature is filled with light, and anticipating the teaching of our Lord on the value of the motive in estimating the act, and on the need for inwardness in the moral life.

We may sum up the Old Testament and later Judaistic ideas as to the perfection towards which man ought to strive thus. (1) No man can live the perfect life except in immediate

[1] Ecclus. xxxviii. 24 ff.   [2] Tobit xii. 8.   [3] Tobit iv. 15.

and continual communion with God. The ideal life was epitomized in the account of Enoch. (2) Stress, however, came to be laid, in the Priestly Code and in such writings as Jubilees, on the observance of the ceremonial law. Hence arose the Pharisaic conception of holiness. (3) It must in justice be added that the ethical ideal gained prominence as well. The ethicizing of the concept of Yahweh went side by side with the ethicizing of the perfection which men might attain through Him. (4) It became clear to the best minds that the early ideal must not be overlaid, but rather enriched by the details of the law. Man could still only reach the goal by an inward communion with God, which would necessarily express itself towards Him by the outward sign of adoring love, and towards one's fellows by the fulfilment of the moral law. 'Love the Lord through all your life, and one another with a true heart.'[1]

4. THE IDEA OF A PERFECT MEDIATOR

As a result of the sense of the Divine Perfection, and of human frailty, the idea of a Mediator became more and more prominent. He might be thought of as prophet, priest, or king.[2] He was a prophet when he mediated God's message to man : he was a priest when he mediated man's approach to God. The king also, in what was always imagined ideally as a theocracy, had a spiritual status. Two difficulties were felt. One was that the claims of the different authorities were often in opposition or in rivalry. The other was that it often became obvious that their claims had no basis in reality. How low the prophetic order might fall is seen in Zech. xiii. 3, where a man's own parents are bidden to thrust through anyone who professes to be a prophet, and wears a hairy mantle to deceive. This decadence was shared by the priesthood and the kingship, and often more evidently, since these orders were fixed and regular, and in more danger of becoming formal and insincere.

This failure led to a longing for the perfect Mediator, the Messiah, the One anointed to fulfil the mediation between God and man. How vague this longing was, how easily it was perverted, what confusions arose between the desires

[1] Test. Dan. v. 3.   [2] Test. Levi viii. 14, 15.

of the moment and the needs of eternity, all this is manifest in any study of the Messianic Hope. Its importance for us lies in the way in which it prepared for the Advent of the Christ. We have already seen how intense was the conviction in Israel of the ineffable perfections of God : if man were to be brought into communion with Him, it must be through one who could speak both to God and man. The following fairly distinct lines of thought may be traced.

(1) *The Perfect Prophet*

It might be conceived that God, who had spoken by divers portions and in divers manners, might speak with a fullness and clearness, which would make a prophetic revelation that might be called perfect. We may ponder such significant phrases as those of the Angel, the Face or Presence, the Glory, and the Name of Yahweh. Very instructive is the account of Hagar in Gen. xvi. (J) and xxi. (E). The Angel of Yahweh saved her, and she called the name of the theophany, El Roi, a God that seeth. Other passages to study are : Exod. xxxiii., Isa. vi., xl. 5, lx. 2 ; Ezek. i., xi. 23, xlviii. 35. From these we gain some idea of the Presence and the Glory ; in Isaiah its abode was in the temple ; in the exilic and post-exilic prophets it was imaged as having left the temple, but as returning. The prophets used these terms as a theologoumenon (a theological formula) to explain the location of the One whom they had fully realized as filling the heavens and the earth. The Presence was often portrayed under human similitudes. Hence arose the conception of the Son of Man, destined to exercise so great an influence on our Lord's utterances. In Daniel He was depicted as the representative of the ideal of humanity, the people of the saints of the Most High. In the Similitudes of Enoch He was invested with superhuman authority : He was the judge of the world and the revealer of all things ; He was also the Messianic champion and the ruler of the righteous. A further development was made by Philo, who has an elaborate doctrine of mediation. The Word of God was the sum of those intermediary powers which proceed from God. There is a great controversy as to the personality of the Logos in Philo ; but there can be no question that he never thinks of an actual human being. It was reserved for the New Testament, in the Synoptic account of the Son of Man, and in the Johannine vision of the Incarnate Word, to make that supreme discovery.

(2) *The Perfect Priest*

From another view-point the offerings and prayers in which man uttered his yearnings towards God might be thought of as presented through a priest on whom rested fully the sign of the Divine approval. The perfect prophet, while he might be human, must necessarily be more than man; but for the priest the one essential was his complete humanity. His true ordination consisted in the fact that he was able to speak with authority as the representative of the people. That the priestly office was conceived as representative is seen from the account of the ideal judgement of Joshua the high-priest in Zech. iii. The true priest must also have something to offer. The first name for consecration was 'filling the hands,'[1] i.e. putting something in the hand for an offering. Man requires a sin-offering to present to his God through his priest. The most elevated expression of this in the Old Testament is in the fourth Servant Song, Isa. lii. 13–liii. The other songs speak of the Servant as proclaiming God's Evangel to mankind, and accomplishing His mission of healing and salvation. But the fourth deals entirely with the Servant's offering to Yahweh. The principle of vicarious suffering is not merely accepted, it is regarded as the ground of our peace and healing. What necessity for this exists within the Divine righteousness and holiness, the prophet can only dimly discern. But it does appear that the Mediator has made, and is making, a perfect offering to God on behalf of humanity. This underlies all vital theories of Christian attainment. The practical aspect is in the fellowship which seekers after perfection strive to attain with that vicarious offering.

(3) *The Ideal King*

A third form which the Messianic Hope took was that of imagining that the theocratic ideal might find a perfect exponent. Josephus gave us the word: 'Moses set forth our

---

[1] Judges xvii. 12.

national polity as a *theocracy*, referring the rule and might to God.'[1] But the thought is implicit in the history of Israel. The historians indeed took opposite views as to the relation of the kingship to the ideal. To some it seemed like a repudiation of the theocracy. Thus Gideon refused to establish a dynasty; and Samuel rebuked the tribes for desiring a monarch. But others considered that the form of government does not affect the question of a theocracy, and that the human monarch was rather to be regarded as the vicegerent of the Divine. It was through those who held this view that spiritual advance was made. The king received his authority direct from God in his chrism; and the phrase ' Yahweh's anointed ' invariably refers to him. Ps. ii. speaks of the futility of rebellion; and in Ps. cx. Yahweh is pictured as acting with such power that the king is almost passive, sitting to await the victory; but this only expresses vividly how the Lord is always at his right hand. In such a king is fulfilled the ideal of a priest-king, foreshadowed in Melchizedek. Hebrew thought naturally dwelt on the dynasty rather than the individual, as, for instance, in Ps. lxxii. The king was further regarded as representative of the secular authority of Yahweh over the nations, and as the embodiment of the secular prosperity of the people of God. Thus Ecclus. xliv. 21 adds to the promise given to the seed of Abraham a verse from Ps. lxxii. descriptive of the king's dominion: ' He will cause them to inherit from sea to sea, and from the River unto the utmost part of the earth.'

In the Testaments, especially Levi and Reuben, the Messiah was definitely proclaimed as prophet and priest and king, and his descent was traced from Levi. This had great influence, particularly in the heroic days of the first Maccabaeans. It was Simon, the second son of Mattathias, who founded the high priestly dynasty of the Hasmoneans. There is a glowing eulogy of his rule, when many thought that the Messiah was indeed come, in 1 Macc. xiv. 4–15. But the glory faded away. There was some hope that it might bloom again in Mariamne, until it was cut off by the ruthless hand of Herod. But this idea of a Messianic priest-king greatly influenced the mind of Jesus. It lay behind one of His keenest temptations. To resist the shadowy crown, pressed upon Him by the popular voice, and

[1] *C. Ap.* ii. 16.

to hold fast to the eternal reality, was not the least of His spiritual victories.

(4) *The Ideal Environment*

In modern thought the environment tends to bulk more and more. We think less of one outstanding leader, and more of the whole people and the conditions of life. The natural tendency is to locate the ideal environment in this world which we know so well. In the early Jewish conceptions of the Messianic kingdom there is no thought of anything more than a happier life, perhaps a somewhat lengthened life, under conditions similar to the present. For a time such a view is sufficient. Yet even as regards this present life it cannot pass unchallenged. To this challenge there came as an answer the idea of a Day of Yahweh, a Day in which He would vindicate Himself in righteousness and judgement. A further development is found in Isa. lxv. 17 and lxvi. 22, which foretell a new heaven and a new earth. This is not intended to indicate a radical change in the conditions of life : only there will be no infant mortality, and men will normally fill out a tale of a hundred years. Later Judaism extended the idea. Sometimes the Messianic kingdom was conceived as enduring for a fixed period, a millennium in 2 Enoch, 400 years in 4 Ezra. In the latter book it was definitely stated that the world would return to the old silence, and that after seven days there would be a restoration from the dust and from the secret chambers[1] to eternal judgement. In Jubilees and 2 Baruch there is also the expectation of a temporary kingdom : in Jubilees it comes gradually in contrast to the usual anticipation of a catastrophic advent. In most of these writings this better time is not in any way final : it is a stage preceding the judgement, and without any clear ethical interest. By some, however, it was imaged as lasting, without end, on earth : as, for instance, in the Testaments, in most of the sections of 1 Enoch, and probably in chapters xvii. and xviii. of the Psalms of Solomon. In the Similitudes there is an interesting and valuable thought, taken from Isa. lxvi, and expanded, that the earth will be renovated, and made fit for an eternal habitation. But it must be noted that ' for ever ' in 1 Enoch is frequently used for a limited time.[2] It must also be noted that another line

---

[1] Cf. Isa. xxvi. 20.   [2] Leckie, *The World to Come*, p. 350.

altogether was taken by those who were convinced of the immortality of the soul alone, and who looked for a purely spiritual blessing.[1]

One difficulty was at once felt : is the perfect environment for the individual, or for the race ? The first idea was that the righteous of old, or at any rate the outstandingly righteous, might be raised to share in the blessedness of Israel. The crudeness of this was soon discerned. Our whole earthly life is inimical to perfection : ' everything that grows stays in perfection but a little moment.'[2] Hence we get the idea of a renovated earth in Isa. lxvi, in the Similitudes, and in the Apocalypse. Though this solution meets the difficulty logically, it is very artificial. Dr. Charles says that the true synthesis is in Christianity; and he is no doubt right. But it is a synthesis which is far from being made clear even yet. Most Christians believe in the perfecting of the individual : the Protestant often conceives that it will be accomplished in some mysterious way at death, while the Catholic believes it will be through the fires of Purgatory. *But we have still to face the question which Judaism left unsettled, how to relate such perfection to that racial perfection which our idealism demands.* Moreover, when we think of the social consummation, we waver between the ideals expressed in the words, The Church and The Kingdom. But these problems had already been indicated in the teaching amid which Jesus grew up and lived ; and we have confidence that in Him, and in His Spirit, the solution is being found.

5. SUMMARY

(1) There are words and phrases in the Old Testament to denote perfection. They are often used negatively of the making a complete end of anything. But they are often used positively of the accomplishment of a Divine Purpose, especially in the characters of men.

(2) The great advance made by Hebrew and Jewish thought was in the knowledge of the perfection of God. It is impossible to over-rate the importance of this for our subject. *We are discussing, it cannot be too emphatically said, not the production of a perfect man, but union with the perfection of God.* The strong ethical bent of the prophets made them insist on holiness

---

[1] Cf. Wisdom, ii. 21–iii. 9. [2] Shakespeare, *Sonnet* xv.

and righteousness as the marks of His Perfection. His dominion also was continually extended, till it embraced the whole earth, the hosts of heaven, and even the uncharted deep of Sheol. This extensive movement was ethical too, since, when fully thought out, it meant the absolute sovereignty of love.

(3) The perfection towards which man ought to strive was regarded as derivative. It came from walking with God, and could only be retained by a ceaseless communication of His Spirit. It was ethical rather than ceremonial, and in the highest and best, in Deuteronomy and Leviticus and the Testaments, it attained to the expression of love towards God and man, on which Jesus has set His seal.

(4) The longing for a perfect Mediator comes from the deepest within us. Such a mediator would be (1) a messenger from God, a prophet but with supernatural endowments, seeing that He would declare the inner meaning of God; (2) a priest, having the right to represent humanity, and to present its prayers and offerings to God; (3) a king, embodying that theocracy, that Divine government, on which all our hopes rest; (4) one who exercised His authority in an ideal environment, in which all attainment might be made permanent, both for humanity and the individual. Many questions inevitably emerged. How, to take one, can the eternal happiness of the individual be combined with the eternal kingdom of Israel, to use the schematism of the Old Dispensation, or of the Church of Christ, to use that of the New? The answer to this question it is difficult for us even to imagine. But behind it lies an ideal hope, divinely inspired, and therefore assured of fulfilment.

Chapter IV

NEW TESTAMENT WAYS OF EXPRESSING PERFECTION

When we turn to the New Testament teaching concerning Evangelical Perfection we approach the heart of the subject. Indeed, we should never have ventured to use a term so liable to misapprehension, and needing such continual explanation, if we had not found it entrenched both in the terminology and in the thought of the New Testament. Modern criticism seeks to discover the meaning of the New Testament phraseology, not only from the Old Testament and the LXX, but also from later Judaistic teaching in the two centuries preceding, and in the century conterminous with, the writing of the New Testament, and from other influences, mainly Hellenic, in the time of Christ and His apostles. This does not depreciate the value and originality of New Testament teaching. We aim at ascertaining the exact sense in which the apostles used their words; and through this terminological exactitude we are enabled to transcend the letter, and to gain a higher appreciation of the spirit. The present chapter will be devoted to a brief study of the words and formulae by which the New Testament expresses the idea of perfection.

1. Words that Convey the Idea of Preparedness

The first word to note is one found only in 2 Tim. iii. 17, where it is said that the inspired Scripture has this profit—that it makes the man of God perfect or complete. This word, ἄρτιος, is derived from the adverbial root ἄρτι, which means 'exactly,' and which is used to denote the exact, present moment. The word as used here signifies the preparedness of one who is fully equipped, and has put on the whole armour.

EXPRESSING PERFECTION

While ἄρτιος itself is only found here, its compounds are of much importance. Ἐξαρτίζειν is found in the verse above-quoted with a word-play quite characteristic of St. Paul. The completeness of the man of God consists in his complete equipment for every good work. The other compound, καταρτίζειν with the nouns κατάρτισις and καταρτισμός, deserves careful attention. The verb is used of the repairing of the nets[1]: and this simple use enables us to understand the technical, theological content. It denotes mending, putting things to rights, so that they may be complete and useful. Once it is applied to the 'vessels of wrath' in that tremendous passage, Rom. ix.–xi., in which St. Paul grapples with the meaning of the Divine Purpose, and the reason for the mercy and the wrath of God. Some purpose there must be in the creation of the spiritual universe. 'By faith we perceive that the Aeons have been framed by the word of God.'[2] The argument of Heb. x. 5–10[3] is that this purpose is manifested in Christ, for whom a Body, historical and mystical, has been prepared. This mystical Body is described in Eph. iv. 1–16. It is one Body, and the Orders of the Church, like the Aeons of Creation, are framed together for the perfecting of the saints. The verb is used predominantly of the restoring grace, by which the Divine purpose of love finds its completion in those who are called to be saints. Sometimes it denotes the repairing of that which has been rent : 'Ye which are spiritual, restore such a one in the spirit of meekness.'[4] Sometimes it marks the fullness of the Divine operation, as in the glorious close of the Epistle to the Hebrews : 'The God of peace and harmony, who has already declared the victory of life and love in the resurrection of our Lord Jesus through an eternal covenant which has been sealed in blood, may He complete you in every good thing, until you have been brought into perfect harmony in yourselves and with one another, because your whole nature is filled with His will, which performs in us that which is well pleasing in His sight, through the same Jesus Christ, always through Him, to whom be the glory through all the aeons of eternity.' This perfection can never be selfish, for it consists in the harmony of one with another ; and its completeness is always in Christ.

---

[1] Matt. iv. 21 and Mark i. 19.
[2] Heb. xi. 3.
[3] Based on a curious reading in the LXX of Ps. xl.
[4] Gal. vi. 1.

2. Words That Convey the Idea of Wholeness or Completeness

The next word to consider is ὅλος, with such compounds as ὁλοκαύτωμα, the whole burnt-offering, ὁλοκληρία, ὁλόκληρος, and ὁλοτελής. These denote a completeness which takes in every part, one which is not only compatible with, but dependent on, variety in the parts. In the healing of the lame man at the Beautiful Gate it is said that faith in the Name had given to the man 'perfect soundness'[1]; i.e. in every part, notably, of course, in that part in which he had been impotent. In 1 Thess. v. 23, which speaks of entire sanctification, perfect health, the work of the God of peace Himself,[2] the apostle shows how it penetrates the whole nature, body, soul, and spirit, our physical form, our personal identity, and our eternal life.

Two of the Master's sayings have standard value in this connexion. In Matt. vi. 22 Christ pronounces that the way to obtain perfection, so that the whole body may be full of light, is to open the eye to the light, that it may stream in, and from within irradiate the whole. This is the only way of attainment. The illumination of one's nature comes, not by minute attention to the details of the law, but by the inward light. The other saying is that in which He set His seal on the old law in Deut. vi. 5 and Lev. xix. 18. In one place—Matt. xxii. 34–40—Jesus gives this as His own finding; in another—Luke x. 25–8—He elicits it by a question from the lawyer. It tells of an endeavour after unification. There is one God, and our devotion to Him should include the whole of our nature, moving under a central impulse.

3. Words That Convey the Idea of Fullness

We now turn to the root idea of 'filling up' in the verb πληροῦν, or its compound ἀναπληροῦν, with the adjective πλήρης and the noun πλήρωμα. The baskets filled with broken fragments after the feeding of the thousands, the waterpots filled with wine during the wedding in Cana—these are simple physical analogues, which form the basis of spiritual conceptions, expressed in the New Testament with much wealth of language.

---

[1] Acts iii. 16.   [2] Cf. Heb. xiii. 21.

OF EXPRESSING PERFECTION

It was natural for the apostles to be impressed by the way in which the word spoken through the prophets had been fulfilled. And they were convinced that there had been a fulfilment, not only of prophecy, but of the law. Gal. v. 14 and vi. 2 reveal the depth of St. Paul's conception of the true fulfilment of the law. He sums it up again in Rom. xiii. 8, 10 : 'He that loves the other (the altruist) hath fulfilled the law . . . love therefore is the fulfilment of the law.' In Rom. x. 4, using another word which we shall discuss later, he says: 'Christ is the end of the law unto righteousness unto every one that believeth.'

> I give you the end of a golden string:
> Only wind it into a ball;
> It will lead you in at Heaven's Gate,
> Built in Jerusalem's wall.

The New Testament is rich in ways of enunciating that wherewith the Christian is 'filled.' Christ Himself, at the very time when He was led into the wilderness to be tempted, was said to be 'full of the Holy Spirit.' The description in John i. 14, 18 of the Face of the Incarnate Word, God the Only-Begotten, declares that the appearance of the earthly tabernacle was 'full of grace and truth.' But all that is in Christ is for His own; 'for of His *fullness* we all received, and grace for grace.'[1] Indeed, similar words are used of the seven chosen for service, of Stephen in particular, and of Barnabas; they are men 'full of faith,' ' of grace,' ' of wisdom,' ' of power,' and ' of the Holy Spirit.' The form varies; but there is a clear idea of a Divine inpouring which fills the whole nature. An evangelical fullness is propounded, which in the Divine intention is not limited to a few, but is the heritage of all Christians. To the very Church which he had to warn against so gross a sin as intemperance, the apostle commends this fullness: 'Be not drunken with wine, wherein is riot, but be filled with the Spirit.'[2] In another place St. Paul speaks of bringing every thought into captivity to the obedience of Christ, and in so doing fulfilling our own obedience.[3] The conception, intensely ethical and spiritual, of the obedience of Christ and of our obedience in communion with Him, is of the utmost value for understanding the Way. This fullness seems

[1] John i. 16.   [2] Eph. v. 18.   [3] 2 Cor. x. 5, 6

always associated with joy. In the sublime assurance of the revelation of the Father in the Son, Jesus 'rejoiced in the Spirit'[1]; and there is a great Johannine view of the fulfilment of joy in prayer and fellowship.[2]

The noun *pleroma* is employed in a remarkable way in the New Testament. In one place it is used of the patch of undressed cloth added to fill out an old garment.[3] This is one of Jesus's homeliest illustrations; and it stands in contrast with the magnificent content given to the word in the mystical epistles to the Ephesians and the Colossians, and still more in the Gnostic systems, especially that of Valentinus. In his earlier letters St. Paul thinks of a Divine purpose which is being fulfilled, age after age, in the coming of the Son, and then in the filling up of the times of the Gentiles. In the later letters he still thinks of an economy of the fullness of the times[4]; but he relates the Divine Pleroma, which fills all in all, to Christ and to the Church. In Christ dwells all the fullness of the Godhead bodily; and by this body is designated the Church; for God has given Christ to be head over all things to the Church, which is His Body, the fullness of Him that filleth all in all.[5]

Two words are used to express evangelical assurance. One is πληροφορία, or, in the verbal form, πληροφορεῖν, found in St. Paul's letters, in Hebrews, and in the opening verse of St. Luke. It is not certain whether it means the fulfilment, the full development of anything, or the full assurance and certainty of it. It is used to describe the strong confidence of Abraham[6]; but for our subject the most significant passages are Col. ii. 2, iv. 12; and Heb. vi. 11, x. 22. St. Paul joins it with the understanding, and Hebrews with hope and faith. Perhaps we shall not be playing with words if we say that this full development, or this full assurance (the two thoughts blend), come to different people according to the variety of their religious experiences, and even in some measure according to their temperaments. The other word, much more common in the New Testament, is παρρησία. It may be used of frank, bold speech, as that of Peter and John before the elders.[7] But there is a noble use of it for that confidence before God,

---

[1] Luke x. 21; cf. Phil. ii. 2. [2] John xvi. 24 and 1 John i. 4.
[3] Matt. ix. 16 and Mark ii. 21. [4] Eph. i. 10.
[5] Eph. i. 22, 23; Col. i. 19 and ii. 9. [6] Rom. iv. 21. [7] Acts iv. 13.

and assurance even in the day of judgement, which comes to those in whom perfect love is casting out fear.[1]

4. WORDS THAT CONVEY THE IDEA OF ATTAINING AN END

The most important root for our subject is τέλος, an end ; from it are derived the verbs τελεῖν and τελειοῦν, the adjective τέλειος, and the nouns τελειότης, τελείωσις, τελειωτής. Three main ideas are associated with this group of words : (1) the idea of perfection as the accomplishment of an end, a purpose ; (2) the idea of maturity ; (3) the idea of full initiation into spiritual mysteries.

(1) The end is sometimes spoken of with a clear reference to the last things.[2] Several times, without such definite eschatology, praise is given to those who endure to the end. Some memorable passages speak of the end as the inevitable issue : for some their end is death or destruction or burning, for others eternal life.[3] A momentous phrase speaks of Christ as the end of the law.[4] Sanday and Headlam insist that this must mean that in Christ law is brought to an end as a method or principle for attaining righteousness. That τέλος, however, may include the idea of fulfilment of a purpose is manifest from 1 Tim. i. 5 ; and only a few chapters before[5] St. Paul had spoken of those whose end or goal was eternal life. I do not dispute that the point contended for in this phrase is that where Christ enters, the principle of ordinances is terminated ; but it is terminated simply because the object of ordinances has been reached in the lifting of the soul into the higher sphere by faith.

It is, of course, from the thought contained in this root that the teleological argument has been evolved. In its highest form it is stated as the evidence of a Divine purpose or will, with which ours has to be brought into harmony. In Matt. v. 48, which some look upon as the base of our whole doctrine, Jesus enjoins perfection, not only before the LORD our God, as in Deut. xviii. 13, but even of the same kind as that of our Heavenly Father. Again in Matt. xix. 21, a passage which has exercised incalculable influence in Christendom, the rich youth is bidden get rid of his possessions, because they were holding him back from perfect union with the Divine Will. In Luke

---

[1] 1 John ii. 28, iii. 21, iv. 17, v. 14.   [2] Mark xiii. 7 ; Rev. xx. 3, 5, 7.
[3] Rom. vi. 21 ; Phil. iii. 19 ; Heb. vi. 8.   [4] Rom. x. 4.   [5] Rom. vi. 22.

xiii. 32, Christ declares mystically that on the third day He is to be perfected ; and the same thought finds utterance in Heb. ii. 10, v. 9, vii. 28. It looks back to the phrase τελειοῦν τὰς χείρας, which the LXX employs in speaking of the installation of priests. The Divine purpose involved the necessity of a limited, progressive experience for the Son. In John v. 36 Jesus speaks of the works which the Father had given Him to do ; and in xvii. 4 He gives thanks for having accomplished them. Further on in the seventeenth chapter He prays that the same perfection which He enjoyed with the Father may be given to His disciples. Several verses in 1 John make mention of the love of God as being perfected, i.e. as finding its full realization in the disciples : the goal of the Divine Love is reached in the mutual love which binds the Church together in communion with God.

(2) Another thought is that of maturity. The adult, fitted for the life of the world, and able to exercise civic functions, represents the end towards which the child is growing. 1 Cor. xiii. 9–12 is instructive in this connexion. There is a crude stage, which passes away as the child passes into the man. Many have thought that the higher stage lies wholly beyond the grave. ' I trust to see my Pilot *face to face* when I have crossed the bar.' But the phrase, πρόσωπον πρὸς πρόσωπον, must echo the Old Testament, פָּנִים אֶל פָּנִים, which is used of the experiences of Jacob and Moses, for example, in this life. Moreover, in several places in St. Paul, and in one in Hebrews, a distinction is drawn between childish Christians and those who have attained maturity ; and stern condemnation is meted out to those who remained childish when they ought to have developed, and taken their share in the corporate life of the Church. They are carnal rather than spiritual,[1] and liable to be tossed about by every wind of doctrine[2] ; in the Galatian Church this had been sadly exemplified in what was practically an apostasy. What was needed was fuller teaching as to the way of perfection.[3] From this it certainly follows that perfection appertains to this present life. Faith, Hope, and Love are natives of earth as well as of heaven. The distinction between 'now' and 'then' is such as Plotinus draws between ' here ' and ' yonder.' Maturity cannot be the maturity of death. It is often suggested, as in *In Memoriam*,

[1] 1 Cor. iii. 1.   [2] Eph. iv. 14.   [3] Heb. v. 13 and vi. 1.

that death brings a spiritual ripeness, so that one comes to the grave like a shock of corn in its season. But this is contrary to New Testament teaching. Not to be in maturity, when it might normally be expected by reason of years, is one of the main causes of Christian failure.

(3) *Teleios* is also used to denote one who is fully initiated into the mysteries. Writers on Church History emphasize the effect of the Mysteries on Christian ritual, life, and doctrine. Forms of Stoicism, Orphism, Oriental cults, and something which may be called an earlier Gnosticism, combined in influencing the mind of St. Paul, and of the Church of his time.[1] That the Mystery Religions stirred intense antagonism in the Christian consciousness is plainly shown in Colossians. But the Christian is never content with a negation. While the leaders in the early Church definitely opposed the mystery cults, which seemed to them allied with daemonism, yet they were careful to point to ' the full assurance of understanding, that they may know the mystery of God, even Christ, in whom are all the treasures of wisdom and knowledge hidden.'[2]

---

[1] Kennedy, *St. Paul and the Mystery Religions*, p. 3.   [2] Col. ii. 2, 3.

CHAPTER V

THE NEW TESTAMENT DOCTRINE OF THE PERFECTION OF CHRIST

IN all study of evangelical attainment ' Christ is the end, for Christ is the beginning ; Christ the beginning, for the end is Christ.' No phenomenon in history can compare in human interest and in spiritual value with the Person and the Work of Christ ; and there is a special aspect in which the doctrines regarding Christ may be considered in relation to the attainment by His own of perfect union with the Father. The following divisions will be made : (1) The perfect revelation of God in Christ ; (2) the perfect obedience of Christ ; (3) the perfect priesthood of Christ ; (4) the perfect dynamic in Christ.

1. CHRIST AS THE PERFECT REVELATION OF GOD

A perfect revelation of God ! It is an amazing claim, which becomes more amazing with the amplifying of our thoughts of God. It is little wonder that many, even among those who desire to do Him honour, rule it out at once ; they cannot conceive that the idea of God should find full expression in any one person. A passage may be quoted from Schweitzer, which states the position of Strauss, with some Hegelian modifications. 'God-manhood, the highest idea conceived by human thought, is actually realized in the historic personality of Jesus. But, while conventional thought supposes that this phenomenal realization must be perfect, true thought, which has attained by genuine critical reasoning to a higher freedom, knows that no idea can realize itself perfectly on the historical plane, and that its truth does not depend on the proof of its having received external representation, but that its perfection comes about through that which the idea carries into history, or through the way in which

THE PERFECTION OF CHRIST 63

history is sublimated into idea.'[1] But in the closing chapter of *The Quest of the Historical Jesus*, which he calls appropriately 'Loss and Gain,' Schweitzer reveals the dissatisfaction which results from this method. ' There was a danger of our thrusting ourselves between men and the Gospels, and refusing to leave the individual man alone with the sayings of Jesus.'[2] This is a momentous conclusion. If the perfection of Christ be regarded as entirely due to man's capacity for idealization, it can never be a revelation of Divine perfection, and can therefore never be a means of leading man into communion with the Divine. We may be able to discern the sense in which it is possible to speak of a perfect revelation in Christ, if we glance at the ideas which underlie the Church's teaching concerning (1) the eternal Sonship; (2) the abiding relation of Jesus to the Church; (3) the Spirit of Jesus; (4) the manner in which He faced the fact of sin.

(1) The earnestness with which the Church insisted on the eternal Sonship sprang from some apprehension of the philosophical objection to the perfection of Christ which Strauss expressed so trenchantly. If we think of the existence of Christ as limited to the days of His flesh, and of His revelation of God as contained within His earthly ministry, we must acknowledge that such a revelation cannot be perfect. To say that God was in Christ fully revealing Himself is to ascribe to Christ an eternal existence. The process of God's self-communication to humanity is through the Word, which has found an utterance in time in Jesus of Nazareth. Such a statement is quite consistent with a philosophical view of the gradual unfolding of the knowledge of God in an endless process, provided the Christian concept be accepted of the continuous life of the Eternal Son.

(2) The full perfection of the Divine revelation in Christ is bound up with the perfection of the Church. It is a thoroughly New Testament idea that the revelation, whereby God is reconciling the world unto Himself, finds in the Church its completeness. We shall have occasion to note later that the individual perfection of the believer can never be rightly attained except in society. In Green's *Prolegomena to Ethics*,[3] he shows that, if moral goodness is devoted to a moral ideal, and if the idea of this end is a Divine principle of improvement

---

[1] *The Quest of the Historical Jesus*, p. 79.   [2] Op. cit., p. 398.   [3] Bk. iii., chap. 2.

in men, then this can only be realized in the progress of humanity towards a perfect society. This is true even of the Christ. The impoverishment of Christ was for the enriching of the Church; that impoverishment was needed in order to reveal through the Church the unsearchable riches of Christ; and that revelation was needed in order to show what was the glory of His inheritance in the saints.[1]

(3) The revelation in Christ, if it is to be perfect, must be such that we are able to discern the Spirit of it apart from the accidents of the time. The Epistle to the Hebrews makes a great effort to disclose this in the phrase: 'Jesus Christ is the same yesterday and to-day, yea and for ever.'[2] Yesterday speaks of the recent mortal life of Jesus, To-day of the conditions under which writer and readers were living and in which they realized the Lord's presence, for Ever of the eternal Being of the Son of God. The thought of God as binding the generations together, and constituting in Himself the perfect environment, had already found utterance in the Old Testament.[3] This thought became prominent in the New Testament: 'I in them, and Thou in me, that they may be perfected into one.'[4] Some earthly habitation is needed; but the true spiritual environment, which alone gives security, is the Love of God.[5] The fashion of this world passeth away. There were advantages about the epoch into which Christ was born which entitled it to be called the fullness of the time; but each era has its peculiar claims; and we can only recognize the perfection of the revelation in Jesus of Nazareth if we discern the Spirit revealed in the details of His life.

(4) A perfect revelation must face the fact of sin. Modern thought, harking back to ways already traversed by the Ophites and Cainites of early Gnosticism, endorses this. Evil appears necessary for the world's progress. The measure of truth in such a view is confirmed by the Cross. That Christ in some way became sin, in the sense that He understood the power of it and felt its attraction at the very time that His whole nature turned away in horror from it, is definitely stated in 2 Cor. v. 21. The absolute sinlessness of Jesus is declared in the New Testament, as Ullmann so beautifully shows. But it is a sinlessness which is associated with the closest

---

[1] Eph. i. 18. [2] Heb. xiii. 8. [3] Ps. lxxi. 1, 3, xc. 1.
[4] John xvii. 23. [5] 1 Pet. v. 10.

OF THE PERFECTION OF CHRIST

possible contact with sin. Schleiermacher, who insisted on the sinlessness, denied the reality of the temptation. But if it were necessary to choose, one would rather accept the suggestion of Irving that the manhood of Jesus included the natural bias to sin, but that it was 'held like a fortress in immaculate purity by the Godhead within.'[1] But we are not shut up to this dilemma. The nature of Christ was pure altogether; but it was a purity which entered into the meaning of sin, and understood the strength of its appeal. A suggestion is thrown out by Dr. Lidgett, to whom I am much indebted in this discussion, that 'The filial spirit, which we have seen to be the distinctive characteristic of His life, was affirmed, and therefore made doubly His own, under the experience of a real temptation.'[2] There must be some value in temptation and suffering. Even Christ learnt by experience. Whatever value for perfection lies in temptation and suffering He garnered. The intensity of His rejection of sin brought with it such an understanding of its attractiveness as to lift Him into a state of sympathy which is only possible to the purity which has surveyed and overcome sin. The true Shekinah is man; and it appears that the experience of man's life is requisite for the fullness of the Godhead. The Divine Kenosis, the self-emptying which was indispensable for the full realization of Deity, involved the closest contact with sin, but it involved it by way of intense and victorious opposition. The intuitions of the spirit lead us to ascribe to Christ the absolute goodness of God. But Scripture dwells on His proximity to sin in all the forms which it took in a world of sinful men.[3] How close that was the cry of the Forsaken on the cross finally revealed. The supreme discovery, which the Resurrection brought to light, was that this close interaction with sin brought to humanity salvation from sin; for in it God revealed His love.[4]

Christ has revealed to us the Heavenly Father—'My Father and your Father, and My God and your God'[5]—with all fullness 'His conception of God was loftier, more tender, more human than even that of the poets of Israel.'[6] He not only taught; His teaching and His life were one, and cannot be separated.

---
[1] Mackintosh, *Person of Christ*, p. 277.
[2] *Spiritual Principle of the Atonement*, p. 343.
[3] John i. 5; 2 Cor. v. 21; Heb. iv. 15.   [4] Rom. i. 4 and v. 8.
[5] John xx. 17.   [6] Gardner, *Explor. Evan.*, p. 185.

The portrait which we have of Him refuses to be placed in any category of religious genius or moral hero. At the same time it possesses that essential unity which belongs only to reality. But to affirm that the revelation of God in Christ is a reality in the highest sense of the word is equivalent, seeing that it is a revelation of God, to an affirmation of its perfection.

2. THE PERFECT OBEDIENCE OF CHRIST

The term 'obedience' is much to be preferred to 'sinlessness.' Ullmann draws out the implications, historical, religious, and theological, of the sinlessness of Jesus; but it is evident, though he has given so much prominence to the term, that he is thinking of something far more positive than mere absence of sin. The term 'obedience' is scriptural, ethical, positive. This obedience is from eternity to eternity; but we think of it primarily as manifested during His sojourn on earth. An attempt has been made to divide it into active and passive—the obedience which He offered during His life, particularly during His active ministry, and the obedience which He offered in death from the time when He surrendered Himself and became passive in the hands of others. Such a distinction is suggested in regard to St. Peter in John xxi. 18-19. It was applied to Christ Himself by Anselm, and elaborated as the centre of his system. The obedience of His life was due from Christ, inasmuch as He was man. But death, inasmuch as He was sinless, was not due; it was therefore something over, an offering, and that of infinite value, which made atonement for the sins of men. The Reformers gave a different turn to the argument. Christ by His passive submission to death satisfied the wrath of God against sin; by His life of willing obedience He displayed a righteousness which was a true energy, whose effect has been felt on all the redeemed.

The New Testament knows nothing of such a distinction; and in this respect its psychology is better than either Anselm's or the Reformers'. In the *Formula Concordiae* it is explicitly stated that 'God, on account of the *whole obedience* of Christ, which Christ *by doing and suffering, in His life and death*, presented to His Heavenly Father on our behalf, gives to us remission of sins, accounts us as just and good, and bestows on us eternal salvation.'[1] To this statement in itself no exception need be taken; but grave errors arose from the dividing, even in thought, of the seamless robe of Christ's obedience. The righteousness of Christ was conceived as imputed to the sinner, laid upon him as a covering garment; and a distinction was made between justification and sanctification. The new redeemed life (*vivicatio et justificatio*) was made to consist in being redeemed without merit, in the non-imputation of sin, and in the imputation of righteousness. Luther himself was not free from this tendency. His bold and confident disposition led him to regard perfection as consisting in the full assurance of the imputation of the righteousness of Christ. ' What enabled Luther to carry beyond themselves, and to bring to finality, all the Reform movements of the Middle Ages, was that he had found what they sought, and was able to express what he experienced: the equivalence of certainty of salvation and faith.'[2]

In the New Testament salvation from beginning to end is through Christ alone. But, just as there are general philosophic objections to a perfect revelation in Christ, so also accusations have been brought against specific actions of His. Most works on the Person of Christ discuss these charges.[3] In some cases, where we are inclined to censure, we are restrained by critical considerations; this or that may be the touch of a disciple mistakenly thinking to add to the Master's glory. Another restraining thought is that He has been so often approved in the very things in which men were ready to judge Him. The supreme instance is in His attitude to the Cross. The difficulty which faced St. Peter is widely felt.[4] Yet it must be apparent that the dynamic of Christianity has come from the decision to go to Jerusalem. We agree that the journey was a pilgrimage towards death, and not primarily for the evangelization of the city[5]; and we agree that the Church has always condemned those who, like Agathonike, have thrust themselves on martyrdom. But the narratives describe Jesus as striving to avoid the issue of death, while convinced that His course must lead to it. The Son of God, who was also the Son of Man, moved forward to a crowning

---

[1] *Form. Conc.*, p. 684.   [2] Harnack, *History of Dogma*, vii. 209.
[3] E.g. Mackintosh, pp. 35-8, and Forrest, *The Christ of History and Experience*.
[4] Matt. xvi. 22.   [5] Schweitzer, p. 389.

act of obedience, which was at once a passive submission to the malice of men and an expression of the wrath of God against that malice; so that from one aspect He was made sin, being sent in the likeness of sinful flesh as an offering for sin; from another He condemned sin, pronounced that absolute condemnation of it which through all the ages breaks down every attempt to make light of its guilt and horror. This experimental obedience of Christ in face of sin has a unique and eternal value for the Christian. A new thought is brought in, that perfection is attained by entering into fellowship with the experimental obedience of Christ, even in the endurance of the Cross.

It is not to be supposed that Christ's obedience ended with the Resurrection. In the New Testament He is represented as seated in glory. But before that Session He went forth to proclaim the Gospel to the spirits in prison. It is difficult to think that this going forth was only once, immediately after death, though that was the conception in the primitive Church. The teaching of the Descent into Hades is plain in 1 Pet. iii. 19-22 and iv. 5-6, and probable in Eph. iv. 9-10. 'This conclusion is, indeed, the only one that can explain the widespread belief regarding this matter which existed in the early Church. Polycarp, Ignatius, Hermas, Justin Martyr, Irenaeus, Tertullian, Clement of Alexandria, Origen, Hippolytus, all refer with more or less emphasis to the Mission of Christ to departed souls.'[1] Dr. Charles also assigns the utmost value to these passages. 'They attest the achievement of the all but final stage in the moralization of Hades.'[2] From other places we see that Christ, even after the Ascension, still turns to earth, as in the martyrdom of Stephen, the conversion of Saul, and the apocalyptic appearance in Patmos; and there is a body of teaching in the New Testament as to the Parousia or future Advent. Gardner, in his discussion of the Descent and the Second Advent, altogether spiritualizes them, and in so doing expresses, I suppose, the common view among cultured Christians.[3] But it may safely be said that in one form or another these ideas, which were embodied in the early creeds, have remained part of the permanent heritage of the Church. They bear witness to a belief in the continued interest of the

[1] Leckie, *The World to Come*, p. 91. [2] *Eschatology*, p. 436.
[3] *Explor. Evan.*, Bk. II., chaps. 21-22.

Son of God in the world which He came to redeem. There is a vista, in 1 Cor. xv. 24-8, of a future submission of Christ in the full surrender of all the rule and authority and power which had been subjected unto Himself. This may be called the End, if we give to that word its full eschatological significance. This ultimate obedience is not limited to His personal submission; for it includes all that rule and authority and power which He has won over to Himself by the spirit of love. The obedience of Christ needs to be perfected in the humanity which He has redeemed. His joy will not have attained full perfection until the consummation of all in the blissful surrender of the whole redeemed humanity to God. The true novelty of the Gospel, as Irenaeus rightly saw, was in the Person and Work of Christ.[1] That New Thing which He brought in, in bringing in Himself, is new with the newness of eternity. His obedience is still, and for ever, finding fresh outlets.

3. THE PERFECT PRIESTHOOD OF CHRIST

The New Testament view of Christ is of One risen, ascended, and seated at the right hand of God. This last phrase proclaims His resumption of the Divine Glory. It is a translation of a phrase in Ps. cx., and is no more to be taken literally by the Christian than by the Jew. It denotes sovereignty, majesty, unique dignity, and honour for one who has accomplished His work. The Session does not imply inactivity, but pre-eminent occupation as King and Priest. Whatever perfection the Christian may strive towards depends on the eternal Session of Christ in these offices. This is the theme of the Epistle to the Hebrews; but it is not only there that this continued activity of Christ is referred to as a source of blessing to mankind. The description of the Son of Man in the midst of the golden candlesticks is that of a king who is also a priest. He is clothed with the high-priestly robe, girt up at the breasts, to show that He is exercising His office.[2]

The author of Hebrews wished to refer to the work of Christ in Heaven under the symbolism of the ritual of the Day of

---

[1] *Adv. Haer.*, iv. 34 : ' Omne novitatem attulit semetipsum afferens.'
[2] Cf. Ecclus. l. 11.

Atonement. He needed, therefore, to speak of Christ, not only as 'priest,' but as 'high-priest,' while at the same time he wanted to break away from the political, Sadducean conception of the office. This he found a way to do through the mysterious figure of Melchizedek in Gen. xiv. and Ps. cx. In Philo, Melchizedek is the true reason, which by its educative work illuminates the soul with the knowledge of God. But in Hebrews he is a real person, who is a type of Christ, even as David was. His name, King of Righteousness, King of Salem, the city of the God of peace, suggests the nature of His person and office. In a Session of perfect glory Christ exercises His functions according to the order of Melchizedek, overpassing the limitations which are inseparable from kingship and priesthood on earth. But the kingship is not even yet in full authority; 'we see not yet all things put under His feet.' It is rather as priest that He is presented to us. His spiritual activity, so far as it relates to our welfare, has a threefold direction: (1) by way of propitiation; (2) by way of intercession; (3) by way of benediction.

(1) *Propitiation*

Griffith Thomas, with whom Westcott agrees, declares that we are to think of an offering made once for all, and of the Blood as a means of access.[1] Yet there is much to be said for Milligan's contention that, though the sacrifice was made once for all in the earthly life and death, there is needed a continual presentation of it in a propitiatory offering. The essence of priesthood is to make an offering[2]; what is offered is a love which bears for ever the experiences of earth[3].

> Thy offering still continues new;
> Thy vesture keeps its crimson hue;
> Thou standst the ever-slaughtered lamb;
> Thy priesthood still remains the same.

After all, if there was need of propitiation, that need has not ceased. Some will deny that there has ever been any need: God has always looked on man with favour. But it is clear that such is not the view of Hebrews[4]; and if we turn to Rom. iii. 25 and 1 John ii. 2 and iv. 10 we perceive that St. Paul

---

[1] *H. D. C.*, ii. 417*b*. Cf. Westcott on Heb. viii. 2, p. 230. [3] Heb. viii. 3.
[2] Moberly, *Ministerial Priesthood*, pp. 244–9. [4] e.g. ii. 17.

and St. John agree with Hebrews that, in spite of the abiding love of God, there is something in man which hinders the grace of God from being shown him. Surely they are right, and surely that hindrance remains. Therefore there is need of a high-priest still, who must show by His offering how great is the sacrifice of which humanity is capable.

(2) *The Intercession*

Westcott considers this the principal part of Christ's present work. It includes, not only praying for men as their representative,[1] but also bringing the prayers and praises of the people to God.[2] The presence of our Lord in Heaven opens the floodgates of Divine Grace. 'We are to understand " Intercession " of every act by which the Son, in dependence on the Father, in the Father's Name, and with the perfect concurrence of the Father, takes His own with Him into the Father's presence, in order that whatever He Himself enjoys in the communications of His Father's love may become also theirs.'[3] We must widen the content of the term ' Intercession ' to cover the securing to the redeemed of access to the privileges of Heaven. Prayer is, of course, included ; but it is such as we find in John xvii., which may be taken as the type of the Eternal Intercession.

(3) *The Benediction*

The work of Christ in Heaven is undivided, except as a concession to human thought. The propitiatory offering, the perpetual intercession, the crowning blessing, are one service of Him who is the surety of the better covenant. From the blessing there ensue peace and prosperity. His Benediction is no mere pronouncement ; virtue goes out of Him. In the Propitiation and the Intercession we think of Him as turning towards God on our behalf ; in the Benediction He turns towards us, and pours upon us the blessing of His Spirit. Thus we think of Christ in His Heavenly Perfection, and thus we are led to understand how that Perfection avails for us. It has come through the experience of His mortal life. He learnt obedience through suffering, and thus became equipped for His saving work. We have next to consider the power which has gone out from Him in blessing.

[1] Heb. vii. 25, 27, ix. 24.   [2] Heb. xiii. 15.   [3] Milligan, *The Ascension*, p. 152.

4. The Perfect Dynamic in Christ

In the endeavour to represent to our thought what is meant by the Holy Spirit, there is always a tendency to modalistic monarchianism, i.e. the representation of God as One Principle operating in various, sometimes successive, ways, But Origen was right in stating that, while the Platonists have attained by the light of nature to a knowledge of the Father, and even of the Son, the belief in the distinct personality of the Holy Ghost is the prerogative of Christianity. The kingdom of the Father is over all; the kingdom of the Son is over all rational creation; but the kingdom of the Spirit is in the sanctified. If the last kingdom is the least in extent, it may be said that it is the highest in thought. We find in Scripture a distinction between the work of the Spirit (1) before the Incarnation, (2) in Jesus the Christ, (3) proceeding from the glorified Christ. This division reveals how important for the operation of the Spirit was the earthly life of the Son.

(1) In the Old Testament the Spirit is regarded as the source of all life and energy. It brooded over the initial chaos, as the wind broods over the deep, or a bird over her nest; and all forms of organization have come from its impact.[1] The phrase Holy Spirit is, indeed, only used twice, in Ps. li. 11 and Isa. lxiii. 10, 11. But it is recognized, especially in the later books, that the highest work of the Spirit is in the inspiration of those who are moved to enunciate the moral truths about God; best of all in the chosen Servant of Yahweh, of whom it is said, ' I have put My Spirit upon Him.'

(2) The action of the Spirit on the Son·of Man is that of a master-power. Jesus declared that the Divine anger was far more deeply roused by blasphemy against the Holy Spirit than by blasphemy against the Son of Man.[2] This passage witnesses to the reverence and awe with which Christ spoke of the Spirit; but it also witnesses to His consciousness that the Spirit was in Him with a fullness which made blasphemy against His Spirit blasphemy against the Spirit of God. Hence Christ spoke with a sense of mastery through His unbroken communion and obedience. Because He wholly obeyed the Spirit's guiding, He obtained authority to send forth the same

---

[1] Dan. vii. 2, 3.   [2] Matt. xii. 31-2, &c.

OF THE PERFECTION OF CHRIST

Spirit. This is the theme of John xiv.–xvi. There we have the clearest statement of the Spirit's personality: He is the Paraclete who will fulfil the mission of the Son of Man. *The authority and mastery of Christ came through His human life; hence the Spirit Himself has been transformed through the humanity of Jesus.* This is the meaning of phrases which speak of the way in which the Spirit was limited, in which Christ Himself was straitened, until the full human obedience had been accomplished.[1]

The subject of the Evangel is not the Spirit, but Christ; it was the capital error of Montanism not to discern this. But the dispensation of the Spirit has definite advantages. The bournes of time and space are transcended. Only of the Spirit is it possible to attach any meaning to the word of Jesus, 'Wherever two or three are gathered together in My name, there am I in the midst.' Only in the Spirit is it possible for Him to promise to all His disciples that He will come again and receive them unto Himself. The explanation of Christ's dealing with the Syro-Phoenician woman is that He was bound by certain limitations; what He gave her had to be taken from those who had a prior claim. But for the Spirit there are no bonds.

In the early Church there was much confusion, some, notably Justin, identifying the Spirit with the Logos. It is suggested that the confusion originated in St. Paul, particularly in 2 Cor. iii. 17, ' Now the Lord is the Spirit.' The apostle, however, is not making an ontological identification of Christ and the Spirit, but is declaring that in Christ is embodied and revealed the Spirit of the New Covenant. The context shows that Christ, who is the Image of God, and in whose Face is the illumination of the knowledge of the glory of God, is the source from which comes all hope of perfection. The Holy Spirit wrought so deeply in Christ, and Christ so fully surrendered Himself to His direction, that no separation can be made. The fruit of that blissful union is seen in lordship, in sonship, in liberty, and in joy. There is a saying in which Jesus gave utterance to His sense of Lordship and Sonship, a saying which has this additional importance—that it adds the witness of Q to the validity of the Johannine interpretation of the consciousness of Jesus.[2] To that saying St. Luke adds a

[1] Luke xii. 50.   [2] Matt. xi. 25–7; Luke x. 21–2.

comment of true spiritual insight : ' In that same hour He rejoiced in the Holy Spirit.'

(3) From the conception of the worth of the experience of Jesus on earth for the work of the Spirit, the Evangel leads on to the revelation of the Holy Spirit as proceeding from the glorified Christ.[1] Before the Incarnation the Spirit entered into man owing to that essential likeness which Westcott calls the Gospel of Creation ; but all was fitful and uncertain. During the days of His flesh, and until He entered into His glory, the work of the Spirit was still ' cribb'd, cabin'd, and confin'd.' The classical passage is John vii. 37-9 : ' This spake He of the Spirit : . . . for the Spirit was not yet given; because Jesus was not yet glorified.'

The Targums used the term Glory as almost equivalent to the Shekinah, the manifestation of God's dwelling among men. In Rom. ix. 4 the apostle enumerates the Glory, the Shekinah, among the privileges of Israel. Heb. i. 3 speaks of the Son as the effulgence of the Glory. In a similar prologue to the Fourth Gospel it is said : ' The Word became flesh, and dwelt among us, and we beheld His Glory.' The fulfilment of the glory anticipated in the Incarnation is the office of the Spirit ; it is, therefore, essentially ethical. For those living under mortal conditions it is necessary that the full Glory should be veiled, and only revealed normally in the Church. In John xvii. the first few verses deal with the way in which the Son had glorified the Father, and His prayer that the Father should glorify Him. In vv. 22, 23 He speaks of the glory of the Church, when it has been perfected into one through the indwelling of the spirit of Divine Love. Life in the Spirit is already full of glory. Those whom He foreordained and called and justified, them He also glorified. Two limitations are inevitable—one from the conditions of our present life, the other from the fact that the glory is communal, and awaits the perfecting of the community. The apostles speak of a glory, and even a salvation, still to be revealed.[2]

The presence of the Spirit glorifying Christ brings with it a new sense of sin and imperfection. Yet (the paradox runs through our whole salvation) it brings a new assurance because of the immediate access through the new and living way. To some this full assurance of faith will come through careful

---

[1] *H. D. B.*, Ext. 312b.   [2] Rom. viii. 18; Phil. iii. 21 ; 1 Pet. i. 5, v. 1, 4.

thinking, to others by swift intuition. But if it be truly evangelical, it will come through the Spirit which proceeds from the glorified Christ.

SUMMARY

(1) Our whole conception of possible human attainment looks up to Christ. We recognize in Him a revelation of God which has the highest claim to reality.

(2) This revelation is in man under the common conditions of human piety and obedience. It becomes, therefore, an offering to God of man's righteousness and obedience, to whose value in His sight we can set no limit.

(3) This offering is continuous, though now freed from the conditions of suffering and humiliation. It has, therefore, a perpetual value and an eternal influence within the Divine Nature itself. This profoundly affects the spiritual status of humanity.

(4) This higher spiritual status is realized in us by the Holy Spirit. It is not a mere possibility, showing to what heights human nature can attain; it is not a mere ideal of man, existing in the mind of God. It is definitely set forth as an actual uplift. It takes place within us in full reality. It is all of Christ undoubtedly; but there is a dynamic which comes from Him, and affects us. To what extent this dynamic may move us—whether, in other words, it is possible for the Spirit completely to fill us—is the question which we are endeavouring to answer.

Chapter VI

THE NEW TESTAMENT DOCTRINE OF THE PERFECTING OF BELIEVERS

1. Obstacles to the Perfection of the Individual

THE study of the perfection of Christ leads naturally to a study of the perfecting of those who have come under His influence. The first impression which Jesus made was on the individual. He appears to have had little to say to the political organizations of His day. That may have been due to the domination of Rome (*immensa pacis Romanae majestas*), which gave a security to the world's life such as has never been before or since, but which at the same time crushed out initiative in social endeavour. But the individuals over whom He exercised such an attraction were drawn together in fellowship; and it is impossible to state the doctrine of perfection, except in connexion with the society which they formed. Even those who have sought to find the Way in solitude have done so under an impulse which they received in the Church. We do indeed find, as a mark of the Quest, especially in the early stages, a desire for solitude. But we also find in the higher developments a transcending of that desire, and a return to society. The individual ideal and the social ideal are bound together. I purpose dealing with them separately; but I wish to enter a caveat at once that this is only for convenience, and that I am convinced that there is no attainment, either here or yonder, except as members of a society.

To the perfecting of the individual there are three obstacles which are, in essence, the same to-day as in New Testament times, although our outlook has enlarged so much that we must try to express them in modern terminology: (1) the inherent sinfulness of human nature; (2) the antagonism of our material environment; (3) the antagonism of our spiritual environment.

(1) The Old Testament teaching as to the sinful bias in man's nature has been discussed on pp. 43-4. By the time of the Christian era two fairly distinct conceptions had emerged: one declared that human nature inherited an evil inclination, which involved depravity and corruption; the other turned back to the story of the Fall and that of the Angelic Watchers to explain the entrance of sin into the world. The first of these came through Alexandrian influences, and has been affected by Platonic ideas. The second looked back to a time of innocence and perfection. This also has swayed Christian thought, partly by dwelling on the idyllic innocence which has been broken, and partly by revealing the spiritual dangers by which we are surrounded. In the New Testament we find a sense of sin and a conviction that man has fallen, which would lead to utter pessimism, such as that of 4 Ezra, if it were not for the evangelical hope. The doctrine of original sin is formulated only by St. Paul; but that statement by no means covers the ground. The New Testament is filled with the conviction of the universality of sin, and of man's moral helplessness. Later theologians conceived of the Fall as taking away the *donum supernaturale* or the *dona superaddita*, which had been bestowed upon Adam, leaving his descendants weak and helpless. But even St. Paul gives no rationale why sin is so universal, and why man is so helpless. Whatever the cause, the fact is patent. The first work of Christ's Spirit is to convince men of their sin. Whether Rom. vii. expresses St. Paul's own experience or that of some other man, and whether it is an experience before or after regeneration, are questions which have been much debated. At any rate, the passage well describes the intensity of the conflict. This conflict is all the more intense by reason of the knowledge of the Law. It is the experience of all Christians that it remains after the knowledge of the Gospel.

(2) The second hindrance is in the world of our material environment. We think of it, not without awe, as stretching to an illimitable universe, and as regulated by principles, which we call laws. But it produces in us a feeling of helplessness. The New Testament does not separate the material from the spiritual universe. Cosmos may stand for the world of Nature, or for the social order. Of the former the New Testament conception is by no means pessimistic. The Hellenistic idea

of the evil inherent in matter, which issued in Gnosticism and Manichaeism, found no support in either the Old Testament or the New. We occasionally perceive a sense of the vanity and futility in Nature ; e.g. Rom. viii. 19.

> Blind and dumb
> The whole creation strives in vain
> To sing the song that will not come.

But deeper far is the confidence that all has been created by and for Christ, and that in Him it all holds together.

Yet, when all is said, the vicissitudes of this world do constitute a serious obstacle to perfection. The changes and chances of this mortal life often shake our faith. One psalm says of the good man that he shall not be afraid of evil tidings ; but what Stoic can so guard his heart with triple brass ?

> Will my tiny spark of being wholly vanish in your deeps and heights ?
> Must my day be dark by reason, O ye heavens, of your boundless nights,
> Rush of suns, and roll of systems, and your fiery clash of meteorites ?

(3) The New Testament makes no clear distinction between the world of Nature, in which there is no apparent purpose, and the world of spiritual beings, in which there is manifestly a striving after ends. Modern thought would agree that the two cannot be separated. ' For Nature not only provides the scenery and properties of history ; but the actors themselves seem to have sprung from its soil, to owe their position largely to its co-operation, and to have come into contact with each other solely through its means.'[1] Nevertheless, it is convenient to distinguish between irrational, non-moral forces in Nature, which do, as a matter of fact, obstruct the perfect life, and those forces which, with conscious purpose, set themselves to oppose those who are striving upwards.

The New Testament accepts the current Jewish ideas as to good and evil spirits. Little reference is made to demoniacal possession in the Old Testament, though the story of the Fall and of the origin of the Nephilim both imply evil rational forces. The development of the idea of the Satan is of much interest. But in later Judaism these ideas were greatly extended ; and all human life was conceived as passed under the survey of the keen, malignant eyes of the Watchers, with the Satans behind and above them.[2] The whole world of

---

[1] Ward, *Realm of Ends.* p 3   [2] As in the Similitudes of Enoch.

New Testament times felt the oppression of a belief in hierarchies of evil powers.[1]

The dilemma has been put before us that we must either accept the statement about evil spirits in the Gospels as literally true, or acknowledge that our Lord was accommodating Himself to the ideas of the time. Neither is, however, necessary. The human development of Jesus demanded that He should express Himself in the language of His day. At the same time His perfect presentation of the Father, and His communion with Him, guarantee the ethical and spiritual value of His every act and word. In our Lord's dealing with the possessed there is a shrinking from any ostentation of power coupled with an intense sympathy for the broken human soul. We are far from understanding yet all about the subliminal self, and the possibilities of change of control, and even of personality. We feel the verisimilitude of the Gospel accounts, while we reject some of the explanations. There is in the world a real antagonism to goodness—something more than the non-moral carelessness of Nature. The New Testament indicates an organized kingdom of evil, and there is much to sustain that view. In man at least there is definite opposition to Christ and His Kingdom. In the Synoptics the disciples are called the light of the world, the salt of the earth; but in the rest of the New Testament, perhaps under the influence of the tragic fact of the Cross and of closer contact with heathenism, the view of the world is darker.[2] Especially is this marked in the Johannine writings. The world is in spiritual darkness, with no desire for light. At first the disciples are exempt from its hatred[3]; but the more they enter into the Master's spirit, the more is the hatred of the world kindled against them.[4] While this hostility exists on the part of the world, including in that term man and any other rational being which may be in opposition to Christ, is there not a perpetual barrier to perfection? Whatever effort one may make in oneself, and however one may determine to remain superior to the vicissitudes of the material universe, the fact of this unreconciled enmity is very menacing to our peace.

[1] Kennedy, *St. Paul and the Mystery Religions*, p. 24; cf. Gal. iv. 8.
[2] Consider Rom. i. 18-32, which is related to Wisdom xiii.-xv.; also Eph. ii. 2, Jas. i. 27 and iv. 4, 2 Pet. i. 4.
[3] John vii. 7. [4] John xv. 19.

2. Ways of Overcoming

Having glanced at the difficulties, we may now consider ways of overcoming.[1] On p. 6 there is a definition of Christian Perfection. Whatever that definition may owe to testimony and experience, it is mainly drawn from a study of the New Testament. Within the sacred volume varieties of religious experience, in regard to the ways of attaining perfection, find ample expression. In our analysis we must remember that the ways are not exclusive. In many respects they necessitate each other. Moreover, a final synthesis is possible in which it will be seen that they are aspects of one way.

(1) *The Way of Obedience to the Law*

The Old Testament is full of thanksgiving for the law. ' The Psalms respecting mercy are often sorrowful, as in thought of what it cost; but those respecting the Law are always full of delight.'[2] Throughout the New Testament many passages dilate on its glory. But we turn to St. James principally for the carrying on of that Nomism which at its best was the highest product of Judaism. The law which he upheld was a perfect law of liberty, a royal law of love, in which mercy gloried against judgement. It was not to be satisfied with a formal and outward obedience; it demanded visiting of the afflicted and purity within. It has come from the Father of Lights, the source of every perfect boon. St. James used in one place the old name Lord of Sabaoth; but he used also the name Father in a way wholly distinct from the usage of the Old Testament. From the Father every blessing has come, and to Him our faith should go out. Faith is not disparaged; but it should be of the right kind, not held with class distinctions, nor without its normal issue in a life of loving service. It is a faith that works within through the implanted word. This word is the law of wisdom, which comes from above, and through patience produces perfection. It starts with faith, which, as it is tested and approved, makes a complete man—one who, by his meek and peaceable spirit, has an unshaken victory over the earthly, the animal, and the demoniacal.

---

[1] John xvi. 31-3.   [2] Ruskin, *Modern Painters*, Part VII., ' The Angel of the Sea.'

Such is the teaching of St. James as to the Way. No one can fail to be impressed by its likeness to his Brother's : it is the Galilaean Gospel. The Church has never been satisfied that this is the whole Gospel. It has traits of the utmost beauty ; in some respects it forms the best method of initiation. But it represents too facile an optimism ; for it does not face the fact of the Cross. The Law cannot make perfect, even though it is divinely given, and though it works with interior grace and real cleansing. This epistle will stand, *pace* Luther, even in the fires of eternity ; but it will stand because of a reconciliation of God and man through the Blood of Christ, which St. James had not yet perceived.

(2) *The Way of Self-surrender*

The principle was laid down in a conversation narrated in Mark viii. 27–38. It speaks of a losing in order to find. The loss of the soul-life is the greatest which a man can suffer, outweighing the world. Yet this loss must be undergone for Christ's sake. This cannot mean death, which comes to all without any ethical content. Neither can it mean the loss of personality, as the river is lost in the ocean ; for the promise is of a soul-finding. It must mean renunciation for the sake of a gratification which is suggested to the mind. In all the teaching of Christ the ultimate aim is joy and self-realization. The incident of the young ruler is instructive. Jesus did not regard the observance of the law as a little thing ; but there is a step beyond which means much. We know how the idea of poverty as necessary to perfection has haunted the Church, how it found actual embodiment in St. Francis, and how it always makes a popular appeal. But it is not poverty, but self-surrender, which is demanded. The mammon which disputes with God the worship of the soul must be dethroned. Matthew Arnold said that the law of renunciation was the real secret of Jesus, which gave effect to His teaching. The philosophy of Hegel rested on the assumption that in that is to be found the law of the spirit. ' What Christianity teaches is that the law of the life of the spirit—the law of self-realization through self-abnegation—holds good for God as for man, and, indeed, that the spirit that works in man to die-to-live is the spirit of God.'[1]

[1] E. Caird, *Hegel*, p. 217.

Approximations to this are to be found in Buddhism, Stoicism, and similar teachings.

I am waiting with my all in the hope of losing everything.
I am watching at the roadside for him who turns one out into the open road,
Who hides himself and sees, who loves you unknown to you;
I have given my heart in secret love to him.
I am waiting with my all in the hope of losing everything.[1]

But the teaching of Jesus is of surrender, not to the Universal Reason, nor yet to the Eternal Void, but to our Father in Heaven. Hence if the Buddhist and the Stoic can claim to have made a full surrender, it should not be impossible for the Christian. It is not certain how far the apostles understood the fullness of Christ's teaching; but they had all grasped the idea of a new birth, in which pride and self-sufficiency had no part. They were ruled by the Master's example,[2] most of all in the surrender of His life.[3] The union of the believer with Christ involved a sympathetic participation in that self-surrender. This is that fellowship with the sufferings of Christ, that conformity with His death, which St. Paul depicts with such mystical power as a necessary preparation for conformity with the Body of His glory.[4]

(3) *The Way of Faith*

The Old Testament thought of God as true and faithful; not to believe in Him was the sign of the fool. But it only dimly discerned that faith in itself had any value.[5] This is a New Testament conception; it is so much a New Testament conception that it is hardly found outside. The insistence on faith would be startling, if we were not so accustomed to it. It is no addendum of St. Paul's. Christ certainly demanded faith. Once, after the Resurrection, He asked for love, and then in a searching way, as though he were rather anxious that Peter should learn the poverty of his love. But He continually demanded faith. His gifts were given in proportion to the faith of the recipients, and He was often limited by the lack of it. There is a school, of course, which declares that

---

[1] Rabindranath Tagore, *The King of the Dark Chamber*, xviii.
[2] Rom. xv. 3.   [3] 1 Pet. ii. 21-5.   [4] Phil. iii. 10, 21.
[5] e.g. in Gen. xv. 6 and Hab ii. 4.

OF THE PERFECTING OF BELIEVERS

faith depends for its value on auto-suggestion apart from any objective reality. But in the New Testament, faith is conceived as having so much worth *because* of the eternal reality of its object. The future and the unseen are realized by faith because of their eternal existence in God. In Heb. xi. 1 we have—what is almost unique in Scripture—a definition of faith. This definition, with its philosophical terms—substance, or essence, and test, or proof—must be read in the light of the preceding verses. It is the part of the righteous to press on ; when he shrinks back, he loses hold of God, and is in peril of sinking into the great deep. But faith tends to soul-possession. This remarkable word is used in Eph. i. 14 and 1 Pet. ii. 9 to denote the property which God has in His saints ; they are His in a way which cannot be predicated of creation in general. It is also used of the property which saints have in themselves[1] ; they have appropriated what has been offered in Christ ; they have obtained His glory as the sign of their salvation.

Faith appears from one aspect feminine, intuitive, receptive ; from another masculine, intellectual, apprehensive. It is finely illustrated from the incident inserted in Matt. xiv. 28-31 from the Petrine tradition. The waters on which the saint attempted to walk are representative of the sea of troubles in which he found himself, with the whole Church, and of which he writes in his epistle. It was a great thing that there should be the masculine, energetic outgoing, the intellectual apprehension that lays hold of God ; but it was equally necessary that there should be the feminine, intuitive assurance that God is laying hold of us. With such an assurance we have received the end of our faith, even soul-salvation. Whatever progress may be effected within us, even in eternity, we have already received in faith. ' Our prayer for spiritual improvement, for growth in faith, in purity, in knowledge, in love, is efficacious just because of that deeper conviction on which it rests, and which constitutes the hidden reality of all devotional acts—the breath and life of that sphere into which prayer lifts us—*the conviction that we are already perfect even as our Father in Heaven is perfect.*'[2]

---
[1] Heb. x. 39 ; 1 Thess. v. 9 ; 2 Thess. ii. 14. In the Papyri the word is used of title-deeds (*J. H. Moulton*).
[2] J. Caird, *Phil. of Rel.*, p. 288.

(4) *The Way of Mystical Union*

From faith we pass to mystical union, in which the believer receives as his own the offering which Christ has made. ' By one offering He hath perfected for ever them that are sanctified.'[1] The perfect offering of Christ is imputed to His disciples. It is reckoned that they have made that offering ; but it is so reckoned because of the mystical but perfectly real union between them and their Saviour. ' I have been crucified with Christ ; yet I live ; and yet no longer I, but Christ liveth in me.'[2] The perfecting of man demands a perfect offering from man to God. That offering has already been made by one Man. But all may share in that offering by faith ; and those who do so are accepted as making a perfect offering. This perfection is quite real through the mystical union ; but it is still ideal, in so far as there is need to fill up in actual experience and discipline that which is lacking in Christ's offering.[3] Dr. MacLeod Campbell expressed the idea of the offering with true insight. ' It was a perfect Amen in humanity to the judgement of God on the sin of men.' Especially valuable is the thought that it was an intense contrition in a human being for the sins of men, and a full agreement with the justice of God's wrath against sin which was needed, rather than the endurance of so much suffering. For each believer there is also needed the utterance of that spiritual Amen. But it must be done, as Dr. Campbell hardly brings out, through the union of the believer with Christ in His Church.[4]

It is not only through suffering that the offering is made. We may believe that only such suffering as is needed for our perfecting will come upon us. The Blood of Christ includes the offering of His whole life, which is now being lived in eternal glory. We are redeemed through that Blood ; and the full assurance of this, through mystical union with Him, lifts us into that perfection, which is so wonderfully brought within the compass of sinful men. But it will have to be worked out, not without fear and trembling, through all the unknown ways of eternity.

---

[1] Heb. x. 14. [2] Gal. ii. 20. [3] Col. i. 24.
[4] This is the theme of the mystical epistles, Eph. and Col.

(5) *The Way of Knowledge*

From another aspect we may speak of perfection as initiation into the knowledge of the Divine mysteries. The attitude of Jesus towards ignorance is the same as towards disease and sin. In each case He is dealing with evils, but with evils which it is far easier to cure when they are frankly recognized. It is one of His charges against the lawyers that they have taken away ' the key of knowledge.'[1] In the Fourth Gospel the emphasis on knowledge and on teaching is much greater than in the Synoptics.[2] Throughout the New Testament, we find a contrast between the false knowledge, the philosophy which is but a vain deceit, and the true knowledge, of which the supreme test is this—that it leads to God through Christ. We owe no small debt to the speculations and aspirations which in the multitudinous philosophies of the time had come to a grand climacteric. But they contained grave moral dangers, and it was natural that the apostles and the apologists should, in the main, have looked on them with suspicion.[3] The true safeguard was through initiation into the mysteries of the knowledge of God in Christ. Such knowledge differs from any science in the world in that it is an effort to translate into words the state of the soul in communion with God. Language is strained to the utmost to do this; yet the effort must be made if the knowledge is to be imparted. Such an effort is made in the phrases in which Christ is called the Word of God, or the Effulgence of His Glory, or the Expression of His Essence.

The knowledge of His will and of the mysteries of His grace comes through communion with His Spirit. But this communion is not an intellectual void. All the rich and abundant experience in the spiritual history of mankind gives content to our knowledge of God. There are many sayings in Scripture as to the growth of spiritual wisdom; and they continually receive fresh illustration from the experience of the Pilgrim Church. This growth in knowledge is full of significance for our conception of what attainment means.

---

[1] Luke xi. 52. Plummer considers this the key that unlocks the door of knowledge; but it is more in accord with the general teaching of Christ to take it as a genitive of apposition. Knowledge is not an end in itself, but a key.
[2] John vii. 14–17, viii. 12–x., xiv.–xvii.
[3] 1 Cor. x. 20–1; Forsyth, *The Church and the Sacraments*, chap. viii., p. 157.

G

Even in the Divine Nature perfection cannot be purely static, but must be compatible with progress and experience. Our knowledge of God must grow with the increase of spiritual experience in individuals and in the Church.

(6) *The Way of Love*

When all has been said in praise of obedience to the law, of self-surrender, of faith, of mystical union, and of knowledge, there remains a more excellent way. For Christ, as for all His disciples, love is everything. The love of men ought to partake of the Divine perfection.[1] It ought to have the right ring about it. It ought not to depend on the selfish motive of a future reward, nor ought it to be given only to those to whom we are naturally attracted. To say that the goal is attained by love even more directly than by faith does not make it easier, but infinitely harder. Of course, it must be said all the same; and, of course, there is really no rivalry between faith and love. Love surpasses faith as the end surpasses the means. St. Paul reviews such ways of attaining as we have been considering, and declares that they all come short of the glory of God. Self-surrender, though it meant the sharing out of one's goods, morsel by morsel, and even the giving up of one's bodily life; faith, though it were sufficient to remove mountains; knowledge, though it were to include all prophecy and all mystery—all these come short of the glory of love. They are ways, at their best, by which one may attain. They are dark mirrors, in which we may discern some reflection of the Divine. *But love is, in truth, not so much a way of perfection, as perfection itself.*

Dr. Platt says: 'The closer definition of Christian perfection is almost invariably stated in the New Testament in terms of love.'[2] The Pauline emphasis we have seen; the Johannine is even more obvious: 'Herein is love made perfect with us, that we may have boldness in the day of judgement; . . . perfect love casteth out fear.'[3] It is manifest also in the other writers. St. Peter, while giving many ethical directions, adds: 'Above all things being fervent in your love among yourselves; for love covereth a multitude of sins.'[4] In

---

[1] Matt. v. 48; Luke vi. 36.   [2] *E. R. E.*, ix. 729*a*.   [3] 1 John iv. 17-8.
[4] 1 Pet. iv. 8.

2 Pet. i. 5–7 is an account of the unfolding of the Christian character, in which love is made the crown of all, by means of which is richly supplied an entrance into the eternal Kingdom. St. James dwells on works, but they are the works of love; no one is clearer than he that the royal law is a law of love and mercy. St. Jude, in the noble exhortation of vv. 20-1, puts this as the central word: 'Keep yourselves in the love of God.' Even in Revelation, through all the terror of its apocalypse, there is an upward look to Him who loveth us, and loosed us from our sins by His blood. In Hebrews the whole epistle is full of a sense of the Divine Love, whose energy still continues in the eternal priesthood of Christ. Because of that, His disciples ought to stimulate one another to love and good works.

A few points in New Testament teaching may be summarized as follows:

(1) The New Testament is neither altruistic nor pantheistic in the sense of urging that the natural self-love should be swallowed up. We are to love our neighbour *as ourselves*. The command to love one's self is not stated, because it is not necessary to do so. It is a natural, God-implanted instinct. In all visions of attainment, in this life or beyond, the end is regarded as life increasingly rich in personal expansion.

(2) There is a progressive outspreading of love till it breaks through every barrier. The history of the Church, in its evangelical movement from Jerusalem through Judaea and Samaria, unto the uttermost part of the earth, is typical of the soul as it moves out in love. The disciples had no need to be exhorted to love of the brethren; they had been taught that by the immediate movement of God in their souls when they first learnt of Christ. But this *philadelphia* ought to issue in a supreme love which knows no limit, and which is beyond all imagination and all thought.

(3) It is somewhat surprising to find comparatively few exhortations to love towards God. There are more in Deuteronomy; in fact, the most striking in the New Testament is the one taken from Deuteronomy, on which Christ set His approval. The thought of the New Testament dwells not so much on the outgoing of our love to God as on resting in His love, till it permeates and fills our whole being, and urges forward with the impetus of its own eternal energy. The

88   THE NEW TESTAMENT DOCTRINE

Johannine teaching, both in the Gospel and the Epistle, is particularly full.[1] The charge has been made against the First Epistle of St. John that it deals too much with generalities. The details have to be filled in from the experience of the Son of Man ; and from the external and the inner history of the Church ; and from our own spiritual experience. These are the rich sources to which we have to go to fill in the content ; but the eternal principles are laid down by St. John with matchless power and insight.

3. QUESTIONS WHICH HAVE TO BE FACED

I will conclude this chapter by outlining questions which are likely to arise in the minds of earnest seekers. They are such as these :

Is the teaching of Perfection an essential part of the Gospel as proclaimed by Christ and His apostles ?

Can we find a better term, one less liable to misunderstanding, than Perfection ?

Ought we to describe the state indicated by that term as sinless ?

Is it possible in this life ?

Is it possible to lose this state, either temporarily or eternally?

Will the future life include probation or purgation for those who have not attained perfection in this ?

In the last chapter I purpose summarizing the conclusions to which I have been led. These conclusions will cover the questions specified above, and others which may arise during the investigation. It may be said at once, however, that the conclusions will not be determined by isolated texts,[2] but by an endeavour to understand the evangelical spirit revealed in the New Testament.

---

[1] See especially 1 John iv. 7-21.
[2] Such as Heb. vi. 4-6, which has deeply influenced the answers to the question whether it is possible to lose the state of Perfection.

CHAPTER VII

THE NEW TESTAMENT DOCTRINE OF THE PERFECTING OF THE CHURCH

1. THE ATTITUDE OF THE CHURCH TOWARDS THE INDIVIDUAL AND TOWARDS THE WORLD

UNLESS we quite misread the signs of the times, Christian people are setting an enhanced value on the idea of the Church. At the same time, the alienation between the world and the Church was never more marked. On the part of the world is seen, among a few, bitter hostility; among others, intellectual contempt; among the great majority, sheer indifference, liable, however, to flame up into hatred. On the part of the Church we find doubt and hesitation, not due to cowardice or want of faith, but to a self-distrust, which has its good side, but may easily become morbid. In opposition to this has arisen this vigorous movement, seeking to realize the ideal of the Church. From the standpoint of the individual and from the standpoint of humanity there is, and probably always will be, the keenest criticism of the Church. The individual fears that he will have to surrender his private judgement and right of action. On the other hand, the Church seems to be taking a course quite separate from the national and international relations of humanity; the old charge of hatred of humanity still stands.[1] The burden laid upon the Church is to prove that the individual can realize his full personality within its pale, and that it exercises towards humanity, not an antagonistic, but a priestly function. The Church lays restraints upon the individual in order that through them he may enter into a larger liberty. The Church separates itself from the world, not that it may leave it to sink, but that by its presence and witness it may lift the world into its own sphere of light. Such at least is the ideal.

[1] ' Odium humani generis ' (Tac., *Ann.*, xv. 44).

It became clear in the discussion of individual perfection that the only sense in which the word can be used is of such fellowship with God in Christ that by faith we become partakers of the Divine Nature. This thought applies also to the society; that also has an ideal perfection which at the same time is quite real, has, indeed, the highest mark of reality, inasmuch as it is already realized in God.[1] The Church is not invisible, shadowy, indistinct; it is manifest in actual organizations, in definite creeds, and in assemblies for worship. On these, which have every mark of imperfection, there rests as a benediction that ideal which they have not yet attained. No true idea of Christian perfection can be obtained unless we have in it an idea of ecclesiastical perfection. It will not be needful, however, to do more than state the fact of this essential element in any true conception. All that I shall do is to glance at (1) the ideal of the Church's life and witness on earth, (2) the Missionary ideal of the Kingdom, (3) the eternal life of the Church in Heaven.

2. The Ideal of the Church's Life and Witness on Earth

The New Testament gives a vivid picture of the early life and witness of the Church, ' nothing extenuate, nor aught set down in malice.' We see how the vision fades into the light of common day, how differences arise even between those who have been nearest to the Master, how varied was the expression of their faith. Yet we see from the first the self-consciousness of the Church, and its effort to find itself in organization, in creed, and in worship.

(1) *Organization*

The Church is the body of Christ; it is therefore a visible and complex organism. A good deal is said in the Acts and the Epistles, especially the Pastorals, as to the formation of the Church. It evidently proceeded apace, so that it soon became a matter of admiration even to those who looked upon it with most distrust. During their lifetime the apostles were a bond of union. They were conscious that it was their

---

[1] Green, *Prolegomena to Ethics*, III. ii. 17.

OF THE PERFECTING OF THE CHURCH

part to knit together all the members in one body.[1] But in after years there have been grievous rents. Moreover, the attempt to insist on unity of organization, in order to prevent such schism, has often detracted from the unity of the Spirit.[2] If heretics, it was argued, had true Christian charity, they would never break away from the discipline of the Christian Church. Such logic has weight with many; but it does not make sufficient allowance for the complexity of human thought and the varieties of religious experience.

It may be maintained that the true unity of the Spirit has persisted through all the heresies and schisms.[3] A common ideal of evangelical attainment has arisen, a new and original type of the religious life, which, notwithstanding local, temporary, and accidental variations, has remained true to its pattern through the whole Christian era. There is a growing desire for a manifestation of this deep spiritual unity. It seems to us, indeed, inconceivable that there should ever be one organization for all Christendom. Our model is not the Roman Empire, under whose shadow the early Church grew up, but the League of Nations, which is slowly finding itself to-day. The goal of the Church cannot be reached until there is a manifested unity; but that unity may be all the more apparent and enduring because of the variety in which it has found itself.

(2) *Doctrine*

A casual survey of the New Testament would lead one to say that it is full of teaching, but not in an ordered form of doctrine. But there soon emerged out of the sea of thought a considerable amount of firm ground. The evangelical facts were carefully handed down, and with them definite convictions as to their significance. This the disciples called the good deposit.[4] It was for the Church to guard well this deposit, and to distinguish the true from the false, the genuine from the counterfeit, like expert money-changers.[5] The Church, therefore, rightly attaches high value to the doctrinal expression

---

[1] 1 Cor. xii. 12-31; Eph. iv. 1-16; Col. ii. 19; Swete, *The Holy Catholic Church*, p. 12.
[2] Cyprian, *De Unitate Ecclesiae*, 6: 'Habere non potest deum patrem qui ecclesiam non habet matrem.'
[3] Dale, *Lectures on Ephesians*, Lect. xv.   [4] 1 Tim. vi. 20; 2 Tim. i. 12, 14.
[5] Origen, *In Joann.*, xix.

of its origin, its history, and its consciousness. Nor can this be quite a simple matter. The Church is struggling towards a creed, which shall utter the infinite wonder of the revelation and the salvation which is in Christ in all its fullness and variety. A simple creed will do that; but it should be one whose simplicity is susceptible of boundless expansion.

(3) *Worship*

Jesus and His disciples inherited the forms of Jewish worship. He regularly went to the Temple and the synagogue; and after His departure the disciples were continually in the Temple blessing God. After the destruction of Jerusalem there was a pathetic attempt on the part of the Christians to cling to Judaism and the worship of the synagogues. In Jas. ii. 2 the assembly of Christians is called a synagogue; and in the letter to the Church in Smyrna[1] the true assembly is distinguished from the false, which is really a synagogue of Satan. Hebrews condemns those who neglect such assembling, and gives a glorious picture of the ideal worship, *which is already proceeding*, and which includes choirs visible and invisible.[2]

Of the forms of worship there may be said to be two main types. H. Scott-Holland draws a distinction between them in an address on ' The Worship of the City.' Naturally he glorifies a liturgical service, giving this as its distinctive feature—that it is the spirit of a great action. ' We who enter into such a liturgy find ourselves, as the service proceeds, taken up into a scene, a drama, in which mighty things are happening. Not that it is a theatric display to rouse our emotions; for it is not so much directed towards ourselves as towards God. On Him it is bent. Upon Him it waits. For Him it calls. He is the supreme agent who is immediately concerned. And He is doing something here and now in our midst.'[3] Opposed to this is the idea of worship as centring round the sermon, with its intellectual effort and its personal appeal. This also must have its place; the prophet demands a hearing as well as the priest. However beautiful the liturgy may be, there must be opportunity for fresh statement of the thoughts of men. There should be the appeal to God, which inevitably shapes itself into some ritual; but there should also

---

[1] Rev. ii. 9. [2] Heb. xii. 22–4. [3] *God's City*, pp. 59–85.

be the appeal to the intelligence and the emotion and the will of men.

3. THE MISSIONARY IDEAL OF THE KINGDOM

The perfecting of the Church must include Missionary enterprise. Its type is not a self-contained fortress, but an advancing army. Love for God finds utterance in a worship in which we are assured of His Presence in pardoning and saving grace; and love for man drives the Church forward in evangelical endeavour. The feet of the Christian soldier must be shod with the preparation of the Gospel of peace.[1] We have seen that the end can only be attained as members of a society; and now we perceive that this society itself is not a closed corporation. It is always expanding. The right conclusion from this, however, is not to deny the possibility of perfection, nor yet to shut the Church within a limited area, within which it might at least be conceivable; but to readjust our idea of perfection. We want a new orientation by which to discern that it is greater than we have dreamed. The ways and the thoughts of God are infinitely higher than ours; yet by faith we enter into union with them.

4. THE ETERNAL LIFE OF THE CHURCH IN HEAVEN

From one aspect the eternal life is far more important than the temporal. We must have it always before us for encouragement and for warning. Whatever worth we may set on our attainment in this life becomes lost unless we are able to view it from the standpoint of eternity; for our citizenship is in Heaven. From another aspect we may say that it is not so necessary that we should have definite doctrine. For attainment in this life it is of the last importance that we should clarify our thought and define our aim. But for the perfection of eternity there is no harm in leaving our views vague and undetermined. A few points may be tabulated.

(1) It will undoubtedly be a social perfection in a deepened fellowship. The Church is not to be considered as a temporary institution. Just as marriage foreshadows, in a type which will pass away, a union in eternity, in which the redeemed souls will enjoy an intimacy equal to that of the angels,[2] so the

---
[1] Eph. vi. 15.   [2] Luke xx. 36.

communion of saints, which forms so much of our felicity here, will be transformed into a permanent rapture.[1] In 2 Cor. v. 1 the house eternal in the Heavens denotes the spiritual body ; but it must be thought of, not in isolation, but as part of the City of God. A remarkable phrase is used in Luke xvi. 9, where Jesus speaks of making such good use of the mammon of unrighteousness that they may receive us into the *eternal tabernacles*. The adjective takes away any idea of transience in the noun ; and the whole passage points to the grouping together of local habitations, even in the eternal life.

(2) Will there be any progressive development in the social life beyond? Von Hügel declared that Protestant thought to-day is moving towards conceptions of Purgatory.[2] But the present writer is of opinion that modern thought, so far as it concerns itself with the future life, rather tends to what Dr. Charles calls the ethicizing of Hades, which involves the extension of probation with the continued exercise of ethical judgement and choice into the life beyond.

(3) The question of communion between the Church on earth and the Church in Heaven ' has no place in any of the great Eastern creeds, nor in any Western creed before the second half of the fourth century.'[3] The most pertinent passages in the New Testament are the one in which St. Paul refers to the custom of baptizing for the dead and the prayer for the departed in 2 Tim. i. 18, if we consider it a fair inference that the master of the household was dead. The most striking early instance is the sacrifice offered by Judas Maccabaeus for his men that had fallen.[4] It is evident that no method is suggested in Scripture by which the communion between the Church on earth and the Church in Heaven may find outward expression. This does not exclude the possibility that in the perfecting of the Church such intercourse may not be made feasible. The simple offering of prayer for the dead is not sinful ; but it may easily become so if we attempt to anticipate what is still hidden from us, and to build up a system in ignorance.

[1] Heb. xii. 22–24.
[2] See *Conc. Trid.*, Sess. 25 ; a very careful statement of the Roman Catholic position. For a Protestant view see Wesley, Sermon cxxii. on ' Faith.'
[3] Swete, *The Communion of Saints*, p. 157.   [4] 2 Macc. xii. 43.

PART III
HISTORICAL

CONTENTS OF PART III

VIII. INFLUENCES OUTSIDE CHRISTIANITY WHICH HAVE AFFECTED THE CONCEPTION OF EVANGELICAL PERFECTION

	PAGE
1. PLATO	97
2. ARISTOTLE	102
3. STOICISM	106
4. PHILO	110
5. PLOTINUS	112
6. THE MYSTERIES	119
7. BUDDHISM	121
8. MANICHAEISM	125

IX. THE IDEA OF PERFECTION IN THE EARLY CHURCH

1. CLEMENT OF ROME AND OTHERS	128
2. IRENAEUS AND TERTULLIAN	130
3. THE ENCRATITES AND THE MONTANISTS	132
4. GNOSTICISM	135
5. MONACHISM	138

X. CLEMENT OF ALEXANDRIA AND ORIGEN

1. CLEMENT	142
(1) *Clement and the Orthodoxasts*	142
(2) *Clement's Teaching Regarding Perfection*	143
(3) *The Characteristic Notes of Clement's Ideal*	145
(4) *Conclusions from Clement's Teaching*	147
2. ORIGEN	149
(1) *The Pre-existence of the Soul*	150
(2) *The Consequences of the Fall*	151
(3) *Redemption*	151
(4) *The True Gnostic*	152
(5) *Purifying Fire*	153
(6) *The Soul's Progress*	154

XI. AMBROSE, AUGUSTINE, AND DIONYSIUS THE AREOPAGITE

1. AMBROSE	155
(1) *Ambrose and Stoicism*	155
(2) *The Evangelical Precepts and the Evangelical Counsels*	156
(3) *The Praise of Virginity*	157
(4) *Stages within the State of Perfection*	158
(5) *The Endeavour to Anticipate the Future Life*	160
(6) *Criticism of Ambrose's Teaching*	161
2. AUGUSTINE	162
(1) *The Theism of Augustine*	163
(2) *Augustine's Doctrine of Grace*	166
(3) *The City of God*	170
3. DIONYSIUS THE AREOPAGITE	172
(1) *The Knowledge of God*	173
(2) *The Way of Union with God*	174
(3) *The Hierarchical Systems in Heaven and on Earth*	176

Chapter VIII

INFLUENCES OUTSIDE CHRISTIANITY WHICH HAVE AFFECTED THE CONCEPTION OF EVANGELICAL PERFECTION

THE preceding chapters have dealt with the evangelical ideal, individual and social, as promulgated in the New Testament. It came as an offshoot from Old Testament revelation; but it is essentially a new ideal, whose novelty consists in its dependence on the Person and the Work of Christ. As this ideal spread among men it came under the influence of the general thought of humanity. This does not in the least detract from its true originality. All perfection is realized ' in Christ '; and no movement of human thought, no progress of human knowledge, can lead away from Him. It would be impracticable to attempt here a survey of all the influences which through the ages have affected the Christian ideal; and I will restrict myself to those which were felt in the apostolic and the early Church. This chapter, therefore, will be a link between the Biblical exposition in Part II. and the Historical in Part III. It is scarcely possible to understand the evolution of theology in the early Church, unless we realize the impact of Hellenistic thought, of the Eastern cults and the Mystery Religions, and of world-wide religious movements such as Buddhism and Manichaeism.

1. PLATO

It would be gross ingratitude to overlook the debt which Christianity owes to Plato. ' Plato has done more than any other writer to fill both poetry and philosophy with the spirit of religion, to break the yoke of custom and tradition, " heavy as frost and deep almost as life," which cramps the development of man's mind, to liberate him from the prejudices of the natural understanding, and to open to him an ideal world in which he can find refuge from the narrowness and inadequacy of life.'[1] In regard to our subject we may summarize his influence under the following heads : (1) his doctrine of ideas ; (2) his doctrine of immortality ; (3) his doctrine of a twofold morality ; (4) his teaching as to the freedom and lordship of the soul ; (5) his conception of the perfect society.

(1) Plato's doctrine of Ideas underwent considerable modification. But the Idea was never regarded as simply a representation in the mind : it had objective reality, and exerted a dominating influence. This is one of the chief arguments in the *Phaedo* for immortality : the very idea of the soul rejects the thought of perishing. In the *Meno* all ideas are traced to a kind of remembrance : so that all that is needed on our part is to bring them into consciousness. In the *Phaedrus* a myth is introduced to explain the difficulty of regaining the sight of the Perfect Idea. No myth has impressed the Christian imagination more than this. The effort to gain the beatific vision, and to rise to the perception of spiritual reality ; the difficulties which have to be overpassed, and which are due to the composite nature of the soul ; all this found an immediate response in the Christian consciousness. Truly Christian is the account of the victors who have overcome, the purified souls who have followed the Blessed Choir, and seen the great and holy sight, and been made partakers of the mysteries which it is meet to call most holy, ' which we celebrated, being complete and freed from evil.'[2]

In the *Republic*[3] the Unseen Idea, which nature and art but imitate, is glorified. A gradation of the Ideas is brought forward, the highest of all being the Idea of the Good. Using the analogy of the sun, we may say that the Good is not only the author of knowledge to all things, but also of their being and essence ; and yet the Good is not essence, but far exceeds essence in dignity and power.[4] This Idea of the Good has been transformed in Christian thought into a means of expressing faith in God, as One who is beyond knowledge, and even beyond being, in so far as being is considered to be dependent on some material form, but whose existence is the ultimate reality.

(2) The arguments for Immortality are marshalled by Plato

---

[1] E. Caird, *Evol. of Theol.* p. 58.   [2] *Phaedrus*, 250b.   [3] *Rep.* x.
[4] *Rep.* vi. 509b.

with increasing power. In the *Phaedo*, in spite of its pathetic interest, the argument appears artificial. The fact that we have an idea of the soul as the opposite of death, and therefore unaffected by it, could at the most only prove the permanence of the idea in the universe of ideas. Plato clearly discerned this himself. In the *Republic* and the *Phaedrus* he perceived a diversity within the soul, which did not take away from its essential and immortal vigour. The soul is the source of all energy and motion ; its very sins do not destroy it ;[1] they may impart an additional energy, as we see in some wicked men.[2]

The highest utterance is in the *Timaeus*, where Plato rises to a truly sublime conception of Creation.[3] Immortality, beatitude, and all perfection, whether for gods or men, depend entirely on the will of the Eternal. But even in the procession of gods in the *Phaedrus* ' envy stands far from the Heavenly Choir ' : much more in the Eternal can be neither caprice nor malice : His will is the surest of bonds. In the *Phaedrus* Plato described the soul as having a necessary immortality in itself ; and this became the general belief in Christendom, though it has little support in Scripture.[4] A higher idea is presented in the *Timaeus* of an immortality contingent on the will of God. Such a view is quite distinct from conditional immortality ; and is consistent with a belief in the survival of the wicked after death, provided there is included the idea of a process of correction and purification, the aim of which would be to bring all at last to perfection. Some such view appears to be gaining ground to-day, but with modifications which Christian thought imperatively demands in the Platonic framework.

(3) The idea of a twofold morality was congenial to the Greek mind in the aristocratic states of Plato's time. Plato went beyond the dictum of Socrates, that virtue is knowledge, and declared that the mark was not philosophical knowledge, but a spiritual insight which involved communion with the highest good. On these lines he taught a lower morality, which was incumbent on all, and a higher, which was only possible to the philosopher, who was conscious of his aim, and who had been led on through visions of beauty, first of the

---

[1] *Phaedrus*, 245b. [2] *Rep.* 611.
[3] Pringle-Pattison, *The Idea of God*, p. 345. ' The timelessness of truth as a logical content was the discovery of Plato.'
[4] Hall, *Hist. of Christian Ethics*, p. 13.

body, then of the soul, then of science, until at last he beholds That-Which-Always-Is.

In the *Republic* four faculties are ascribed to the soul, the two higher being dominant in those who have reached the stage of reason, the two lower in those who have obtained some perception of shadows, and who are guided by some opinion or belief which they have.[1] Those who have attained the highest stage are to be Guardians of the State, for the Government should be in the hands of philosophers. They are to be free from avarice or envy : so that the knowledge which has come through being ' spectators of all time and all existence ' will be used for the general good. This idea of service to the community, which was natural to Plato, robs the teaching of the twofold morality of its greatest peril. ' The victory which they have won is the salvation of the whole state ; and the crown with which they and their children are crowned is the fullness of all that life needs.'[2]

(4) In his later writings Plato tended to speak not so much of the idea of the soul as of the soul itself. It is impossible to exaggerate the effect of this on the Christian conception of the End. The soul was thought of as indissoluble, either owing to its own nature or to the unchanging will of God ; and the end which it sought was in itself. This was not all gain. The spiritual was placed in antagonism to the physical ; moral improvement was conceived as desensualization ; and the body was regarded as a grave, to escape from which was like coming out of a den into the light. These ideas are alien to the Old Testament, and to the teaching of Jesus ; but they found a ready entrance into the early Church. It would be a mistake to lay the blame for this aberration altogether on Plato ; but the very enthusiasm of early Christianity created a rarefied atmosphere, in which his teaching easily became dangerous and misleading.

An unqualified gain is in his insistence on the Freedom and Lordship of the soul, as for example in the story of Er at the close of the *Republic*. The central thought is that the soul chooses its environment, like Lot when he went towards Sodom, and by that choice becomes responsible for the character which of necessity evolves from it. ' To be free is to be a continuously existing, self-affirming, environment-choosing personality.'[3]

[1] *Rep.* vi. 511.   [2] *Rep.* v. 465.   [3] Stewart, *Myths of Plato*, p. 171.

A further development is found in the eschatological myths of the *Phaedo* and the *Gorgias*. The necessary immortality of the soul gives it an awful freedom for all eternity. 'The danger would appear to be dreadful, if one should neglect it.'¹ Judgement is the inevitable issue of the soul's own choice. 'The evil soul is carried of necessity to an abode suitable for it; but the soul which has passed through life with purity and moderation, having obtained the Gods as its fellow travellers and guides, settles in the place suited to it.'² The aim of the Gorgias myth is to bring home the conviction that judgement will be according to reality, and not according to appearance. 'This word stands firm that we must be on our guard against doing wrong even more than against being wronged.'³ This is a noble conclusion to a great argument. When we strip off the mythical form of the judgement by Minos and his peers on the naked soul before them, we discern an endeavour to articulate the divine and unerring judgement which comes in eternity.

(5) The influence of Plato's sketch of the ideal state is shown in St. Augustine's *City of God*, and in Sir Thomas More's *Utopia*. He conceived of it as coming through an ideal education. It is because they have been rightly trained in all ways that the guardians are able to be true leaders; and it is because the people have been trained, though in a less degree, that they are able rightly to follow. The purpose of philosophy is to bring healing to the soul, in order that citizens may excel in virtue. The doom of the wicked is to be shunned; but philosophy is the bond of the State; for society depends on virtue, as virtue on right knowledge. The knowledge of right and justice Zeus bestows on all; but it remains a love of opinion, of custom, use and wont, unless men attain to that true wisdom which comes through a perception of the Absolute, the Eternal, and the Immutable.⁴

A strain of pessimism in Plato made him regard the ideal society as a pure fabrication of the mind. In the beautiful close of the Ninth Book Glaucon says that such a man as they have depicted will be no statesman. By the dog of Egypt he will, said Socrates, 'in the land which is his own he certainly will, though in the land of his birth perhaps not, unless he have a divine call. You mean, said Glaucon, that he will be a ruler

---

¹ *Phaedo*, 107.   ² *Phaedo*, 108.   ³ *Gorgias*, 527b.   ⁴ *Rep.* v. 479.

in the city of which we are the founders, and which exists in idea only; for I do not believe there is such an one anywhere on earth. In heaven, I replied, there is laid up a pattern of it, methinks, which he who desires may behold, and beholding may set his own house in order (or, take up his abode there). But whether such an one exists, or ever will exist in fact, is no matter; for he will live after the manner of that city, having nothing to do with any other.'[1]

To sum up, it is easy to see how congruous was the teaching of Plato with the ideals which were native to the Christian Church. In some ways he led later thinkers astray, especially by the pessimism which regarded the body as the prison of the soul: so that the soul's attainment was to be reached in escape from the body.[2] Nevertheless he made a great contribution in enabling the Church to develop its ideal, and to show that that ideal was in accordance with reason, and was essentially ethical and social. The further conception that both reason and ethics were means to an end, the end of ecstatic union with the Divine, is already implicit in Plato, and was fully unfolded in Plotinus.

2. ARISTOTLE

Aristotle agreed with Plato as to the soul's longing for unification; but he dissented as to the way of attainment. The fact that he ascribed a more definite reality to matter and to the individual organism led him to make a greater gulf between God and the universe. 'In God is life: for the activity of intelligence is life, and He is that activity. Thus His essential activity constitutes a perfect and blessed life. We speak of God therefore as a living being, perfect and eternal; for to Him is ascribed a life which is continuous and eternal: it would be still better to say that He is eternal life.'[3] This noble thought was vitiated by the fact that he could not perceive any bond between the self-regarding God and the world. He did not deny the possibility of our knowledge of God and union with Him; but such union can only be transient, seeing it consists of a conscious contemplation of

---
[1] *Rep.* ix. 592 (Jowett's trans.).   [2] *Phaedo*, 114.
[3] From *Met*. XI. vi.-x., of which E. Caird says that it has influenced theology more than any other philosophical writing.

the Divine, to which we can rise only for a brief time. ' The life of God is of the same kind as those highest moods which in us are but for a little while. It is eternally so with Him, although with us it is impossible, since the active exercise of His self-consciousness is an ever-present pleasure.' In relation to our subject Aristotle's influence may be traced in four distinct ways : (1) his conception of the Soul; (2) his doctrine of the End; (3) his doctrine of the Way; (4) his praise of the contemplative life.

(1) His conception of the Soul, to which he gave the whole strength of his analytical intellect, was non-animistic, and to that extent had a beneficial effect on Christian thought. In one famous passage[1] he speaks of the creative reason in the soul, and also of the passive. The creative reason exists apart from all matter : it is, therefore, immortal. The receptive or passive exists only in the temporal, individual form : it perishes, therefore, with the form. The higher the receptive power, the more does the soul become conscious of itself; but the only immortality is in the creative reason apart from the individual soul. This leads to a doctrine of the absorption of the individual in the universal. But Aristotle does not dwell on the question. He conceived of the soul as able to attain a fixity of virtue, which he calls habitude; but he was not interested, as Plato was, in following the argument from the fixed condition of the soul to its eternal state.

(2) The End bulks large in his writings. Indeed, his whole view of the universe was teleological : there is an end for all things. But he uses this not as a proof of the Divine existence, but as showing the creative reason which works in all. It should be the aim of all to discern their proper end ; and ethical philosophy consists in realizing this.[2] Thus a single act of courage only has value as it tends to the formation of a fixed character. So for Aristotle the End is quite definite, actual and realizable. As regards material things, including the vegetable and the animal, while it is true to say that the end is regulative, yet it is an end which can only be contemplated by minds ; but rational beings are able by contemplation to assist in the realization of their own ends. For a rational being the end may be considered subjectively as happiness; objectively it may be defined as the morally

[1] *De An*. III. v. 2.   [2] *Eth*. III. vii. 6.

beautiful. Aristotle's thought is moving in the direction of the great definition that man's end is to know God, and to enjoy Him for ever. But it should be noted that in his thought God is One whose moral beauty attracts man, but from whom there is no outgoing of saving love.

(3) As to the method of attainment his teaching is of the utmost value, especially because of its sobriety. He was far from the idea that perfection was purely a matter of the soul. A man might be virtuous, and yet be unsuccessful, or inactive, or beset by misfortunes, and no one would call such a man happy, unless he were endeavouring to prove in an academic thesis some paradoxical position.[1] Perfection cannot be separated from the search for bodily health and well-being. But these are obviously things not altogether in our power. Hence he is careful to discriminate as to the sense in which the end can be said to be reached.

In fact, Aristotle's whole doctrine is based on limitations; the Infinite is not by any means to be desired. The life of the good man is happy just because it is finite. Frankly recognizing this, we are led to see that the wise course is the way of the Mean. This is often considered the distinctive Aristotelian contribution to Ethics.[2] It is characteristic of the Hellenic temper, as in the famous saying, Nothing too much, on the temple of Delphi. It appears definitely opposed to the Christian spirit, especially in its early enthusiasm. But this is not quite just to Aristotle. The Mean is connected with Plato's *Harmony*, and denotes that equipoise of the nature which only comes when the will follows right law, and is not led astray by the extremes of desire. It is almost equivalent to Temperance which forms so important a part in the Christian's development. The danger is in regarding the method of self-restraint and moderation as an end in itself, as though the Mean represented an ideal of moral beauty. We can understand how Aristotle failed to reach any conception of Love. He comes nearest in his account of Friendship.[3]

(4) While in practical life the only method of attainment is by a careful following of the Mean, in which we must not expect more than a measure of success, and in which we are

---

[1] *Eth.* I. v. 6.   [2] Cf. Aquinas, II. ii. Q. 186. A. 3, referring to *Eth.* II. vi.
[3] *Eth.* VIII. and IX.

liable to suffer 'the slings and arrows of outrageous fortune,' yet there is a way in which we may pass beyond this; and that is the way of Philosophy, of Contemplation, and Speculation. It is strange that Aristotle should have been led to such a conclusion, which seems a reversal of the aim of a moderate and restrained enjoyment of the opportunities of life. But it came through the dualism into which his logic had forced him. The life of God was a life of self-contemplation, a purely intellectual activity, which was also the truest repose: His thought may be best described as a thinking about thought. Between such an existence and any mortal a gulf is fixed which the lower, practical reason can never cross. The lower reason is bound up with man's composite nature, and is dependent on external circumstances: it is, therefore, altogether unlike the life which we must attribute to God. But the higher reason transcends this in philosophy.[1] It is the higher, because it is the activity of the highest in man; because it affords the purest pleasures; and because it is self-sufficient, and is its own end, and not a means to something higher. Hence it produces a spiritual rest which is nearest to the life of God. 'A moment of contemplative thought is most perfectly and absolutely an end. It is sought for no result but itself. It is a state of peace which is the crown of all exertion. It is the realization of the divine in man, and constitutes the most absolute and all sufficient happiness, being as far as possible in human things independent of external circumstances.'[2]

The influence of Aristotle was dominant in the Middle Ages. Aquinas, indeed, made large modifications, doing away with the empiric method by which Aristotle sought to find the golden mean, and making the contemplative life consist in a spiritual union with God rather than an endeavour to imitate the Divine self-contemplation. The aristocratic tendencies of the Greek found a higher expression in the Catholic. The contemplative life was still only for a few; but those few were marked out not by worldly advantages, nor even by intellectual capacity, but by the earnestness of their spiritual endeavour. Moreover, the Christian hope made possible an expectation of its glory hereafter for the many.

The objections to this exaltation of the contemplative life

[1] *Eth.* X. vii.–viii.   [2] Grant, *The Ethics of Aristotle*, i. 228.

are very cogent. It makes a mischievous distinction into
two classes, for one of which only is possible the higher blessing.
It makes an unreal distinction within the life of the individual
as though it were possible to cut it into sections. But attainment must apply to the whole life, considered as a whole.
It cannot even be said that spiritual progress tends to make
life more contemplative, or that the eternal life is one of
pure contemplation. The full-orbed life towards which we
are striving demands practical activity as well as spiritual
contemplation.

3. Stoicism

When St. Paul came to Athens certain of the Epicurean
and the Stoic philosophers encountered him. Of these the
Epicureans had little influence on Christianity. Their mental
detachment, their geniality, their love of ease and comfort,
their freedom from vindictiveness, present features which
require increasing attention from ethical teachers. But the
Church rightly discerned the lack of iron in their teaching:
above all it was alienated by their denial of Providence. Even
those who sought to discover the good in philosophy turned
away in indignant contempt from the godless Epicureans.
The tranquillity to which Epicurus invited, in order to enjoy
during this brief life as much as may be of serene intellectual
pleasure, seemed the antipodes of the rest that remaineth to
the people of God.

On the other hand Stoicism exercised an immediate and a
permanent influence. The Stoic idea of the relations between
God, the world, and the individual is expressed in terms which
appeal to the Christian conscience. We may gauge the effect
on the evolution of the doctrine of perfection under the following heads : (1) the victory over the world by faith ; (2) the
higher and the lower way ; (3) the cosmopolitan ideal.

(1) *The Victory over the World by Faith*

The Stoic, following Heraclitus, imagined the world as
fashioned by a fiery breath, or a creative fire. In seeking for
a monistic formula he tended to Pantheism : thus in the hymn
to Zeus, quoted by St. Paul on the Areopagus, the God is
defined as equivalent to Fate or Nature. His teaching was also

strongly materialistic, and has likenesses in this respect with the theology of Tertullian. The proclivity of such a doctrine is towards pessimism or fatalism. ' Lead me, O Zeus, and thou, O Destiny, in the work to which I am divinely chosen, and I shall follow, not unwilling ; but, even if I refuse and become evil, no less must I follow thee.'[1] With all this Stoicism inherited the intense individualism of Cynicism. The work which Ezekiel did for Hebrew prophecy in proclaiming the value of the individual, Antisthenes accomplished in the next century in Greek philosophy. But to the latter the only way by which a man could assert his individuality was by a rough breach with the social order. Zeno, with much greater breadth of vision, sought to find a way by which the individual could come to his own, consistent with the Fatalism and Pantheism which were bound up with his system. He found it in the formula, to live in harmony or conformity : to which was added in further definition, to live in conformity with nature. If it be asked, with what nature ? two answers are possible : one's own nature or universal nature. Chrysippus, it is said, stressed the first, and Cleanthes the second. But both finally would say (and this is the paramount message of Stoicism) that the answers are really one. Between the microcosm and the macrocosm there must be substantial conformity. In all nature is the working of Mind, of the constructive Reason, of the germinative Word. To know this is to attain man's end. ' For there is no greater thing, either for mortal men or for Gods, than to sing rightly the universal law.'[2] ' No one can stop you from living according to the principle of your own nature : nothing will happen to you contrary to the principle of the universal nature.'[3]

Our admiration is evoked by such utterances. What we are concerned to note, however, is that the result was gained by a dogmatic faith. We do not find anything like the connected argument of Plato or Aristotle. The Stoics content themselves, as a rule, with intuitive statements. It is only by faith that they perceived that the rational principle in man is also the principle in nature. But this faith was necessarily directed purely within : from the dweller in the innermost alone they expected to find confirmation of their trust. This is not intended as a condemnation of Stoicism : its failure was

[1] Hymn to Zeus. [2] Cleanthes. [3] Aurelius.

inevitable, and no doctrine will justify the ways of God to men unless it finds room for such heroic efforts. At the same time the failure must be discerned, and its inevitableness.

(2) *The Higher and the Lower Way*

When the Stoics painted the equanimity of the Wise Man, infallible, impassive, invulnerable, they readily admitted that it was an ideal portrait. In some respects it was not even an attractive one; and additions were made by the later Stoics to soften its sternness. But all agreed that the Wise Man had reached a higher stage than the Golden Age. He had come to a full consciousness of himself, and of the meaning of virtue; and thus he had acquired complete freedom. He was in the best sense king and priest; for he could do what he pleased; and nothing that he did could be wrong, since he was above law. It was also agreed that a distinction must be made between those who were in the way towards that ideal, and those who were content to follow the round of commonly accepted duties. They used the word ' Progress ' to denote the Way into which those had entered who were seeking the Ideal, the only Way in which is was possible to make true advance. With this profound and ethical notion we may compare Bunyan's phrase, The Pilgrim's Progress.

While the Stoics accepted from Plato the division into four cardinal virtues, they summed them up under one guiding formula. ' The life according to Nature is that virtuous and blessed flow of existence which is enjoyed by one who always acts so as to maintain the harmony between the God within and the will of the Power that orders the Universe.'[1] All else is to the wise man a matter of indifference; and he will school himself to an utter insensibility, thereby surpassing the temperate indulgence which the Peripatetics had learnt from Pythagoras. This is not an ideal which we can accept, for it leaves life a blank. The Stoics, though they did not penetrate to the fault of their ideal, felt that it needed some accommodation. The Perfect Duty (*officium perfectum*) goes according to a straight rule. But they allowed a measure of praise to the Ordinary Duty (*officium medium*), that which is fitting according to the custom of men. This distinction was taken over

[1] *Diog. Laert.* vii., i. 53.

by Ambrose from Cicero, and, in conjunction with one aspect of Platonic teaching, became the source of that view of a double morality which brought a train of evils into the Church.

(3) *The Cosmopolitan Ideal*

To bring the idea of Humanity into consciousness was a real achievement on the part of Stoicism. It came quite legitimately through their premisses. The world is a rational and intelligible unity. To all men there come certain innate ideas; these ideas come from Nature, and are therefore catholic, being involved in the universal reason. Zeno dreamed of a world federation, in which every man should exercise his citizenship; and the events of history assisted this conception. The empire of Alexander, and then still more decisively and permanently the Roman Empire broke down the barriers of nationality, and swept away the patriotism which makes even Plato and Aristotle imagine the ideal city in the forms of Athens and Sparta. We cannot assign to Stoicism the whole credit for formulating the idea of humanity; but we can see how it helped by giving some philosophical sanction to the conception of the *jus gentium*, which underlies so much of the Imperial legislation, and which found expression later in the code of Justinian. Chrysippus, the most systematic of the Stoics, says: 'No ethical subject can be rightly approached, except from an antecedent consideration of Entire Nature and the ordering of the Whole.' In this way a conviction of the individual's worth was coupled with a sense of the solidarity of humanity.

If this could have been fully worked out, it would have saved Stoicism from some of its chief perils. One of these was spiritual pride. Zeno's equanimity, the even flow of life which he urged, might easily turn to a cold self-sufficiency. Moreover, this self-sufficiency often issued in a deep sadness, especially in the noblest souls. By a curious paradox Stoicism, which conceived of all things as governed by reason, nevertheless had so strong a materialistic bias that it inevitably tended to pessimism. Marcus Aurelius, while he acknowledged the sway of universal reason, had little hope for the State or for mankind. The Stoics had the idea of a universal kingdom of righteousness: if they had been able to add the sanction of a Divine Presence and the hope of immortality, they would have come very near Christianity; but they had no sanctions, and no sure ground of hope.

4. Philo

In Philo we have a definite attempt to harmonize Judaism and Hellenism. A belief in one God had become axiomatic with the Jew; but Philo admitted the right to demand arguments to justify such a faith. He found such argument in the nature of man himself, in his rational powers and his ethical sense[1]; but he was anxious to keep clear of anything like anthropomorphism. He had drunk so deep of the Pierian spring of Plato's muse that materialism in any form was abhorrent to him. ' In attributing all perfection to God Philo uses at times expressions which denote the perfect in man.'[2] For example, He is called blessed, happy, the only wise, the only free, the only citizen, the only king. But, while he acknowledged the Divine Immanence, he insisted on the Divine Transcendence, which he found easier to harmonize with Hebrew thought. In reality God is beyond all knowledge; the deepest significance of His Name is unknown; and we can only speak of Him by negatives. In all this Philo was re-treading in his own experience the path which Israel had traversed. Philo's influence on the Doctrine of Perfection may be seen in two ways: (1) in his teaching of the manner in which knowledge of the Divine Perfection is conveyed; (2) in his conception of the method of human attainment.

(1) It might seem that Philo's premisses involved an impassable gulf between God and the world; but his Jewish training forbade such a conclusion. His account of creation is a curious mixture of Genesis and the Timaeus; but he enriched the Platonic conceptions of the derivative gods and the derivative world, by Jewish speculations in angelology, and by Stoic dogmas. Matter was regarded as eternal, and evil in a negative way. Between God and the world, therefore, there must be mediators[3]; but it is significant of Philo's thought, and greatly to his credit, that he steadily endeavours to sum up all the mediators in one. All the Powers, Ideas,

---

[1] S. Pringle-Pattison, *The Idea of God.* Lect. VI., ' Man as organic to the world.'
[2] T. H. Billings, *The Platonism of Philo Judaeus*, p. 22.
[3] *De Op. Mun.* 21–25.

Angels are grouped together under two, Goodness and Sovereignty; and these two find their fullness in the one Logos. It is impossible to think of this Logos without remembering the Prologue to the Fourth Gospel. Westcott, Drummond, and Harnack are agreed that there is no direct relation, and that it is probable that the extraordinary resemblance is due to the fact that both writers are uttering thoughts that were current at the time. This may be so; but if we cannot trace any relation between Philo and the New Testament, at any rate his influence on the Church through the Christians of Alexandria is apparent. His doctrine of the Logos has affected the whole statement of the communication of the Divine Perfection. Many translations may be given, such as Word, Reason, or Thought. Drummond prefers Thought as the best representation of the variable applications of the term. The Logos, while in one sense the Vicegerent of God, is in another and higher sense God Himself, as His Thought goes out from Himself. Philo could well have used the twofold statement, the Logos was with God, and, the Logos was God.

The Logos was conceived as the ideal High-Priest, and also as the ideal Man, the archetype, in whose mould man has been formed, by participation in whom man becomes a rational spirit. Philo allegorizes Adam as the incarnation of the Divine Archetype, but not of the perfect Logos, inasmuch as he was led astray by Eve, the sensational part of man. He never thinks of the Logos as a true Redeemer. There is indeed a hope of restoration; but it is due to man's not having entirely lost the Divine Nature. In man's return the Logos works as a suppliant, crying out in man after God; but there is not, nor could there be, any idea of the Logos becoming incarnate for man's salvation.

(2) In considering the method of attainment, Philo makes due allowance for the diversities of human dispositions. Some, like Abraham, have to learn from the beginning, through contemplation of the world and of self; others, like Isaac, have a natural bias towards the good; others, like Jacob, have to be fitted for the higher life by painful discipline.[1] It is to be noted that Philo was no ascetic. This painful discipline is not an end, but a means, and one which is not always necessary. The end which a man should set before himself

[1] Bigg, *Christian Platonists of Alexandria*, p. 46.

may be termed happiness or blessedness. This denotes the state of one endowed with a good genius : ' His bosom's lord sits lightly on his breast.' His opposite is one who like Orestes is haunted by the Furies of remorse, the dreadful sisters, the Eumenides, ' so called by antiquity in shuddering propitiation.' But the man who has attained eudaimonia is in perfect peace, for his mind is stayed on God. This experience came to Philo in ecstasy, frequently while studying the Word, or endeavouring to express his thoughts on it, as for instance in considering the account of the Cherubim at the Gate of Eden. Already we see the suggestion, which later writers greatly developed, that, while this state comes to the pure in heart and those who have studied the heavenly wisdom, it is not in itself connected either with holiness or knowledge. It comes by ways that cannot be discerned, and it is the highest to which man can attain.

5. PLOTINUS

More than two centuries elapsed between the birth of Philo (30 B.C.) and that of Plotinus (204 A.D.). During that time the Christian Church had taken root. It had attracted sufficient attention to be definitely proscribed as a *religio illicita*. Persecution, which from time to time broke into flame, smouldered throughout the Empire. Nevertheless, Christianity continued to increase ; and its fellowship was steadily knitting together a strong organization. Plotinus was an Egyptian by birth ; but it is the opinion of most scholars that, in estimating the influences which acted upon him, we need ascribe little to the Eastern. He was steeped in Plato ; and his philosophy may be described as an extension of one aspect of the master's teaching. The influence of Aristotle can be plainly traced ; but it is quite subsidiary. With Christianity, so far as we know, he came in contact mainly in the form of Gnosticism. It was against the Gnostics that he directed his only polemical work, *Ennead*, II. ix., in which he declared that there were three doctrines which were repulsive to him : (1) that the world had been made evil by an evil demiurgus, not the Supreme God, but the demiurgus who had been efficient in creation ; (2) that the soul of man was more important and higher than the world soul, or the souls of the sun and the stars ; (3) that a redeemer had come from a higher sphere, entering into the world of sense in order to bring man back to the fullness of God. Of these (1) is peculiar to Gnosticism, and has always been repudiated by the Christian Church ; but (2) and (3) are truly Christian. They propound a belief in the Incarnation of God in man, and in the redemption of the world by Christ, which seemed the climax of absurdity even to such a noble soul as Plotinus. One may judge how great was the gulf which separated Neo-Platonic thought from Christian. It was a gulf which needed bridging ; and we shall have to examine the first attempts in Clement-Alex., Origen, and Augustine. Perhaps Plotinus is referring to Origen when he says : ' We are ashamed of certain of our friends who before they were intimate with us were conversant with these opinions (i.e. of the Gnostics or Christians) ; and who still, I know not how, persevere in them, and endeavour to render them credible.'[1] If any charge of inconsistency is suggested it is groundless, for Origen walked in the light of Christ. But this quotation shows that the Platonists themselves deemed it incredible that their teaching should be amalgamated with the Christian.

Yet the amalgamation took place, with lasting effect on the Christian aim. It is, therefore, of the utmost importance that we should understand the method of the soul's upward movement, according to the conception of Plotinus. Three stages may be traced, perhaps four : (1) the stage of purification ; (2) the inner life of the contemplative, self-conscious spirit ; (3) the ecstasy of the God-conscious. Von Hügel tells us that St. Catherine of Genoa made a similar division of spiritual experience into three categories, according to the three prepositions, in, out of, over ; but they do not quite correspond with the three stages of Plotinus. Stage 1 she takes for granted. The category, In, includes recollection, concentration, introspection, and corresponds with Stage 2. The category, Out of, denotes the ecstasy of liberation, when the soul loses sight of itself in God. ' I see how all the sanctity which all the saints have is outside of themselves, and all in God.' This corresponds with Stage 3. The experience which St. Catherine utters in the third category, and which she designates by the preposition Over, seems to have nothing correspondent in

[1] *Enn.*, II. ix. 10. Cf. the account of Origen by Porphyry given in *Eus.*, *H.E.*, vi. 19.

Plotinus. It is, however, just to say that Thomas Taylor, commenting on *Ennead*, II. vii. 15, writes : ' The most sublime of the arcane dogmas of the Platonic Theology is this, that the ineffable principle of things is something even beyond the One.' This is the passage on which he relies : ' Such a nature all beautiful and eternal subsists about the One, proceeding from and with it, and in no respect departing from it ; but it always abides about and in the One, and lives according to it. Hence I think it beautifully and with a profundity of decision said by Plato that Eternity abides in One ; that he might not only lead it to the One which is in itself, but that he might lead it to the life of being about the One.' If we may take it that Plotinus is declaring an experience even beyond that of communion with the One, the Alone, then he is uttering a truth which Plato foreshadowed in his Idea of the Good in the *Republic*, which Numenius elaborated in the hypostases of his *Triad*, and which is fully enunciated in the Catholic doctrine of the Trinity, and of the Eternal Church of Christ. We will, however, confine ourselves to the three stages which are plainly set forth in his works.

(1) *The Stage of Purification*

We have seen that Plotinus was indignant with the Gnostics for saying that the world had been made by an evil demiurgus. He followed the *Timaeus*, agreeing that there was a receptacle into which the supreme God put form and life and beauty. Aristotle first used the word matter to designate this infinite, continuous, unshaped receptacle. It is the rough block in which the sculptor has to fashion the Divine image : it is the dark mirror which has to be cleared till it reflects the face of God. This world of matter has a certain reality : it cannot be said to be nothing. But it has not the highest reality : it does not exist for thought. There is an intelligible world, however, of which this is a pattern. ' For since we say that this All is framed after that Yonder as after a pattern, the All must first exist Yonder as a living entity, an animated being ; and, since its idea is complete, everything must exist Yonder.' [1] Purification is needed from the defilement which the soul has contracted from matter. Plato also speaks much of purification,

[1] *Enn.*, VI. vii. 12.

which he extends into many lives. The soul is sown in the body from its native star, and has to recover from the effect of that sowing. 'Chisel away from thy soul what is superfluous, straighten that which is crooked, purify and enlighten that which is dark, and do not cease working at thy statue, until virtue shines before thine eyes with its divine splendour, and thou seest temperance seated in thy bosom in its holy purity.'[1] Plotinus was no ascetic, and does not advocate mortification : plain living and high thinking are sufficient. In order that the soul may be raised from the miserable state into which it has fallen it must be convinced of the baseness of the attractions of earth, and must learn to despise sensual pleasure ; but it is still more important that by high thinking it should understand its own worth and dignity. The motive for purification can only be made intelligible to rational beings through the perception of the higher life. The soul finds it necessary to detach itself, and to become a stranger and sojourner on earth, not because the world is evil, but because it is confusing. ' Just as a singer who wants to catch a note must shut out all other notes, and strain his ear to catch the true note when it comes, so in this world we must shut out physical sounds, except so far as is necessary, and help the apprehensive power of the soul, and be ready to hear the voices from above.'[2] This is all the Neo-Platonic purification actually involved ; but in practice it tended to include detachment from the interests and work of the world.

(2) *The Inner Life of the Contemplative Spirit*

From the outward glance by which we perceive the baseness of material things, we turn to the inward gaze by which we discern the preciousness of the spiritual. This little preposition, In, will lead us from things Here to things Yonder. Plotinus used the distinction between Here and There as equivalent to a distinction between the world of sense and the world of thought, the spiritual universe. Following Aristotle, he declared that the only way is through the contemplative life. Our first need is Recollection and Quiet, for the voice of God speaks in silence, when His Presence illuminates the house. ' Then it is proper to think that He is present, when,

[1] *Enn.*, I. vi. 9.   [2] *Enn.*, V. i.

like a God entering the house of some one who invokes Him, He fills it with splendour.'[1] The reference is to a passage in the *Odyssey*, xix. 29–45. Ulysses and his son were secretly removing the weapons from the armoury in preparation for the day of vengeance on the morrow. Pallas Athene preceded them; and from the golden lamp which she bore there radiated a soft splendour which filled the chamber with a beautiful light. Telemachus cried out in wonder and delight; but Ulysses bade him be silent and put a wise restraint upon his speech, whenever he perceived a Divine Presence. This passage exactly shows the idea of the contemplative life, and the purpose for which it is enjoined. God is within; and in order to perceive Him the soul must retire into the silence of contemplation. ' Go to Him who is Yonder. Surely thou wilt find Him not far from thee, for there is not much between.'

Man is drawn to the upward way by the attraction of beauty, which is from God, we may even say, which is God. The soul, having by its discursive reason wandered over the world and seen the lower forms of beauty, now turns inward and intuitively perceives. This distinction between the discursive reason and the pure or intuitive intelligence comes from Aristotle's *De Anima*, and has received prominence in the modern philosophy of Bergson. Aristotle considered that the higher intelligence was eternal, but that it had no individuality, no content, no interest : the lower was extremely interesting, but it was only for a brief moment. Now Plotinus, with his Platonic interest in immortality, was anxious to safeguard the soul's individuality.[2] The soul discovers its error in thinking of mine and thine; but it does so because it learns that its true individuality is found in God. As in the old story, Psyche turns from her deceitful sisters, Desire and Anger, and yields herself to her true lover; the soul, however, in yielding finds itself. All that it has learnt through art and earthly love and philosophy becomes as nothing before the Divine contemplation. The discursive reason is our messenger; but the intuitive intelligence is our king. God has been with us all the time, though we have not recognized Him.

' The whole difficulty that besets us in considering the world of sense arises from our first setting up space as a kind of Chaos, and then, when we have set up this notion of space in

---

[1] *Enn.*, V. iii. 17.   [2] See the whole discussion in *Enn.*, V. iii.

our imagination, bringing God into it. Then, when we have brought Him in, we begin to ask whence and how did He come : as if He were a new arrival, we wonder how He got here and what He is, as though He had suddenly emerged from some abyss or dropped down from the clouds. It is needful, therefore, to cut away the cause of all this perplexity, and to cast space away altogether from our thought of Him ; and not to suppose that He is in anything, or lies or is seated in anything, or that He came at all ; but just that He is, and as reason proves Him to be ; and that space, like everything else, is after Him, and that space is after everything else.' The contemplative faculty needed to discern this truth belongs to all, but in only a few is it developed by use. The life of the spirit is one of pure contemplation, in which the dualism between the subject and the object is fused into a perfect unity. Spirit and reality, or, we may say, spiritual thought and the real object of spiritual thought, become fused in the act of contemplation. ' For nothing Yonder has passed away, but all things abide in an ever-present Now ; since they are of such a nature as to be satisfied with thus existing. But each of them is spirit (or intellect) and being. And the Whole is every spirit and every being. Spirit, therefore, derives its existence as spirit from the perception of being ; and being exists as being through becoming the object of spiritual perception to spirit, and through imparting to it intellection and existence.'[1] As we ought to strive to think of God apart from any notion of space, so we should receive the conception of the timelessness of eternity : the power to receive these conceptions will come through developing the faculty of contemplation. When Plotinus says, ' Instead of time Here, eternity is Yonder,' he is not separating Here from Yonder by death, but by the difference in spiritual condition due to contemplation.

(3) The highest stage (or almost the highest) is that of ecstasy or the Beatific Vision. Plotinus followed Plato rather than Aristotle in describing the soul as the very principle of motion, and as having life in itself ; and also in his account of the Blessed Vision. But from Aristotle he learnt to think of those highest moments in which the divine activity of the soul is no longer latent, a mere possibility, but an actuality : so

[1] *Enn.*, V. i. 4 (Taylor's trans.).

that the soul enters on a realization of the eternal blessedness of God. Porphyry says that his master four times enjoyed this state; but for the best it is extremely rare. The soul has simply to wait for this highest state, and must not even desire or pray for it. It may not be good that it should come; and when it does come it will be only for a brief visit. This state is, therefore, clearly distinguished from the ecstatic states of which Philo speaks, when in a very placid way he felt thousands of times during his study of the Word a transporting influence which unfolded its inner meaning. But for the Neo-Platonist the experience is extremely rare, and always ineffable. It is noteworthy that here for the first time Plotinus discovers a Divine Helper. It is alien to his thought to imagine that a Redeemer should descend to the soul in its weakness: indeed he is angry with the Gnostics for suggesting anything so unseemly. But, when the soul has raised itself by purification and contemplation, then at last it meets with One who is waiting to welcome it home.

He learnt from Plato[1] that there is One, who may be called the Good, beyond being and essence. Any intellectual perception which involves spiritual exercise is just this, viz. a motion towards the Good or the One.[2] But this energetic movement towards God is not God; for God is energy in the sense that He always enjoys perfect self-communion; and why should such an energy wish to energize? All the strife and strong energy which moved up to God is of untold worth; but in the moment of actual fusion, as there is a hushing of the tumult of the flesh, so also there is a cessation of the activity of the discursive reason.[3] For by the reason we analyse and perceive the many, but never the One. The One comes last in the procession which passes before the soul. ' After all these the King Himself appears suddenly, and all pray and do Him obeisance; all, that is, who have not gone away satisfied with the glorious pageant which preceded the King.'[4] The path of virtue leads to the path of intellectual freedom, in which we know God, but we know Him as another: we see Him in images, as we see the statues outside the Temple. But when we pass within we see no more the images, for we become inspired and possessed to discern that which is higher

---

[1] *Republic*, vi. 509. [2] *Enn.*, V. vi. 5.
[3] Cf. Augustine's experience, *Confessions*, ix. 25. [4] *Ennead*, VI. v. 3.

than ourselves, and yet which is ourselves at our highest and best.

Is there a further stage? Yes, there is one, the greatest of all, though only dimly perceived by Plotinus. He has a glimpse of it when he asks why the soul does not abide Yonder ; but he does not follow the clue. He answers by saying that it is because the soul has not yet wholly migrated from Here ; but she will when her vision of God is no longer impeded by the body.[1] He is thinking of the description in the *Timaeus* of the Lonely One, who is the source of all, and whose kindness is the only, but sufficient, security for all. To return from the bodily form to Him is true blessedness. ' This then is the life of the Gods and of Divine and happy men, a liberation from all earthly concerns, a life unaccompanied by human pleasures, and a flight of the alone to the Alone.'[2] What he fails to discover is that the movement from the loneliness of God, which must have come by His will, is not destined to be simply negatived. To come back after the hour of vision to the world in which the discursive reason acts is not necessarily a downward step. God loves the world because of His eternal need of it, and a return to His loneliness is by no means the end of creation. But Neo-Platonism was never able to lay hold of that ; and Christianity itself is far from having perceived the full implications of the Divine Kenosis.

6. THE MYSTERIES.

The Mysteries originated in Nature-Myths and the cults woven around them. This is clearly seen in the story of Demeter and her daughter, which formed the basis of the Eleusinian Mysteries, and which arose from the burial of the seeds in the dark, and their resurgence in vegetation and flower.

> O Proserpina !
> For the flowers now that, frighted, thou let'st fall
> From Dis's wagon.

The fertility of nature, her recovery from winter's darkness, then by a natural transition the reproductive powers in man, and the exhilaration that comes through wine, all these seemed to speak of God. If the Mysteries gave a warmer tinge to

[1] *Enn.*, VI. ix. 10.   [2] *Enn.*, VI. ix. 11.

religion than philosophy had done, it was a warmth fraught with grave dangers of sexual irregularities and excesses, and of orgies of Bacchic revelry. These dangers were kept in check by an earnest effort after salvation, together with a strong conviction that salvation could not be limited to the present, and that it was dependent on purity. This desire after purity came partly as the result of the social warmth kindled in the fellowship of those associated in mystic brotherhood, for it was apparent that fellowship could only be retained through purity. It came also by the awe induced by a belief in immortality, and by the contemplation of the heavens. The belief in immortality became more potent through the growth of the Isis-Serapis cult; for Egypt had been the pioneer of the life immortal.[1] The contemplation of the heavens also had a purifying effect.[2] 'Like draws to like. The rapture of contemplation becomes a real communion. The gazer is possessed by a Divine love. He cannot rest until he participates in the divinity of those living, sparkling beings above. Thus the astrological writer, Vettius Valens, page 242, 15 (ed. Kroll): "I desired to obtain a Divine and adoring contemplation of the heavens and to purify my ways from wickedness and all defilement." '[3]

In some respects these cults were the keenest rivals of Christianity; in some they smoothed the way for its progress. The Fathers were often startled to note resemblances. 'Mithra signat illic in frontibus milites suos; celebrat et panis oblationem et imaginem resurrectionis inducit.'[4] St. Paul was interested in the Mysteries; but he was alive to the dangers. 1 Corinthians was written in opposition to those who would reconcile allegiance to Christ with participation in idol feasts. Over all the world hung a belief in daemons: to many earnest minds the way of salvation was by initiation into the Mysteries. Few believed in the idols as having power in themselves; but behind the idols lay daemoniacal forces. The Mysteries taught the use of symbolism, of which the Church availed itself. A resolute endeavour was made to keep free from the evils of heathen worship. But the sense of mystery in life, the use of symbolism to express that sense, and the feeling of

---

[1] See *Timaeus*, 22b. Kennedy, *The Mystery Religions*, p. 99.
[2] Posidonius, who combined Platonic and Stoic teaching, popularized the astrology of his day in a way that made it suitable for amalgamation with the Mystery Religions.
[3] Kennedy, op. cit., p. 7.   [4] Tertullian, *De Praescr.*, 40.

brotherhood which comes to those who have been initiated into a great secret, all these were freely and rightly utilized by the Church.

The perfection which shone before the Church had been seen by many earnest souls outside. The stages of progress in the Eleusinian Mysteries were similar to those which Clement-Alex. outlined in his three books; first Purification, then Illumination or Initiation, then the Vision in which the whole drama is re-enacted in the experience of the soul. But what gives distinction and originality and splendour to the Christian message is that it is based on no drama, but on an actual life, not on the yearnings of men, but on the revelation of the love of God. The sacrament was a symbol, but it was much more than a symbol. That which was so crudely shown in the taurobolium was fulfilled in Christian Baptism, and in the communion of the Body and the Blood of Christ; just as the instinct which unites the sexes is purified and uplifted till it finds its spiritual fulfilment in the mutual love of Christ and His Church.

7. BUDDHISM

A great likeness exists between the teaching of Christ and that of Buddha, and particularly in regard to the way of perfection.[1] The ideal of a gentle ascetic, which for many centuries prevailed in Christendom, is precisely that of Buddhism. It stands in marked contrast, for instance, with the ideal of Mithraism, which had such an attraction for the Roman soldier. Probably one reason why Mithraism failed was because it disdained the service of women and neglected the feminine virtues. But consider the following description of Buddhism: 'It exhibits in the most striking manner all the gentler virtues. It is simply amazing how far on this side it transcends the Platonic, Aristotelian, Stoic, and Epicurean ideals of the sage, and how mean and superficial even it causes the boasted wisdom of the classical world to appear. Among its features are a love without limit, self-sacrifice, justice, purity.'[2] This tribute is all the more impressive because it is part of a mordant criticism of Buddhism as the supreme

[1] See art. in *H. D. C.*, ii. 287-8, which discusses the attempt of Seydel and Pfleiderer to trace a direct influence of Buddhism on Christ.
[2] R. Flint, *Anti-Theistic Theories*, p. 298.

instance of Pessimism. It will be of service to the investigation of this subject to consider the following points in which the Buddhist ideal has contact with the Christian.

(1) In both much stress is laid on ethics; and in both the ideal is defined as love even more than as righteousness: so that the feminine ideal, with its insistence on the passive virtues, appears to take precedence of the masculine. It may be noted, however, that Christianity was formed on the basis of Yahwism, which was eminently a masculine religion. For the fulfilment of Yahwism it was necessary that it should be rounded off by the addition of the more gracious and gentler virtues. But the masculine virtues of wisdom, justice, courage, and self-command remained still, though they were crowned with the feminine graces of faith and hope and love. To some extent the same comment applies to Buddhism, which grew out of Brahmanism. One vital difference, however, may be noted. In the earlier Yahwism and in later Judaism man's relation towards God is always intensely personal. In the higher forms, as in the Deuteronomic school, it is a relation of personal, loving devotion. When we turn to Jesus we find that He practically discarded all other names for God that He might use the intensely personal one of Father. Now in Brahmanism, as it is set forth in the Upanishads, 'the ordinary name for the World-soul was Brahman, a neuter noun which expresses the common thought of the time, that the World-soul is an impersonal essence, present in all things. There were many speculations as to its nature; until some wise thinker called Brahman the *ātman*, or self, of the universe. Then, as the soul of the universe was *ātman*, and the soul of the individual was *ātman*, the conclusion was soon drawn that the two were identical. The great affirmation was made, My self is the infinite Self; the soul of the universe, whole and undivided, dwells in me. Thus self-knowledge is knowledge of God; and as the knowledge of God leads to Release, the man who realizes the identity of his soul with the World-soul is thereby set free from the cycle of births and deaths; he will never be born again. The great phrases used are, Thou art That, I am Brahman, and I am He. This is the Vedanta philosophy in its earliest form.'[1] It is manifest that Buddhism, which was founded on such a base, and which

---

[1] Farquhar, *Primer of Hinduism*, p. 41.

set before itself such an ideal of Release, could attach no meaning to what Jesus called the first and the great commandment. Consequently, the influence of Brahmanism on Buddhism in retaining the masculine virtues was by no means so effective as that of Yahwism on Christianity. Even the feminine virtues cannot be said to have any logical place in the scheme: love for one's neighbour, which is certainly inculcated, comes by way of intuition rather than deduction. Logic, of course, is not everything. The perfect man, *arahant*, is one who is worthy to enter Nirvana; but there were those, known as Bodisatwas, who postponed their entrance into the final stage, in order that their accumulated merit might be of service to the world. But, interesting and beautiful though this is, it cannot hide the fact that Buddhism depends on a pessimistic logic, and that in that chain mercy has no real connexion. *Pessimism and love are ultimately incompatible.*

(2) Perfection is not purely a question of ethics. In one place, indeed, Jesus speaks as though it were. When the lawyer rightly defined the essence of the law as love to God and man, Jesus answered, ' This do and thou shalt live.' But the ethical word love must designate a spirit founded on knowledge, on intelligent observation, and on active interest. It is a just, even an obvious, deduction to say that it involves faith. Similarly, Buddhism transcends the purely ethical, but with different issues, in so far as it is founded on different premisses. The finding of the Path by the Buddha, which is the type for all his followers, comes at last through perfect insight into the relation between life and suffering, cause and effect. It is plain that the knowledge which leads to insight through meditation, and the asceticism by which desire is restrained, have a more logical place in the scheme of Buddhist perfection than those ethical and social virtues which are brought in by a *tour de force*. It is plain also that such attainment is not open to those engaged in the world's work. Hence the monk is essential to the whole scheme. It is not necessary for us to decide how far Christian monachism was affected by Buddhist teaching. Its first development was in Egypt, and we know that the teaching of Buddha was promulgated there in the time of Clement-Alex. But the human mind runs easily into certain grooves. If with Aristotle and Buddha we consider contemplation as the highest life, the recluse or

the monk seems inevitable. The Greek mind never seriously turned to asceticism, as the Hindu did ; but asceticism is a logical conclusion, if we regard the body with its desires as the chief restraint on the soul, or as keeping it back from the final release. These ideas have had a great and mischievous influence on the doctrine of perfection. The *arahant* attained perfection as the crown of long effort ; but it was effort in which benevolence and service had only a subordinate part, and that without any logical connexion. The real effort was within his own self, in discipline, in subjugation, and finally in something very like self-annihilation. All this has entered into Christian thought to an extraordinary extent. It still largely represents the popular ideal of saintship. But the difference is enormous between this and the true Christian ideal as expressed in St. Paul's : ' I have been crucified with Christ ; yet I live ; and yet no longer I, but Christ liveth in me.' The difference is due to the Christian's faith that in losing himself in Christ he is finding himself in the eternal love.

(3) ' In no religion is the perfection of the saint as something won and realized during life so emphatically conceded and insisted upon as it is in early Buddhism.'[1] This appears to me the matter in which we can learn most from the Buddhist idea of perfection. Death in itself brings no deliverance. Even the hope of the materialist,

> That no life lives for ever ;
> That dead men rise up never ;
> That even the weariest river
> Winds somewhere safe to sea,

—even this hope is groundless. Release can only come by a spiritual effort in which the soul attains freedom. ' Not to seek for anything, O monks, is to be free ; to seek for anything is not to be free. . . . If passion for form . . . for sensation . . . for perception . . . for the predispositions is abandoned, then through the abandonment of passion the support is cut off, and there is no resting-place for consciousness. When that consciousness has no resting-place, does not increase, and no longer accumulates Karma, it becomes free ; and when it is free, it becomes quiet ; and when it is quiet, it is

[1] Rhys Davids, *E. R. E.*, ix. 727a.

blissful; and when it is blissful, it is not agitated; and when it is not agitated, it attains Nirvana in its own person; and it knows that re-birth is exhausted, that it has lived the holy life, that it has done what it behoved to do, and that it is no more for this world.'¹ Such a condition is not only possible during this present life, it must be accomplished during some one or other life in the flesh. When attainment has been fully reached, death may be said to have some slight value in snapping the last thin link.

The teaching of Christianity is much less dogmatic: its only unqualified dogma is its invincible optimism. It is not committed to an assertion of the continued existence of all the souls born into this world, though I suppose that might be called the orthodox view. Neither is it committed to a denial of re-birth, although few Christians would admit the possibility of it. The point of contact between the Evangelical Ideal and the Buddhist is in regard to attainment in the body. Where such attainment has not been reached during any particular lifetime, the Buddhist conceives that it will have to be during some future existence into which one will be re-born in this world. But Christian thought is dominated by the Gospel of the Resurrection, which on the one hand has set such a seal on the body of our humiliation as to make it no longer incredible that it should be the temple of the Holy Ghost, and on the other hand has opened illimitable possibilities of ethical activity for the glorified body in other spheres.

8. MANICHAEISM

The influence of Manichaeism on the formation of Christian doctrine was *sui generis*.² In spite of Catholic opposition, it had a profound effect in making perfection, Divine and human, consistent with a belief in the eternity of evil. The aetiology of Mani, that evil had an original eternity co-equal with good, has been generally rejected; but his eschatology, that evil would last as long as good, has been as generally

¹ Warren, *Buddhism in Trans.*, 162-3.
² Harnack, iii. 316-36. Mani (*circa* A.D. 215-77) was a Persian who elaborated a new system, at once philosophical and ethical, under the influence of Mazdeism, but on a basis of the old Babylonian nature mythology. Christian and Buddhist influences may also be traced.

accepted throughout the Church. He taught that there always has been, and there always will be, Good and Evil, both materialistic, and the one as necessary as the other, and he recognized in both a spiritual principle. The rage of Evil against Good finding expression in Satan, its spiritual head, war broke out. Victory remained with Good, but not without loss; for man fell under the dominion of Satan. Hence there came a mixture of good and evil in the world. The Light was submerged in the Darkness, as we might imagine sunshine buried in coal. But the God who is Light is continually seeking to release this buried sunshine; and the agent of redemption may be called Jesus, not the historical Jesus, but a docetic Saviour incapable of suffering.[1] After him came others, such as Paul, who was always honoured in Manichaeism. The last and the greatest was Mani himself.

It may be noted in this system that, while it admits an irreconcilable dualism of good and evil, it transcends the dualism of spirit and matter. But two results followed; the first, that redemption was conceived primarily as asceticism, a separation from the evil in the world, the second, that as this was only possible for a few there must be a double standard. These results, which are always cropping up, are defined with unusual clearness in Manichaeism because of the frankness with which it faced the problem of evil. There ensued a rigid asceticism, marked by the three famous signs or signacula: *signaculum oris*, by which the mouth was to be sealed against unclean food or speech; *signaculum manus*, by which the hand was to be kept from unclean occupation; *signaculum sinus*, by which the breast was to be guarded from impure thought, including desire for sexual intercourse even in marriage. How strict this was may be judged from the fact that a fourth part of the year was set apart for fasting. Naturally this could not be demanded from the whole community. From those who were called *catechumeni* or *auditores* there was only required observance of Mani's ten commandments, abstinence from idolatry, fornication, magic, lying, &c. Those who professed themselves able to bear the whole yoke were called *electi* or *perfecti*. They were not only perfecti but perfectores; and it was this belief which made Manichaeism so attractive. The electi attained a high degree of saintship, as people commonly

[1] Jesus impatibilis.

understood it, and their attainment had a redemptive power even for those who had no mind to seek such heights.

We find Manichaean influence in the saying of Lactantius that evil was needed to reveal good by way of contrast. It can be traced for many centuries, down to the Middle Ages, in such sects as the Cathari, the Paulicians, and the Bogomiles.[1] But its main effect on Christianity was through Augustine. For nine years he was an auditor; and he had considerable intercourse with the Manichaean Bishop Faustus, whose intellectual honesty he greatly admired. After he entered the Catholic Church he gave his whole strength to pointing out the errors of the system. It has been said that he opposed an aesthetico-metaphysical optimism, which he had learnt from Neo-Platonism as well as from the Catholic Church, to the Manichaean pessimism. But that is only one side. There is a deep-rooted pessimism in Augustine. When he speaks of the mass of perdition, even though he always confronts it with the sovereign and over-ruling grace of God, he never escapes the sense of its stubborn and eternal reality. He became a Manichaean, because of his sense of sin, and because 'he did not get past the idea that Catholic doctrine held God to be the originator of sin.'[2] Even after his return he never altogether threw off the effect of those years. This was probably the main reason which led him, in spite of his conviction of the harmony and beauty of the universe and of the absolute goodness of God, to acquiesce in a final statement of unending evil.[3]

[1] Hagenbach, ii. 110.   [2] Harnack, v. 110n., also v. 253n.
[3] *Civ. Dei*, xxi. c. 9ff.

CHAPTER IX

THE IDEA OF PERFECTION IN THE EARLY CHURCH

THE course of our investigation has followed the idea of perfection as it is found in the Scriptures, and as it arose outside Christianity. I have included in the latter some account of Plotinus and also of Manichaeism, though both these occur in the Christian era, and must have been affected by Christian teaching. They are essentially non-Christian, and may be fairly distinguished from such movements as Montanism and Gnosticism, which, however heretical, would not have arisen if it had not been for the teaching of Christ and His apostles. These, therefore, come under the subjects to be considered in the present chapter.

Noteworthy expressions occur in the early Fathers as to individual and ecclesiastical perfection, but unsystematically, and without any attempt to pursue the conclusions deduced from them. Certain movements—e.g. Montanism and Gnosticism—have a clear conception of the way of attainment. In most cases these were condemned by the ecclesiastical authorities; but the movement known as Monachism, or Monasticism, received the imprimatur of the Church. Then some of the leaders of Christian thought set themselves to work out a scheme which should justify the attitude of the Church. The great names in this connexion are Clement of Alexandria, Origen, Ambrose, and Augustine, to whom it will be necessary to pay special attention. In the present chapter I purpose dealing with the early, unsystematic endeavours to define the Christian's aim.

1. CLEMENT OF ROME AND OTHERS

Of the simple and undeveloped statement of Christian Perfection the Epistle of Clement of Rome is an excellent example. In the opening paragraphs he reminds the Corinthian

Church of its former glory : ' Who did not honour you for your faith . . . your piety . . . your hospitality . . . your perfect and sound knowledge ? '[1] But above all he sings the praise of love. ' The height to which it exalts is unspeakable. What man is able to tell the excellence of its beauty ? Love unites to God. *By love all the elect of God have been made perfect ;* without love nothing is well pleasing to God. Those who have been perfected in love through the grace of God attain to the place of the godly. . . . How great and wonderful a thing is love, and there is no declaring its perfection.'[2] Here we have the characteristics of perfection truly set forth. It is nothing else but love ; only it is love founded on Christian knowledge ; not a mere natural growth, but the fruit of Divine Grace. Its stability is due to the fact that it has its root in faith in Christ. It might be deemed wise to remain content with such simple and unthought-out statements ; but the history of the human mind shows that it cannot rest without pressing on to some more elaborate and reasoned utterance.

Another letter of singular beauty and charm is that to Diognetus by an unknown writer.[3] It gives an idealized picture of Christians in the world as having a citizenship of their own, which surpasses expectation.[4] The writer is thinking, with St. Paul, of the heavenly citizenship, which found expression in the earthly constitution, which was already knitting itself together. He makes the famous comparison of Christians in the world to the soul in the body. It is a witness to the growing power of the Church that he was able to say that as the soul, being enclosed in the body, holds it together, so Christians, kept in the world as in a prison, are the true source of its consistency. We may compare Col. i. 17, in which there is the same spiritual intuition to discern the force by which the world coheres. Similarly, in the Shepherd of Hermas the Church is shown as having an ideal existence, so that it may even be said that the world was made for the Church.[5] But Hermas has no sense of that which is so beautiful a feature in Diognetus, the conviction of the untold blessing which the Church brings to the world. In the Apologists we find both views—that the Church brings a blessing to the world, and that it stands over against it for condemnation.

---

[1] *Ad Cor.*, c. 1. [2] *Ad Cor.*, cc. 49–50. [3] *Circa* 130–50 A.D.
[4] *Ad Diog.*, 5. [5] *Vis.*, ii. 4.

If we speak in any way of the early Church as perfect, we know that it was an ideal perfection; but we know also that it was an ideal which came sufficiently near realization to constitute a great victory.

2. IRENAEUS AND TERTULLIAN

The attitude of the early Church towards the Christian aim may be illustrated from two writers of very different temper. Irenaeus (*ob.* 202) is of much importance for the doctrine of Redemption in regard to its purpose in man. His great word is *Recapitulatio*, the summing up of all in Christ. God, who alone hath immortality, of His goodness designs to bestow on man this gift. Man is by nature capable of receiving it[1]; but until He is redeemed He has only the potentiality. Man's nature had to be taken into the Divine by adoption in order that this potentiality might be realized. The original capacity in man has never been lost, but it has never been fulfilled until all things have been summed up in Christ.[2] One of the chief categories which Irenaeus uses to declare man's original destination for perfection is that of an immortal life with God. He has some exquisite sayings as to the way in which Christ recapitulated in Himself the stages and processes of human development. 'For He came to save all through Himself; all, I say, who through Him are reborn unto God, babies and little ones and boys and youths and older ones.'[3] He proceeds to show that this included even the experience of death.[4] A good deal in Irenaeus is rudimentary, and makes no appeal to us; but his central thought is also central to any true conception of evangelical attainment. 'Jesus Christ became such as we are, in order that He might make us such as He is.' This recapitulatory work has no limit. It goes back, without doubt, to Adam, for it would have been a great victory for the Devil if the first head of humanity had been lost. It goes forward into Hades, whither Christ descends to redeem. Those who are united to one another in faith and love through Him form the true Church, the real humanity which has been perfected in Christ.

In Tertullian we have one who attracts by his earnestness,

---

[1] 'Capax incorruptionis et immortalitatis.' [2] Eph. i. 10.
[3] *Contra Haer.*, ii. 22, 4.
[4] Recapitulans autem universum hominem in se ab initio usque ad finem, recapitulavit et mortem ejus' (op. cit., v. 23, 2).

vigour, and single-mindedness, but who repels by his intolerance, and sometimes even by his callousness. The following estimate is taken from a Roman Catholic historian : ' Our author's exaggerated severity on the question of second marriages is but one particular feature of that severity which permeates all his system of ethics. True, in theory, he distinguishes between precepts and counsels ; but when he comes to deal with the practical cases of conscience, which Christians living in the midst of pagans had every day to face and settle, he seems to forget this distinction, and ordinarily requires nothing short of the extreme.'[1] At any rate, he may be taken as a proof of the Church's confidence in its moral superiority. The Christian must aim at perfection ; and in such a world as Tertullian's it might well be thought that the only way was by complete renunciation. Tertullian never dreams of the Church redeeming the world. Only by the most austere discipline could the Christian guard himself from the thousand snares in the world. ' It is a great defect of heretics that they allow catechumens to enter the state of perfection before they have been grounded in Christian knowledge.'[2] One curious result of this attitude of the great African doctor was that he deprecated infant, and even early, baptism. ' Why should an age which is innocent hasten to the remission of sins ? '[3] We should have expected an opposite conclusion from his realistic traducianism ; the soul, he says, is generated in the womb equally with the body, and equally bears the marks of its parentage.[4] Evidently he does not consider that this inherited tendency to sin constitutes guilt in the sight of God, or brings down His condemnation. Christ alone is altogether pure through His Divinity.[5] The soul is reckoned in Adam until God accepts it in Christ ; and until that revaluation it is impure and sinful, receiving ignominy from association with the body. This shadow falls on humanity by reason of its creaturehood ; it has been deepened by man's impatience, grasping too eagerly at equality with God ; but it can never become a total eclipse, since, after all, man has come from God.[6]

[1] Tixeront, *Hist. of Dogma*, i. 324.
[2] 'Ante sunt perfecti catechumeni quam edocti' (*De Praescr.*, 41).
[3] 'Quid festinat innocens aetas ad remissionem peccatorum ?' (*De Bap.*, 18).
[4] *De Anima*, cc. 19, 36.   [5] *De Anima*, 41.
[6] 'Potest enim obumbrari quia non est Deus, extingui non potest quia a Deo' (op. cit., 41).

This is a weighty statement of the factors with which we have to deal. The perfection set before man is compatible with his creaturehood, and with the tendency to sin which he has inherited. Whatever penalty might come on man as the result of the impatience which had brought about his fall had been taken away through Christ.[1] The baptized believer has entered into a new state in which he is revalued in Christ instead of in Adam; but it is expected that he should keep himself unspotted from the world; and that can only be done by the most diligent watchfulness. Whatever is not expressly allowed must be considered as forbidden.[2] Tertullian shows that the Christian is well able to attain his goal, and is on the right road to it, though he will need the utmost care in order to win through. Two defects in this teaching may be named. One is that the world is simply abandoned; 'leave the poor old stranded wreck, and pull for the shore.' The other is that the sanction to which he appeals is largely external, a custom which had been handed down in the *Regula Fidei*, and which had no doubt much ethical value, but which was not necessarily a spiritual principle derived immediately from the Atonement in Christ.[3]

3. THE ENCRATITES AND THE MONTANISTS

The question of the Christian attitude to the world greatly exercised the early Church.[4] How far should one who was seeking to follow Christ with a perfect heart withdraw himself from the world of his day, with its secular interests? Many answers were given; nor could any one be always consistent. The close of the Didache is very instructive: ' If indeed thou art able to bear the whole yoke of the Lord thou wilt be perfect; but if thou art not able, do what thou canst. And as regards food, bear what thou canst; but against idol offerings be exceedingly on thy guard, for it is a service of dead gods.' This is the soil from which sprung the conception of a double morality. The Church was not prepared to follow the Encratites,

---
[1] 'Exempto reatu eximitur et poena' (*De Bap.*, 5).   [2] *De Corona*, c. 2.
[3] When Tertullian lapsed into Montanism, the first of these defects became accentuated, but the second was lessened.
[4] The subject is discussed by H. H. Scullard in *Early Christian Ethics in the West*, Part I., c. ii., from the standpoint of the scientific conception of the world and its creation. Dr. Scullard rightly dissents from Harnack's statement that this must be put aside as an intellectualism which interferes with our placing Christian morality on a stable basis.

Montanists, or Novatians. '*The Church resolutely declared war on all these attempts to elevate evangelical perfection to an inflexible law for all, and overthrew her opponents.*'[1]

The attitude adopted by the Encratites and Montanists, and later by the Novatians, was no ignoble one. It was that of a withdrawal from the world, and from anything that could minister to the lust of the flesh, the lust of the eyes, and the vainglory of life. Tatian, the best known of the Encratites, wrote a book entitled, *Concerning Perfection according to the Redeemer*, setting forth a strict asceticism, which included abstinence from marriage, from wine and flesh, and from earthly possessions, as the only true following of Christ. This undoubtedly represented a widespread feeling in the early Church. ' Die to the world, renouncing the madness of its pursuits ; live to God, renouncing thy old nature through the knowledge of His Being. We are not born for death ; we die through our own fault ; freedom has completely undone us. We have become slaves, we who were free ; on account of sin have we been sold. Nothing evil has been created by God ; it is we who have produced what is bad ; and what has been thus produced we can again renounce.'

The Montanist movement had a much wider scope than the Encratite. Besides its first leaders, Montanus and the two prophetesses, Priscilla and Maximilla, it numbered two who will always have a place in Church history—the mystic and martyr, Perpetua, and the great Tertullian. Gwatkin compares them with the early Methodists for their essential sanity and earnestness.[2] This is a suggestive comparison, though we may note that they had still closer resemblances with the Quakers ; it may be added that, like the Quakers and the Methodists, they laid stress on the teaching of Perfection. The two main questions which Montanism raised in an acute form are these :

(1) Is the Church a pure body of those who have been fully redeemed and who have entered into the spiritual life, or is it an organization in contact with the world, a field in which wheat and tares grow close together ? The Montanists looked for a visible Church, whose centre would be in Phrygia ; but they believed that such a Church must be pure from all defilement.[3] This is what gives such genuine indignation to

---

[1] Harnack : *Hist. of Dogma*, ii. 123n.   [2] *Early Church History*, ii. 88.
[3] ' Vera, pudica, sancta, virgo ' (Tert., *De Pudic.*, 1).

Tertullian's protest against the edict of Bishop Calixtus, allowing even adulterers, if penitent, to be received back into the Church. He was angry because this power to bind and loose was assumed, not through spiritual grace, but through ecclesiastical position; it appeared more akin to the authority of a *pontifex maximus* than of a minister of Christ. But his main indignation was at the thought that such an edict should be read out in the Virgin Church. ' Sed hoc in ecclesia legitur, et in ecclesia pronuntiatur, et virgo est.'[1] To us it seems that there is a good deal to be said for Calixtus, whose action has an obvious likeness to Christ's. But a large section of the Church had become convinced that for gross sins, such as idolatry, adultery, whoredom, murder, there was no penance which made possible a return to the fold. With this there was a growing conviction that salvation was not possible outside the Church.[2] The Montanists held this firmly, and all the more insisted that the Church must be pure, not having spot or wrinkle or any such thing.

The possibility of a Church forgiveness of heinous sins was further raised in the Novatian controversy, though there the sin particularly dealt with was not adultery, but idolatry following betrayal or denial. The firm yet wise and temperate attitude of Cyprian during the keen controversies on discipline, which resulted from the persecutions under Decius and Valerian, proved a great blessing to the Church. Nevertheless, we note the beginning of an idea, which wrought much harm, that unity was more essential to perfection than sanctity. The thought also emerged that those who were fulfilling the ideal of holiness were doing more than was necessary; they might be said not only to satisfy the Divine requirements,[3] but to merit a reward from God.[4,5] Cyprian regarded Tertullian as his theological master; but he diverged widely from him, and in ways which show some of the dangers against which Montanism was a protest.

(2) The second question raised is this: Is the revelation which has come through Christ complete, or are we to look for developments under the ministration of the Spirit? Montanism said that there were three epochs, that of the Law and

---

[1] *De Pudic.*, 1.   [2] ' Extra ecclesiam nulla salus.'
[3] ' Satisfacere Deo.'   [4] ' Promereri Deum.'
[5] The titles of Cyprian's works, *De Unitate Ecclesiae* and *De Opere et Eleemosunis*, show clearly the trend of his teaching.

the Prophets, that of Christ, and that of the Paraclete, each of which marked an advance. *Prima facie* there seems a good deal to say for this. Unless we are to think of Christianity as a closed system, without any intellectual future, it seems fitting that there should be progress in the knowledge of God still. But Montanus and the prophetesses claimed that in them the Paraclete found full expression. Hence they had authority to rectify and complete the Evangel. Moreover, this completion was always by way of limitation; they admitted that the Church had authority to forgive sins; but the Paraclete refused to ratify that authority lest it should lead to an outbreak of sin. One notes, with all its apparent boldness, a real timidity in Montanism, the mark of good people who have lost some of their confidence in Christ. The great truth declared in Montanism was restated in modern times in Quakerism, whose strength also lies in its insistence on the immediate and continuous and progressive witness of the Spirit, and whose weakness also lies in underestimating the historic revelation in Jesus Christ, and its corporate expression in the Church.

4. GNOSTICISM

Side by side with Montanism was another movement, which had much to say as to the Way of Attainment; it lacked cohesion, but all its varied forms may be included under the category of Gnosticism. It was based on the idea that besides the open evangel, which might be proclaimed in the marketplace, there was a secret doctrine which had come down from Christ and the apostles, but which was only to be made known to the few, lest it should be cast as pearls before swine. This doctrine is that true knowledge which is able to make men wise unto life eternal. Those to whom it might be revealed were the *pneumatikoi*, the spiritual, predestined to eternal life; ordinary Christians, who only knew the Gospel, might be described as *psychichoi*, possessing a soul and capable of salvation, but never of entering into the Pleroma, the Fullness; for the rest of mankind they might be called *hylikoi*, materialistic, earthy, without God and without hope.

Here we have a clear-cut scheme into which all that is most objectionable seems to be concentrated. Perfection is predestined, and impossible for the bulk even of Christians; its apprehension is predominantly intellectual, and it ministers inevitably to spiritual pride. ' Most of them, *as though they were already perfect*, call themselves spiritual, and say that they already know the place of rest which is theirs within the Pleroma.'[1] Moreover, it tended to indifference to ethical values. Redemption came through the *gnosis*, which, being communicated to the *pneumatikoi*, elevated them to perfectness, and which demanded utter contempt for matter. Among the nobler Gnostics this was shown by asceticism, or by absorption in intellectual effort. But it is easy to see how readily such teaching lent itself to antinomianism. The world of matter, they said, had been made by a Creator, or Demiurge, the God of the Old Testament, who is quite distinct from, and in many ways antagonistic to, the Good God who has been revealed to us in Christ. Is not the best way of showing our contempt for matter that of repudiating the laws of the Demiurge, and defiantly breaking them ? Carpocrates and his son Epiphanes carried the doctrine to its logical conclusion. Until all laws of the Demiurge had been broken, and every fetter snapped, the soul would be in the prison of the body, where it must remain until the last farthing had been paid.

With all these defects, Gnosticism possessed a great attraction in the fact that it provided some satisfaction for man's intellectual interest in redemption. It is true that redemption can never be purely a matter of the intellect ; but unless it be presented in a way intelligible and interesting to the reason it cannot be full redemption. There is ground for the Gnostic statement that perfection comes when the true knowledge has been imparted to the spiritually minded. Only we should demur to their conception of what that knowledge is ; and we shall be sure that its apprehension is never purely an intellectual process.

Of much significance was the doctrine of the Pleroma, and the place of Jesus in it, the meaning of which we may best perceive in the fascinating and influential system of Valentinus. Victorinus says that he taught a Pleroma and thirty Aeons arranged in syzygies, or couples. Evil came through the desire of the Aeon, who was farthest away from the Eternal Depth and Silence. Her grief and passion and

---

[1] Irenaeus, *Contra Haer.*, iii. 15, 2.

terror because she failed to gain the sight of the Source of all is the cause of misery and wretchedness. Redemption came through the mercy of Christ, who beheld the struggles and sorrow of this Aeon, whom one may call Sophia, or Achamoth. He sent Jesus, whom one may call the Paraclete or Saviour, and who is the consummation of the harmony of the Pleroma, as it is written, ' In Him dwelleth all the Pleroma of the Godhead.'[1]

In such speculations there seems to us much that is offensive, and much that is simply absurd. Yet we must remember that these syzygies and aeons and monads and ogdoads are not mere fantastic inventions. They had come down from antiquity as one of the forms in which religious speculation had found utterance.[2] Valentinus clothed them with the splendour of his imagination. In the philosophies and mysteries of his day he seemed to hear the wail of Achamoth as she sought for the light. He recognized in Jesus Christ, who had come from Monogenes, the Only Begotten of the Father, the One who might be described as the Light-Bringer, the Initiator into the Mysteries. In spite of his docetism, and of his curious distinctions between Monogenes and Jesus and Christ, he made a true confession of Jesus Christ as the Light of the World.

One characteristic of Gnosticism, which was a great stumbling-block to Irenaeus and Hippolytus, appears to us marked by insight and fraught with possibilities of spiritual knowledge. I refer to the conception that the disturbance arose within the Pleroma. It is true that it came from the outskirts, and not from the centre; still, Sophia, or Achamoth, was a true Aeon, and necessary to the Fullness of the Godhead. Modern thought, which is striving to combine Pluralism with Monotheism, finds in this much that is suggestive. The idea, of course, is one which has found expression in many ways—as, for instance, when Milton expands into the sixth book of *Paradise Lost* that mysterious saying in the Apocalypse, ' There was war in heaven.' Valentinus does not speak of war, but of disturbance and unrest within the Pleroma. He seeks to safeguard the central peace by means of the Horos, or Stauros, the Fence, or Cross, which no disturbing power might pass; but he has the sense of a supreme tragedy and a supreme hope.

---

[1] Col. ii. 9.   [2] Hall, *Hist. of Eth. in Organized Christianity*, p. 134.

He places both the tragedy and the hope within the Godhead, and he connects both with the Cross of Christ. The loss which had come through sin is a loss, not only to humanity, but to Deity; and to make up that loss requires the perfecting, not only of man, but of the Divine Pleroma. In *Paradise Lost* the heavenly hierarchies are thus addressed:

> Hear all ye angels, progeny of light,
> Thrones, dominations, princedoms, virtues, powers.

But Milton never suggests that they form part of the Deity. Valentinus, however, perceived that the ruin or the ignorance of the progeny of heaven must bring loss to the fullness of the Godhead. Man's perfection is bound up with God's, and with that of the whole spiritual universe. Therefore it is such a great thing, and must be placed in the eternal future; but there is a true sense in which it may be realized in the present by knowledge and faith.

Before turning from Gnosticism, we may glance at the unique position taken by Marcion. He had little speculative tendency, and based his Gospel, not on any esoteric knowledge, but on an open and confessed faith. Like Montanus, he strove for a perfect Church; but the decisive factor with him was St. Paul's interpretation of the Scripture, rather than the immediate witness of the Spirit. He also distinguished between the catechumens and the perfect. In these directions he approached the Catholic position, by recognizing the value of an historic standard of the faith, and by making concessions to human nature in order finally to win the world to the asceticism of the Church. He failed, however, to understand how deep were the roots of the Gospel, and how necessary it was to retain the results of the long revelation of God in the Old Testament.

5. Monachism

It is a curious question why the same Church which condemned Montanism and Gnosticism, and which saw in the ascetic Church of Marcion the Church of the first-born of Satan, should have given its enthusiastic approval to that movement known as Monachism, or Monasticism, a movement which apparently denotes just as much alienation from the

Church, just as severe a condemnation of it, and a still more rigid asceticism. The answer may be suggested that the Church had learnt wisdom. Just as later colonies have been more wisely dealt with owing to the experience which Great Britain had gained through errors in dealing with earlier ones ; so the Monastic movement was favoured by the fact that the Church had learnt that it was impossible to repress the longing in many hearts after the perfect way. The movement did not attract attention until the fourth century, by which time, we may say, the Church had learnt its lesson. Though there is something in this answer, it is by no means adequate. What we have to account for is the fact that the Church not merely acquiesced in Monasticism, but was enthusiastic in its support. Those who attempted criticism, such as Jovinian, Helvidius, Vigilantius, could scarcely obtain a hearing. Even to-day the Monastic ideal is dominant in the two largest divisions of Christendom. ' If we ask either the Roman or the Greek Church wherein the most perfect Christian life consists, both alike reply : In the service of God, to the abnegation of all the good things of this life—property, marriage, personal will, and honour ; in a word, in the religious renunciation of the world ; that is, in Monasticism. *The true monk is the true and most perfect Christian*. Monasticism, then, is not in the Catholic Churches a more or less accidental phenomenon alongside of others ; but, as the Churches are to-day, and as they have for centuries understood the Gospel, it is an institution based on their essential nature ; it is *the* Christian life '[1]

If we admit that so large a part of Christendom has confessed that the way of the monk is the way of Perfection, it is still a matter of surprise that it should have tolerated what seems like an implicit condemnation of the way of the ordinary Christian. The answer is that a conviction arose, very crudely expressed by some, very profoundly by others, that those who attained by this arduous and distasteful way brought a blessing on the whole Church. Ecclesiastical statesmen perceived in the monk a spiritual energy which might be used in disciplining the Church and in subjugating the world. But this was an after-thought. The energy itself arose from the belief, almost universally held, that the life of renunciation laid up

[1] Harnack, *Monasticism*, pp. 10–11.

a store of blessing in the treasuries of Heaven which would be available, not only for the monk, but for many besides.

The name monk means the lonely or solitary one. Plotinus taught that the final stage in the soul's journey is the flight of the alone to the Alone; but he thought of that loneliness as purely spiritual, and consistent with a citizen's life. The monks went further; they desired absolute loneliness, a complete withdrawal into some desert place. Hence they were called anchorites, or hermits. They sought to satisfy the instinct for solitude which comes to all who have felt the world's vanity. The luxuriant civilization of the third and fourth centuries intensified this desire. The deserts of Egypt offered an escape from the empty pomp of this unintelligible world. Most of all, deliverance was sought from the unbridled lust which had settled on the world during the long years of the Pax Romana. From this sprung that insistence on chastity, and even on complete continence, which led to chastity being considered the distinctively Christian virtue. 'It is our exclusive possession,' says St. Ambrose.[1] The Incarnation, and the fact that the body was regarded as the temple of the Holy Ghost, caused a shrinking from all impurity. Ignatius writes to Polycarp (5): 'If any one is able to abide in chastity in honour of the Lord's flesh, let him do so without boasting; for if he boast he will perish.' Here chastity means complete abstinence from sexual relations, even in marriage. From this impulse came the monastic flight. There was a desire to be alone, away from the allurements of the world, the flesh, and the devil. The mirage of a solitary life in which the soul should be absorbed in devotion to God alone shone from the deserts of Egypt.

Practical necessity led to the next step, in which the anchorites began to form themselves into bands or monasteries. This was not done without hesitation. It must be remembered that the flight was not only from the world, but from the Church. The very success of the Church in producing an organization which was the envy of the world constituted an offence to these zealous souls. Celsus had noted how rapidly and efficiently the Churches were being knit together; and he coveted their energy and enthusiasm, and especially their bond of brotherhood, for the task of saving civilization.

[1] *De Virginibus*, i. 3.

Others from within the Church had noted the same phenomenon, but had regarded it as a sign, not of success, but of declension from the true ideal. Hence Monachism was essentially a lay movement, a protest against the organization of the Church under strong episcopal and priestly government, as a form of secularization, of conformity to the world, which the apostle denounced. But, if the solitaries became organized into communities under discipline, would there not be a danger of treading the same path ? There *was* such a danger, as history has amply proved. Nevertheless, practical necessity prevailed ; and soon there were societies stretching from Leontopolis to the famous Pachomian Monasteries in the Thebaid. On the whole this was a great advance. The heathenism of St. Simeon Stylites has always attracted some admiration ; but it was a great boon when it was superseded by the sane and moderate Benedictine rule.[1] If men are to live under the unnatural conditions of celibacy and poverty, it is good that there should be over them a strong rule, to which they are expected to render unconditional obedience. Under such it is perfectly possible for them to live healthy and useful lives in the worship of God, in reading and study, and in manual labour. As a matter of history, no impartial observer can fail to see the enormous benefits which the monasteries rendered during the breaking up of civilization.

[1] *Regula Monachorum*, drawn up by St. Benedict of Nursia in the sixth century 515 or 527 A.D. Workman, *Church of the West*, i., pp. 255 ff.

CHAPTER X

CLEMENT OF ALEXANDRIA AND ORIGEN

1. CLEMENT

(1) *Clement and the Orthodoxasts*

FROM the study of the idea of perfection as it developed in certain historical movements we turn to consider it as it found utterance in certain great men. The outstanding names are: Clement of Alexandria, Origen, Ambrose, Augustine, and the so-called Dionysius the Areopagite.

The character of Clement is very attractive; there is a winsomeness about his joyous confidence in the Gospel. He is charged with a lack of energy and of orderliness. In reply to the former, we may point to the examples of noble effort which he has left; but the latter he himself acknowledges.[1] Some excuse may be found in the fact that he was doing pioneer work; yet it must be confessed that he might have done better; and there is little doubt that part of the lack of order was intentional. He was convinced of the need for reserve in doctrinal teaching. He learnt this partly from the parables and a few sayings in the New Testament, but principally from contact with the Mysteries. This reserve is not, of course, peculiar to the Alexandrians. Many felt the need for fencing round the central doctrines and services. Nothing, after all, was concealed, except what every one might learn who had a true desire. Where this is plainly shown, as in the Parables of Jesus, the reserve is, in effect, a challenge to arouse the sluggish. But it has been misused in the Church; and of blame for this Clement cannot be altogether acquitted.

Clement, more fully than any before him, drew up a doctrine of the Perfect, to whom the mysteries of the Kingdom might

---

[1] In *Strom.*, vi. 2, he compares the studied disorder of his Miscellanies to the variegated appearance of a meadow.

CLEMENT OF ALEXANDRIA AND ORIGEN 143

be revealed. The importance of this for our subject may be realized from the fact that it was through the reading of the seventh book of the *Stromateis* that John Wesley was led to a clear view of the goal before him. It was the first attempt to represent to the reason the ideal of the Christian life. Many denied that such an attempt was needed at all. Clement several times refers to this party in the Church; it was so prominent and powerful as to be identified with the whole Church by Celsus.[1] They were called Orthodoxasts, seeing that they repudiated reason, and declared that the one thing needful was to have the right faith, though they were able to give no rational proof why it was the right faith. On the whole, Clement's action was abundantly justified, for it was only through reason that the leaders of the Church could make good their appeal to the whole man. ' Unless they had presented to the thinking part of mankind a system of the world and of human life which they felt to be higher and truer than others, it must have failed to make its way. For if the emotions are the sails of life, the intellect is the rudder. . . . Religion is more closely connected with the emotions and actions than with thought; yet, if we love religion, we must think about it. And if we think about it at all, it is of the utmost consequence that we should think rightly.'[2] But it was impossible to rationalize the Christian ideal without taking account of the magnificent results of Greek philosophy. In spite of the vehement opposition of men like Arnobius, Tatian, Theophilus, and Tertullian, the Church followed the lead of the Alexandrians in this matter. The gain was great beyond all calculation; but it was not achieved without some loss, which it should be our aim to perceive and remedy. The instructed Hellenist conceived of the High God as passionless; and when this idea was brought into Christian teaching, not only was the last injustice done to the Divine character, but the absence of passion was set up as the Christian's mark.

(2) *Clement's Teaching Regarding Perfection*

The Lord Himself, when He took our flesh, since that was by nature subject to passion, trained it to impassibility.[3] But

---

[1] *Contra Celsum*, iii. 44-78.   [2] P. Gardner, *Exploratio Evangelica*, p. 324.
[3] *Strom.*, vii. 2. 7.

He must be free from envy if He be eternally free from passion. Therefore He has no envy of us, but desires that we should come into the same blessed condition. One who knows this, and who may be described as the true Gnostic, becomes, as the result of careful training, assimilated to God. 'This he effects by undisturbed intercourse and communion with the Lord. Of this Gnostic assimilation the canons, as it appears to me, are gentleness, kindness, and a noble devoutness.'[1] We honour Him by taking Him at His word, and by consecrating ourselves to His will, until we are enabled to press on ' to ever higher degrees of freedom from desire and passion.'

The goal can never be reached simply by intellectual perception, apart from love and communion. One who is joined with the Lord in the full union of the Spirit becomes a spiritual body, one with the Lord. Those who are called by the Name of Christ, but do not live according to His Spirit, constitute the fleshly part of His Holy Body, which is the Lord's Church. But those who only eat to live, and who make even living subordinate to the pursuit of knowledge, these are the true, inner, spiritual Church.[2] One who belongs to this inner band ' is entirely a son, a holy man, passionless, Gnostic, perfect, being formed by the Lord's teaching, in order that he may be brought close to Him in deed and in word and in His very Spirit, and may receive that mansion[3] which is due to one who has thus learnt the meaning of his manhood.'[4] From this passage we perceive that, when all is said as to Platonic and other influences, the dominant factor is the Lord's teaching. The form may be philosophical, but the matter is essentially Christian. Its basis is the saying, ' Be ye perfect, as your Father is perfect.' That saying is uttered in the form of an ellipsis ; and we fill it in, not from Greek philosophy, but from Christian consciousness. Clement vehemently dissented from what he called the impious opinion of the Stoics that our virtue is identical with God's. We cannot be perfect as He is ; but we may fulfil what He wishes us to be. Who shall lay anything to the charge of His elect ? ' It is the Father's will that we should become perfect, so that no charge may lie against us,[5] by living in obedience to the Gospel.'

---

[1] *Strom.*, vii. 3. 13, 14.   [2] *Strom.*, vii. 14. 84–8, a passage of deep insight.
[3] John xiv. 1.   [4] Mayor translates : ' one who has thus approved his manhood.'
[5] 1 Tim. vi. 14.

Many would dissent from Clement's statement that this second stage is attained by knowledge rather than by faith. In this he seems to be following Plato more than the apostles. The Gnostic, he says, arrives at the goal by the very fact that his obedience is intelligent, and based on a full understanding of the rationale of the commands. The simple believer may attain to some extent; but he has no reasoned ground for his faith. Clement speaks with enthusiasm of this possibility of Divine knowledge. ' If any one were to put it to the Gnostic by way of hypothesis whether he would wish to choose the knowledge of God or eternal salvation, and if these could be separated (though in reality they are identical), he would have no hesitation in choosing the knowledge of God.'[1] But, after all, what is this distinction between knowledge and faith? There can be no faith which does not seek for confirmation; and there can be no knowledge which does not presuppose faith. In one passage[2] he speaks of Greek and Barbarian as attaining perfection by faith; to the Greek philosophy, to the Jew (i.e. the Barbarian), the law had been preparatory. ' But if one will, one may dispense with the preparation of philosophy, and may take *the short cut to perfection, that of salvation by faith.*' Clement, however, rightly considers that any one who is in earnest will press on to make stable the gains of faith.

(3) *The Characteristic Notes of Clement's Ideal*

(1) The note of Joy was very marked in the first century, but not nearly so prominent in the second and third. A certain pessimism crept over the Church, partly through the strain of the long conflict with the Empire, but mainly through the increasing conviction of the power of sin. Clement, more distinctly than any other in the early Church, struck the note of Joy. Indeed, he made a scale of it.[3] The lowest is the voluptuous pleasure which may be predicated of the heathen; then comes the joy of strife, which is the mark of the heresies; above these is the joy and gladness which belongs to the true Church; and even there we may distinguish between the joy which we may ascribe to the whole Church, and the festal gladness which can only be rightly imputed to one who knows.

---

[1] *Strom.*, iv. 22. 36.   [2] *Strom.*, vii. 2. 11.   [3] *Strom.*, vii. 16. 101.

When the higher knowledge comes to any one in Christ, it brings with it a richer melody than poet or philosopher dreamed of :

> Untwisting all the chains that tie
> The hidden soul of harmony ;
> That Orpheus' self may heave his head
> From golden slumber on a bed
> Of heaped Elysian flowers.

These closing lines from Milton's *L'Allegro* may be compared with the opening of the *Protreptikos*, where the new song in Christ is shown as having a greater power to charm than any fabled of Orpheus or Eunomus. Gleams of truth are to be found in poet and philosopher ; but in Christ they have been gathered into one, the sight of which, and the knowledge of which, is the source of endless joy and gladness. Clement is the least ascetic of the Fathers.[1] It has been charged against him, as against Boethius, that he was more philosopher than Christian ; but it is not a just charge. His soul was filled with a sense of the blessing which Christ had brought ; and it has been to the Church's loss that this gladness in Christ was for long overshadowed by the asceticism of Origen and Augustine.

(2) A further note is that of Freedom. Clement was entirely opposed to the Gnostic Determinism ; but he was not content to show that man is free ; it is part of his message that progress in knowledge enables men to realize their freedom. Sin becomes identified with ignorance, which binds men as with a chain. The Holy Spirit's influence draws men, even though they be far away, as the spirit of the magnet attracts the distant particles of iron.[2] But this attraction is not an overwhelming force. The wicked may resist; and then they simply fall away, having no consistency. But the more one knows the more one realizes the meaning of human liberty. Such knowledge in its fullness only comes through Christ, and, coming through *Him*, brings with it freedom from sin. It is probable that the apathy on which so much stress is laid means no more than this full consciousness of freedom. ' Whatever is lovely has power to draw to the contemplation of itself

---
[1] The *Paidagogos* gives a most interesting account of the quiet, dignified happiness which is natural to the Christian.
[2] *Strom.*, vii. 2. 10.

every one who through love of knowledge has applied himself wholly to contemplation.' In the setting of his whole nature towards God the true Gnostic finds perfect freedom.

(3) The last mark on which we need dwell is that of Progress. The Higher Life is a definite stage; but within it there is continuous, and, so far as we can learn, endless, progress. 'At first the seeker will pray for faith, and then for more faith; but as he presses on to know more he will ask for the perfection of love.'[1] As a man naturally asks for health, so he will ask for a continuance of the power of contemplation; for he is well aware that even some of the angels have stumbled through carelessness. Therefore there is always a blessed necessity for prayer. *The true Gnostic would rather not have a blessing than have it without prayer.*[2] Clement well describes this as the utmost attainment, the hyperbole of the life of holiness, that one would prefer to pray, and fail, than not to pray, and succeed.

(4) *Conclusions from Clement's Teaching*

From this survey of Clement's conception of the state of perfection, and of its characteristic features, some conclusions may be drawn which illuminate our view of the future life and of its relation to the present.

(1) The period of probation cannot be confined to this present life. Clement follows Plato in teaching that the end of all punishment is purification. There is a fire—not the devouring fire of common life, but a wise fire, which searches out as with a sword of flame. That fire it is good for us to pass through in this life. ' The Gnostic pities those who undergo discipline after death, and are brought to repentance against their will by means of punishment, while he himself is of good conscience as regards his departure, and is ever ready for it as being a pilgrim and a stranger.'[3] Through this purifying fire all must pass; but the wise man endures it now, for he makes what St. Catherine of Genoa called a plunge into Purgatory. The man who has obtained the higher knowledge, through which he has a true view of the Divine purpose, may be said to co-operate with God.[4] Those who

---

[1] *Strom.*, vii. 7. 46. [2] *Strom.*, vii. 12. 73. [3] *Strom.*, vii. 12. 78.
[4] *Strom.*, vii. 16. 102.

through ignorance or wilful refusal fail to attain to this knowledge in this life will have to suffer chastisements hereafter ; not vengeances, for that would be a retaliation of evil, and unbefitting God, but less satisfactory forms of discipline.

(2) While there is a definite state attainable in this life, which may be rightly called a state of perfection, and which means deliverance from purgatorial discipline hereafter, this must not be taken to mean that there will be no further advance possible Beyond. On the contrary, the perfection attainable in this life must not be identified with the Divine, as the Stoics impiously say. The soul passes through many abodes before it comes to the highest. ' At any rate, after he has reached the final ascent in the flesh, he still continues to advance, and presses on through the Holy Hebdomad into the Father's House, to that which is indeed the Lord's Abode, being destined there to be, as it were, a light standing and abiding for ever, absolutely secure from all vicissitudes.' This is the conclusion of paragraphs 55–7 of the seventh book of the *Stromateis*, in which there is a magnificent description of the soul's progress : to him that hath shall be given, knowledge added to faith, and love to knowledge, and to love the heavenly inheritance. At last the soul swings to its place in the Hebdomad, the Sabbath Rest in the Father's House. It has passed through the mystic stages, till it comes to the crowning abode of rest, where the Pure-in-Heart look upon God Face-to-Face with understanding and full assurance. This phrase Face-to-Face denotes a stage not possible in this life.[1] ' The cause of these things is Love, surpassing all knowledge in Holiness and Sovereignty. For by it the Gnostic, owing to his worship of the Best and the Highest, whose seal is Unity, is made at once friend and son, a perfect man indeed, grown to the full measure of the stature. Aye, and concord also is defined to be agreement about the same thing, and by the same thing we mean unity ; and friendship is brought about by similarity, because fellowship lies in unity. The Gnostic, therefore, being naturally a lover of the One, which is indeed God, is truly a perfect man and God's friend, being counted in the order of a son. These are names expressive of noble origin and knowledge and perfection, according to the vision

---

[1] But on p. 60 I have given reasons for dissenting from the view that the contrast in 1 Cor. xiii. 9–12 is between the present life and the life beyond the grave.

of God, which the Gnostic soul receives as its crowning achievement, having become perfectly pure, and being counted worthy to behold for ever Face-to-Face, as they say, the Almighty God. For having become entirely spiritual, and having passed away to its native sphere in the spiritual Church, it abides in the Rest of God.'[1]

This is the ideal which is set before the Christian, to be fully realized in eternity, to be apprehended in a measure now. To many it will appear too slight and fragile to influence human conduct. If we put away the natural ambitions of a man for self-expression and self-realization we lose the energy needed for progress. Even the Church looked with suspicion on the teaching of absolute passivity towards God, which, though it has a spiritual sough, might easily be made an excuse of laziness, and might result in mental degeneration. There was reason for the condemnation of the Quietism of Molinos and of Madame Guyon. But it would be very unjust to blame Clement for the aberrations of those who had learnt from him. His own sane and well-balanced mind has set before us a noble ideal, which he had learnt from St. Paul, of a glorious consummation, when God shall be all in all, finding Himself in us, as we find ourselves in Him.

2. ORIGEN

Those qualities which were, to some extent, lacking in Clement, intellectual energy and constructive capacity, were found in plenitude in Origen. For our special subject he is not so important, or perhaps, we may better say, he is not so distinctive; his doctrine of perfection may be deduced from his general theology, but it is not, as with Clement, the centre around which all revolves. Origen, following St. Paul and the Epistle to the Hebrews, agreed with Clement that a distinction must be made between the immature and the perfect. The former must be taught as children, for sayings will have one meaning to them and another to those who can understand. Scripture corresponded to man's nature. It might be like the body, obvious, grammatical, literal; or it might be like the soul, conveying moral instruction; or it might be like the spirit, with a hidden, mystical meaning, only to be discerned by those

[1] Mayor's translation.

whose eyes were opened. This threefold interpretation must always be borne in mind in reading Origen. He proclaims a Gospel for all; but there is in it a secret meaning which will have a subtle message for those who have ears to hear. But the distinction between those who can hear and those who cannot is not one pre-destinated and permanent.

Some outline of his teaching on our subject may be put together from a consideration of his theological conceptions: (1) of the soul's eternity, including its pre-existence; (2) of the Fall from the Image of God, and the effort needed to regain it; (3) of redemption through the sinless Jesus, and what it means to all creation; (4) of the knowledge of the Higher Christ, and the superior benefits which it brings; (5) of the purifying fire in the realm of the Spirit, both in this life and beyond; (6) of the soul's eternal freedom, with its apparently necessary conclusion of eternal hope and eternal fear.

(1) *The Pre-existence of the Soul*

The idea of the soul's pre-existence sprang from Pythagorean and Platonic teaching. It came into prominence in some of the later Jewish schools, as in Wisdom viii. 19, 20, where Solomon is represented as saying: ' Now I was a child of parts, and a goodly soul fell to my lot. Nay, rather, being good, I came into a body undefiled.' That the effect of pre-natal behaviour on present conditions was discussed among the Jews is shown decisively by John ix. 2. The opponents of Origen declared that his doctrine of pre-existence involved Metempsychosis[1]; but this is no more a necessary conclusion from the idea of an existence in the past than it is from the idea of a resurrection body in the future. What may certainly be inferred is that he did not regard this life as the only period of probation. There had been probation before as there will be after. ' In the beginning, when God created what He pleased to create—that is, rational natures—He had no other cause beside Himself—that is, His own goodness.'[2] This creation was free and eternal. It was not God, but it was necessary to the self-realization of God.[3] Origen could not conceive of God as inactive; He must be operative through all eternity in

---

[1] C. Bigg, *Christian Platonists*, 241n.   [2] *De Prin.*, ii. 9. 6.
[3] We may note approximations to the Pluralism and Pan-Psychism of our day.

creature souls.¹ There is an original equality among these souls, and any distinction that has arisen between them must be due to their free choice. However, the best came first. They belong to the Earliest Creation; and they are elder and higher in honour, not only than man, but also than all the universe created after them.²

2. *The Consequences of the Fall*

Though all souls inhabit eternity by reason of their relation to God, yet there has been among them all a Fall. The account in Gen. iii. is symbolic of what occurs, not only in human souls, but in the whole spiritual universe. Origen's thought, like that of Celsus, revolves round the idea of the soul rather than of man. All souls had participated in a Fall; but some had fallen farther than others. Lowest of all are the demons—dark, gloomy bodies, to whom the disorder of creation is due. Creation may indeed be described as Manifestation.³ The whole free spiritual creation ' surrounds the Deity like an ever-living garment'; those which are highest manifest Him most clearly; and of these some have never lost their first estate, and may be called the stars of glory. But all which may be called souls, with one exception, have fallen. Man stands midway, for he has lost the Divine manifestation, and spiritual death has come upon him. He retains the image of God, which, indeed, he cannot lose; but he has so fallen under the power of material things that the utmost effort will be needed to accomplish the potentialities of his spirit, and to consummate the Divine likeness in himself.⁴

(3) *Redemption*

Origen was one of the first to attempt a theory of Redemption. Christian teaching was filled with the thought that, whatever human effort might be put forth, all salvation, from beginning to end, was the result of a Divine movement. The advent of Jesus meant that God came into immediate

¹ *De Prin.*, iii. 5 : ' Otiosam enim et immobilem dicere naturam Dei, impium simul et absurdum.'
² Comm. in Matt. xv. 27.
³ Compare Pringle-Pattison, *The Idea of God*, pp. 307-8.
⁴ *De Prin.*, iii. 6. 1 : ' In fine demum per operum expletionem perfectam sibi ipse similitudinem consummaret.'

contact with the sinful life of the world; and His sinlessness brought a purifying and redeeming influence into humanity.[1] But Origen grappled also with the idea of redemption through the shedding of the Blood of Christ, and offered several suggestive explanations of it.[2] It was a sign of victory, exposing the weakness of the demoniacal powers, and showing the futility of sin. It was also a price paid to Diabolus, the chief of the demons. He had a claim on mankind through their sins; but he was willing to relinquish that claim if he were paid the price demanded, namely, the Blood of Christ. But in seizing his price Diabolus overreached himself; he discovered that the presence of the soul of Jesus was a torment to him, and he lost the wish to retain Him.[3] Origen at times speaks as though God had deceived Diabolus, seeing that He knew well that it would not be possible to retain the soul of Jesus. But I imagine that this is just an attempt to express the thought of Acts ii. 24: ' Whom God raised up, having loosed the pangs of death: *because it was not possible that He should be holden of it.*' Moreover, it must be remembered that Origen is as much interested in cosmic redemption as in the redemption of humanity. This includes the final restoration of Diabolus himself. The last enemy that shall be destroyed is Death—that is, Diabolus—whose destruction means, not his annihilation, but his destruction as an enemy, his ceasing to be an enemy.[4]

(4) *The True Gnostic*

Most significant for our subject is the fact that Origen regarded the true Gnostic, the perfect man, as reaching a stage where Jesus the Crucified has no longer any meaning for him.[5] He made an earnest endeavour to avoid separating the Eternal Word from the historical Christ, and at the same time to avoid including the Logos altogether in the human form. He was very definite as to the human soul of Jesus, the one soul out of all the multitudinous creation of souls which had never fallen. To know Him as Physician, able

---

[1] Hom. in Lev. viii.   [2] Harnack, ii. 367.
[3] Hom. in Rom. ii. 13: 'Tenebat autem nos Diabolus, cui distracti fueramus peccatis nostris. Poposcit ergo pretium nostrum sanguinem Christi.'
[4] *De Prin.*, iii. 6: 'Destruitur ergo non ut non sit, sed ut inimicus non sit et mors.'
[5] Bigg, *Christian Platonists*, pp. 207-12; and Harnack, ii. 342n.

to heal the sick, as Shepherd, and as Redeemer, is the first step upward.[1] But blessed are they who need Him no longer under those names, but as Wisdom and Word and Righteousness, or any other name by which they are able, through the attainment of perfection, to receive the supreme truths about Him. Both in this teaching and in his insistence on the subordination of the Son Origen was guided by Scripture. He strove seriously to understand what St. Paul meant by the distinction between knowing Christ according to the flesh and according to the spirit ; and what he meant by the subjection of the Son in the final act of the eternal drama. He somewhat fails, however, to realize the abiding value of the sacrifice on the Cross.

(5) *Purifying Fire*

The realm of the Spirit is less in extent than that of the Father or the Son ; but in it is seen the highest development of creation. Philosophy had gained some knowledge of the Father and of the Word ; but only through the Christian revelation had there come any knowledge of the Holy Spirit.[2] The Spirit's work is peculiarly that of sanctification, the best symbol of which is fire. Origen regards all punishment as remedial. The annihilation of a soul is not really conceivable. The action of the Divine Spirit must be uplifting ; and if its effect in any case, as in the hardening of Pharaoh's heart, is injurious, that must be through the evil will turning even the good to harm. Origen dwells on 1 Cor. iii. 12–15, giving to it an eschatological content. There is a mystical, purifying fire at the end, through which all must pass. Not even such saints as Peter and Paul will be able to evade it ; but to them it will cause no pain ; ' though they walk through the fire they shall not be burned ; neither shall the flame kindle upon them.' To others there will be intense pain as they pass through this baptism of fire, but it will be purificatory. Although the reference is eschatological, there can be little doubt that he considered this fire as burning even in this life. He was convinced that the fire of Hell was not material, but resembled rather the angers and lusts that burn in the

[1] In *Joan.* i. 22.
[2] *De Prin.*, i. 3. The office of the Spirit is emphasized in Origen's account of the *regula fidei*.

hearts of wicked men. And I think his whole teaching showed that he made no distinction between the fire of Purgatory and the fire of Hell. It is the same fire; but for some it smoulders in the fuliginous gloom of the Abyss; for others it shines with the pure light of Heaven.

(6) *The Soul's Progress*

Behind all Origen's doctrine is his Platonic view of the soul as being, by nature and origin, immortal and free. The apparent conclusion would be that there can be no finality either in good or evil. It has always been one of the strongest arguments of those who have insisted on eternal punishment that if any term be placed on the sufferings of the damned, there must also be on the joys of the blessed; if it be possible to pass the great fixed gulf from one side, it will be possible from the other. Therefore, it would seem that if we speak of eternal hope, we must speak also of eternal fear. But there is a great thought in Origen's mind of the superior reality of the good. The victory of righteousness cannot be doubted, for it is bound up with the essence of things as they are. It found expression in the victory of Jesus over Diabolus, which came, not through any contrivance of force or skill, but through the facts of existence. Because Jesus was what He was He could not fail to win. There is not in Origen the serene assurance of Clement, for his temperament was darker; but he had a strong confidence in God, which he had learnt, not from Plato, but from Christ.

CHAPTER XI

AMBROSE, AUGUSTINE, AND DIONYSIUS THE AREOPAGITE

1. AMBROSE

AMBROSE occupies a position of his own in the development of the doctrine of perfection. He was a noble example of a Christian bishop, a man of action, having at times to confront emperors and people, yet never allowing himself to be swayed by base motives of gain or fear. He was a man of his age, not rising above some of its prejudices, but guided by a kindly and generous spirit. Thus he well defended his action in selling sacred vessels to redeem captives.[1] It was this humanity which kept Ambrose sound amid the dangers of sacerdotal arrogance and ascetic bitterness which were threatening the Church, and from which he himself was far from free. It is well known how deeply St. Augustine was affected by the sermons and the personality of St. Ambrose.[2] The dignity of the Church, as expressed in the person of the great bishop, fascinated him; for it was a dignity founded altogether on righteousness and benevolence. Those ideas, which were afterwards expressed in *The City of God*, stirred in St. Augustine's mind as he marked the political and social carriage of a man of whom it might truly be said that his citizenship was in Heaven.

(1) *Ambrose and Stoicism*

The idea of *The City of God* was the more explicit in Ambrose's teaching because he had turned to the Stoic philosophy in order to formulate a Christian ethic. He modelled his chief

---

[1] *De Off. Min.*, ii. 28. 136–7. He imagines the Lord rebuking him if he had refused to give up the metal vessels in order to redeem the living. 'Melius fuerat ut vasa viventium servares quam metallorum.'
[2] Harnack, v. 34–5.

work, *De Officiis Ministrorum* (*On the Duties of the Ministry*), on the *De Officiis* of Cicero, even as Cicero had modelled his on the work of the Stoic philosopher Panaetius. Varied estimates have been made of the extent of the Stoic influence. In discussing the question, Professor H. H. Scullard finds reason to dissent from the position taken up by Hatch, and more moderately by Ewald; he points out that the distinction between the ordinary and the perfect morality is such a natural concession to the frailty of human nature that we find it almost everywhere.[1] At the same time the great Stoic philosophers drew out the distinction more definitely than any one else; and their system enabled them to express it in a reasoned formula. But this is precisely what gives such significance to Ambrose's teaching. He was the first Christian leader to take this common concession to human infirmity, and express it in a philosophical form; and he did so under Stoic influence and in the Stoic terminology. But his outlook was entirely Christian. Any proposition which came to him he consciously and earnestly and sincerely referred to Christ. ' Whatsoever ye do, in word or deed, do all in the name of our Lord Jesus Christ, giving thanks to God the Father by Him. Let us then refer all our words and deeds to Christ, who brought life out of death, and created light out of darkness.'[2] Stoicism at most is only the form in which he utters his conviction of full salvation in Christ.

(2) *The Evangelical Precepts and the Evangelical Counsels*

The *locus classicus* for the distinction between the duties is *De Off. Min.*, i. 11. 36. ' Every duty is either ordinary or perfect (*medium aut perfectum*), as we can prove by the authority of Scripture.' After referring to the Stoic division,[3] he discusses with much acuteness the account of the rich young man in Matt. xix., and the exhortation to be perfect in Matt. v. 48. To keep the law, as the young man had done, was to fulfil ordinary duties in which something is lacking; but in performing perfect duties one goes beyond what is absolutely required. He appears to recall the similar counsel in Luke vi. 36, for he adds : ' Mercy also is good, which in itself makes

---

[1] *Early Christian Ethics in the West.*   [2] *De Virginibus*, iii. 5. 24.
[3] See pp. 108–9.

men perfect, because it imitates the perfect Father.' The
first exercise of mercy is towards the poor, to show that you
judge them to have a common inheritance in the produce of
Nature, which brings forth the fruits of the earth for the use
of all; and also by your largess to prove that you regard the
poor man as your kinsman, sharing in the same Nature as
yourself. He proceeds to show that we receive more from
the poor man than he from us, since he makes it possible to
exercise that grace of mercy which brings us near to the
Heavenly Father.[1] The argument continues to unfold the
blessedness of one who never turns away the poor and helpless.
'In the day of judgement he will receive salvation from the
Lord, whom he will make His debtor through the mercy
which he has shown.'[2] The phrase is not clear; it seems
to mean that as we are indebted to the poor for full salvation,
so by the exercise of mercy we put the Lord in our debt to
show mercy to us. That this teaching tended to develop
kindliness and goodwill is beyond doubt; but it had grave
defects. One was that poverty was praised as a good in itself,
instead of being looked upon as something to be remedied;
another was that the carrying out of the evangelical counsels
came to be regarded as involving a claim for reward.

(3) *The Praise of Virginity*

Of all the evangelical counsels, most stress was laid on
virginity. Ambrose was a man of affairs, who knew well how
to order a diocese; and these mundane interests kept him from
some of the extravagances of Jerome. But we see even in
such a well-balanced mind the morbidity which comes from
undue exaltation of celibacy. The titles of many of his books
sufficiently show how large this bulked in his teaching of the
Way. The beginning of this praise of virginity is found in the
New Testament; but by Ambrose's time it threatened to
overshadow everything else. He was careful not to disparage
marriage. 'I do not, then, discourage marriage, but recapitulate the advantages of holy virginity.'[3] The emphasis, however, on virginity was such as to make earnest seekers shrink

---

[1] 'Ad haec plus ille tibi confert, cum sit debitor salutis.'
[2] 'In die judicii habebit salutem a domino, quem habebit suae debitorem misericordiae.'
[3] *De Virg.*, i. 7. 35.

from marriage. All this was quite contrary to the Roman ideal, which enacted laws against celibacy as injurious to the State. Ambrose had enough of the old Roman character in him to understand this view; and his breach with it is significant of the intensity of his conviction of the value of celibacy. He had learnt this partly from St. Paul, but, more than he would admit, from heathen, non-Roman sources. It swallowed up even his sense of humour, as in his story of the kinsman whose early death was due to his hindering a maiden from taking the veil. 'So the other kinsmen, each fearing for himself, began to assist and not hinder as before; and her virginity did not involve the loss of her property. . . . You see, maidens, the reward of devotion, and do you, parents, be warned by the example of transgression.'[1]

(4) *Stages within the State of Perfection*

While Ambrose exalted the evangelical counsels, especially that of celibacy, he never identified them with the state of Perfection. He discourses on the cardinal virtues in a truly Christian spirit. Indeed, he so treats of Justice, and so unites it with Benevolence, as almost to make it equivalent to Love. It is a noble thought that love is a kind of justice. The Christian, who is in the Way, is to be identified with the Wise Man of the Stoics, but with important modifications.[2] The wise man thinks of what is for the common good in this life; but the Christian has a wider outlook. Ambrose instances Cicero's casuistical question whether a wise man might not take a plank in a shipwreck from a fool, since his life was more valuable to the community.[3] He decides that a Christian cannot save his life at the expense of another's. He goes further, and declares that a Christian must not even defend himself against a robber. What robber could be worse than the persecutor who came to kill Christ? Yet Christ refused to be defended from him; for it was His will to heal all by His wounds.[4] From this instance it is manifest that he brought to the consideration of the question new motives derived from Christ's example. The Christian, even if he be a wise man, must not count his life of too much value. Whatever we may

---

[1] *De Virg.*, i. 12. 66. [2] ' Vir Christianus et justus et sapiens.'
[3] *Cic.*, *De Off.*, xliii. 89. [4] *De Off. Min.*, iii. 4. 27.

think of the conclusions, we cannot deny the earnestness of the endeavour to fashion his life according to the Master's pattern.

From David's attitude towards Shimei, not rendering cursing for cursing, and thus acting in the true evangelical spirit, Ambrose leads up to a description of the Higher State.[1] *Though David was perfect, he kept seeking after higher stages of perfection.*[2] So he cries out : ' Lord, let me know mine end and the measure of my days, what it is : that I may know what is lacking to me.' Then Ambrose refers to 1 Cor. xv. 23 : ' When the kingdom is delivered up to God, even the Father, and all the powers are put down, as the apostle says, then perfection begins. *Here, then, is that which entangles and weakens even the perfect; there full perfection.* Thus it is he asks for those days of eternal life which are, and not for those which pass away, so that he may know what is wanting to him, what is the land of promise that bears everlasting fruit, which is the first mansion in the Father's house, which the second, which the third, wherein each will rest *according to his merits*. We then must strive for that wherein is perfection, and wherein is truth. Here is the shadow, here the image, there the truth. *The shadow is in the Law, the image in the Gospel, the truth in Heaven.*[3] . . . Here, then, we walk in an image, we see in an image ; there face to face, where is full perfection. For all perfection rests in the truth.'

This sublime passage shows how Ambrose turned to Christ, to whom David and St. Paul bear witness. It also shows his belief in stages within perfection, whose end is the Supreme Consummation. He regards the end which David desired to know as being in eternity, in that spiritual life which is reality, not the passing show, but that which is, the truth itself.

Similarly, in Book III., chap. ii., he delineates the way in which human perfection here is related to the Divine, and also to the perfection possible for humanity hereafter. Goodness and wisdom may be predicated of God and of man, but not in the same way. Even with men there are differences ; and there is a broad distinction between what is possible now and what may come hereafter. ' I read that Paul was perfect and not perfect. For when he said : " Not as though I had already

[1] *De Off. Min.*, i. 48.
[2] ' Sed tamen quamvis perfectus adhuc perfectiora quaerebat.'
[3] ' Umbra in lege, imago in evangelio, veritas in caelestibus.'

attained, either were already perfect, but I follow after, if that I may apprehend it ": immediately he added, "We then that are perfect." There is a twofold form of perfection, the one having but ordinary, the other the highest worth; the one availing here, the other hereafter; the one in accordance with human powers, the other with the perfection of the world to come. But God is just through all, wise above all, perfect in all.' This is a notable endeavour to rise above the difficulties of language. To any one who conceives of an end in life, a purpose to the fulfilment of which humanity is straining, it is natural to speak of the attainment of that end as perfection. Nor can such attainment be put altogether in the future; tomorrow, even if it be an eternal to-morrow, can never be the day of salvation. Yet one may think of future progress even in the rest that remaineth.

(5) *The Endeavour to Anticipate the Future Life*

The purpose of the evangelical counsels is to anticipate the conditions of the future life. It has never, I think, been suggested that they constitute an ideal in themselves; but they are considered as advantageous for the development of the spiritual. Ambrose carried on the distinction in Cicero between the virtuous (*honestum*) and the useful (*utile*); but he saw that in the light of eternity they become one.[1] There was a state possible in this life, which was an earnest of that which is to be. It did not contain the fullness, but it was a true foretaste, and to enter on it now meant deliverance from painful purgation in eternity. The evangelical counsels were not absolute commands; they were not necessary for salvation; they were not even necessary in order to enter on this blessed earthly condition; but they were advantageous for this reason —that they anticipated the conditions of eternity. *There* they have no property, they neither marry nor are given in marriage, and their whole will is surrendered in glad and free obedience to the Father in Heaven. To prepare for this by rejecting those earthly blessings which are *pro detrimento sub specie aeternitatis* appeared to Ambrose the highest wisdom. In his heart he was against all private ownership, not on communistic principles, but because it alienated from God,

[1] *De Off. Min.*, iii. 2. 9.

who is the source of all natural right.[1] In the same way he praised virginity, because it brought Heaven to earth. 'That which is promised to us is already present with you, and the object of your prayers is with you; ye are in this world, and yet not of this world. This age has held you, but has not been able to retain you.'[2] From this standpoint the evangelical counsels appeared superior to the precepts; for, whereas the precepts dealt with the conditions of earth, the counsels anticipated those of Heaven. 'A command is issued to those who are subject; counsel is given to friends. Where there is a commandment there is law; where counsel there is grace. A commandment is given to enforce what is according to nature, a counsel to incite us to follow grace.'[3] Those who have fulfilled the precepts are like unprofitable servants, who can only say that they have done that which was their duty to do. 'The virgin does not say this, nor he who sold all his goods; but they rather wait the stored-up rewards, like the holy apostle, who says: "Behold, we have forsaken all and followed Thee. What shall we have therefore?"' Merit is laid up, like treasure in Heaven, by those who have followed the evangelical counsels.

(6) *Criticism of Ambrose's Teaching*

I have dwelt at some length on St. Ambrose's teaching, because it is so significant of the strength and beauty of the ideal which was unfolding itself before the Christian consciousness, and because it is equally significant of the ethical perils which so easily beset it. Ambrose saw clearly that to transfer the ideal to some future life, of which the imagination cannot conceive, was, in fact, to abandon it altogether. He saw also that the realization must not be purely a matter of faith; there must be a perfecting in love. But it seemed to him that the only way in which this could be done was by ante-dating the environment of Heaven; and that any one who did so, seeing he was doing more than was commanded, would acquire merit and earn a reward. But if it be right to say that the realization is possible in this life, it must be possible under the conditions which are normal to the life of

---

[1] 'Natura jus commune generavit, usurpatio jus fecit privatum' (*De Off. Min.*, I. 28. 132).
[2] *De Virg.*, i. 9.   [3] *De Viduis*, chap. xii.

this world. If it be essential to the world's life that business should be done, and that there should be marrying and giving in marriage, these must constitute the normal sphere in which the ideal is to be realized in this world. And, further, if it be the centre of the evangelical faith that salvation is altogether by the grace of God through Christ Jesus, that must be true of the higher stages as well as of the beginning of the Christian life. All the way through, the idea of merit, on which Ambrose undoubtedly dwells, and which so easily arises in connexion with the evangelical counsels, must be firmly excluded.

2. AUGUSTINE

If we judge by the extent of his influence, St. Augustine will rank as the greatest of the doctors of Christendom. Roman Catholic and Calvinist find a common ground in admiration of him. We must seek to estimate the effect of that influence on the Christian ideal. It may be said at once that he definitely transferred it to the future life. 'The daily prayer which Jesus Himself taught, and which is therefore called the Lord's Prayer, does indeed destroy the daily sins, when the words are daily said, "Forgive us our debts," and when the clause that follows, "As we forgive our debtors," is not only said but done. . . . But what is the meaning of "your sins," unless it means sins without which you will not be, even you who have been justified and sanctified?'[1] We find it necessary in this subject, perhaps more than in most, to guard against disputing about words. Those who speak of attainment in this life must be prepared to define it in a way which shall be consistent with the daily utterance of the Lord's Prayer. On the other hand, Augustine himself declares that in the prayer for forgiveness the daily sins are destroyed; so that in that moment, at any rate, there is perfect cleansing. His temperament and experience led him to emphasize the persistence of sin; but no man ever made a more strenuous effort to attain the state of perfection.

We may contemplate his spiritual effort under three aspects: (1) he made a great intellectual and spiritual attempt to find in theistic philosophy the basis for a life which should be at perfect unity with itself; (2) he sought to express in theological

[1] *De Civ. Dei*, xxi. 27.

doctrine the resultant of the actions and reactions between the sins of men and the grace of God ; (3) he endeavoured to show that the ideal life was that of the City of God ; not purely one of unification through the mystical theism, nor yet purely one of reconciliation through the Divine grace, but one of fellowship in the redeemed Church of Christ. The controversies in which he engaged with Manichaeism, Pelagianism, and Donatism were due to the firmness with which he held certain tenets, philosophical, theological, and ecclesiastical, which underlay his magnificent endeavour to realize the full, many-sided Christian ideal.

(1) *The Theism of Augustine*

In Augustine, love of truth was combined with an equal love of order. Sin, even when it led him astray through ambition and passion, always appeared as lawlessness ; and he always had the desire to escape into the well-ordered life. But at first he could not find in philosophy, nor indeed in the Gospel, that which satisfied his desire for the truth. The attraction in Manichaeism was the sincerity with which it grappled with the facts of sin and evil.[1] Its dualism and materialism appeared to the young inquirer signs of reality.[2] What also weighed with Augustine was the readiness of its teachers to enter into debate.[3] The separation between the Elect and the Auditors was a further inducement to throw in his lot with them. Augustine was content to remain an Auditor, just because he was not then in earnest in seeking to escape from sin. He, with others, used to bring food to those who were called elect and holy, and thus obtained cleansing, or, rather, freedom to wallow again in sin.[4] The elect among the Manichees were never more than a few. To them Heaven would open at once ; but for the rest there would be a long purgation. But this motive was not strong enough for ordinary human nature, to which the future life is never clear and certain. It became especially weak when it was further taught that the virtues and renunciations of the Elect would avail for those who were content to remain Auditors.

The permanent effect of the nine years of bondage may be summed up thus : (1) the twofold morality strengthened its

[1] See p. 127.   [2] *Conf.*, iii. 6.   [3] *De Util. Cred.*, i.   [4] *Conf.*, iv. 1.

hold on the Church; (2) an idea of merits developed, as we have also seen in the case of Ambrose; (3) a deep pessimism was engendered, which acquiesced in an eternal domain of evil; (4) by way of reaction, faith was conceived as having virtue in itself, apart from its expressing real conviction.[1] These ideas were not, of course, peculiar to Augustine. Tertullian was well aware of the distinction between the *praecepta* and the *consilia dominica*; and he also deduced the meritoriousness of keeping the *consilia*. Cyprian, in the *De Opere et Eleemosynis*, enlarged on it. The eternity of evil, as regards the future, was accepted by the majority of Church writers, though by no means universally. But Augustine's great and well-deserved authority clinched the mind of the Church on many points; and his views on some of the most important were determined by his Manichaean experiences.

Such a religion, however, could not permanently claim him; the demand for unification was too insistent. 'Peace of mind,' he says, 'is the sign of our secret unity.' He broke with the idea that there could be two equal principles; but for a time he resigned himself to an Agnostic position.[2] But Agnosticism, when all is said, is selfishness—not necessarily ethical selfishness, but metaphysical. The very strength of his animal nature prevented him from resting in that metaphysical indolence. The loss of a dear friend troubled him greatly. 'I became to myself a great enigma; and I asked my soul, Why was she so sad, and why did she disquiet me so sorely; but she was able to give me no answer. And if I said, Hope in God, she quite rightly obeyed me not; because that dearest friend whom I had loved was truer and better as a man than the phantom on which she was bidden to set her hope.'[3] Like Job, his soul recoiled from an unreal conception of God, and preferred even the blank of Agnosticism; but it was pain and grief to him. 'And now to feel that nothing can be known, this is a thought that burns my heart.'

The way out, for Augustine, was through Neo-Platonism. He realized that the objections of the Academics to the validity of knowledge obtained by the evidence of the senses

---

[1] Harnack says that Augustine was the father of the conception of *fides implicita* 'by associating with the individual believer the Church, with which he believes and which believes for him, in as far as it takes the place for him in many points of a psychological element of faith, namely inner conviction' (v. 81).
[2] See the fourth book of the *Confessions*.
[3] 'Factus eram ipse mihi magna quaestio' (*Conf.*, iv. 4. 9).

do not cover the whole ground. We are able to reason about numbers; we are able to draw out a logical argument; and we understand the distinction between right and wrong. None of these kinds of knowledge comes through the senses. Moreover, we need not be browbeaten, even when the Academics point out the many sources of error, saying that we may be deceived about anything. We cannot be deceived about our own existence.[1] This remarkable anticipation of Descartes shows the honesty with which Augustine grappled with his problem. From this firm ground of certainty he sets forth in Platonic language his conviction of the intelligible world, of which this world of sense is but as a dark mirror.

Then by a supreme spiritual effort he rose to the thought of One in whom and through whom is all our knowledge of the intelligible world, without whom it would be impossible to put together any rational thought. In this he was following the argument of Plotinus[2] that the great, eternal principles cannot be bound up with the individual soul, since the discursive reason may be directed towards them, or may not. This fickleness of the soul's discursive reason proves that the principles of eternal beauty and justice must have their basis in that which is Unseen and Eternal. But it proves also that there is in the soul, for all its fickleness, that which keeps turning to God. The conclusions arrived at are that the reason is a true guide leading to God; but that the full vision is discerned, not by reason, but by intuition, which must come as a direct gift from God.[3] Moreover, the soul is so mutable during this mortal life, owing to the disturbing influence of the flesh, that it can never enjoy this vision for more than a brief period. *In some ways this close following of Plotinus led Augustine astray, especially in identifying perfection with vision, and in regarding the sensuous frame as the chief hindrance.*

These statements are illustrated by two experiences, narrated in the *Confessions* (vii. 17 and ix. 25). The second represents a higher experience. The soul is turning more and more steadily to God; and it is doing so because it has moved beyond the mystical, Neo-Platonic ideal of union. There is something even beyond knowing that the Word was with God and that the Word was God. The supreme statement is this—

---

[1] *De Civ. Dei*, xi. 26.   [2] *Enn.* v. 8. 11.
[3] See the seventh book of the *Confessions*.

the Word was made flesh and dwelt among us. It is this which turns into a real City of God that which we saw only in a mirage. In the close of ix. 25 Monnica and Augustine agreed that, if but that moment could have been prolonged, it would have been nothing less than the fulfilling of the word, ' Enter thou into the joy of thy Lord '; but that would only be when we shall all rise, though we shall not all be changed.[1] We need not pause over the curious variation in I Cor. xv. 51; it is noted again in *De Civ. Dei*, xx. 20. Manifestly, Augustine conceived of this experience in its fullness as reserved for the future life. It can be only a transient gleam in this. We must distinguish, however, as he does not, between evangelical perfection and the beatific vision. His Neo-Platonism prevented him from perceiving that Christ has brought a salvation which is appropriate and sufficient for a life in the world and in the flesh, whatever further salvation, beyond the world and apart from the flesh, may be implicit in it. I am not suggesting that the Incarnate Christ was not central to all the thought of Augustine. The verse which gave final relief to his soul was this, ' Put ye on the Lord Jesus Christ.' But his long spiritual vagaries hindered him from realizing how complete and immediate was the salvation which Christ had brought.

(2) *Augustine's Doctrine of Grace*

A perfect union with God must be the aim of every Christian. Are we to think of such union, or of the imperfect image of it which we have in this life, as attained by the free gift of God, or by man's effort, or by a combination of both? This was the question which flamed up in the Pelagian controversy. The Pelagians did not deny the reality of sin, nor its punishment; but they conceived that each sin stood by itself. Pelagius thought that concupiscence had come to be evil, because it was so often used as a snare of the Devil. Julian took the more genial view that it was only wrong in excess, or when it led to injuring another. But they agreed that sin did not affect the whole nature. Hence the sins of humanity did not oppose an obstacle to union with God of such a nature as to nullify human effort.

---

[1] Nonne hoc est: intra in gaudium domini tui? et istud quando? an cum omnes resurgimur, sed non omnes inmutabimur?'

The value of Pelagianism as a protest is great; but, when viewed as ultimate, it cannot stand. For it is among the ultimate facts that each sin does not stand by itself, but works itself into nature ; moreover, the whole of humanity is affected by the sin of one. It is this which makes sin so terrible ; but it is this also which makes redemption possible. Logically Pelagius's system demanded that every sin must receive its punishment. Pelagius certainly believed in Hell ; and on his premisses it seemed as if every sinner would be doomed to it. Of course, he did not follow this logic. He held by the Divine grace and the possibility of redeeming power. Before the Synod in Palestine in A.D. 415 he accepted that as his belief, so that they said, ' Now that Pelagius with his own voice has anathematized the groundless nonsense, answering rightly that a man can be without sin with the Divine help and grace, let him reply also to the other counts.'[1] But, in spite of this disclaimer, the system of Pelagius is atomistic, individualistic, and therefore ultimately hopeless.

When the Church has had to choose, it has always turned rather to Augustine. There is more hope in any doctrine, however stern its view of human nature, even if it treat it as a mass of perdition,[2] if only it treat it as a whole. If the angels were entirely separate creations, without mutual interactions (as to which, of course, we have no evidence), it would not be possible to conceive of any redemption for them. Augustine regarded evil as the deprivation of good, the falling away from the immutable.[3] ' Let no one seek the efficient cause of a bad will ; for it is not efficient, but deficient ; for there is no effectiveness in it, but rather defect.'[4] When the will chooses the lower in preference to the higher it becomes evil ; not because that is evil to which it turns, but because the turning away from the best is itself a piece of perversity. He who in a perverse and vicious spirit loves even that which is good in itself and relatively, becomes evil even in the good. Evil springs, not from the eternal goodness, but from a perverse defection from the good, beginning with the angels and spreading to man. Even where the will is good, it is ineffectual to carry out its own desire, except through His help, who is the only cause that there is a good will at all. Through His

[1] Harnack, v. 179. [2] ' Massa perditionis.' [3] *Conf.*, vii. 12.
[4] *De Civ. Dei*, xii. 7 : ' Quia nec illa effectio est sed defectio.'

inspiration the will may be so strengthened and uplifted that men may live the life of communion with Himself. This summary of the argument in the twelfth book of *The City of God* shows that Augustine did justice to the will, and that we must not identify his teaching with later developments in Calvinism.[1]

The question of original sin and of total depravity is very pertinent to our subject. Does Evangelical Perfection mean freedom from the inner corruption as well as from the sinful act? Augustine's own experience led him to trace sin back to the unconscious age; and he was confirmed in this by the practice of infant baptism and by the theory current in the Church concerning it. He taught that sin before baptism was due to the corruption entailed by Adam's Fall, and that it was transmitted, like a disease, from parent to child. In Adam's sin all possible sins—pride, envy, disobedience, sensual lust, and all others—were contained; and the Fall was all the worse because it was so easy for Adam to have avoided them. From Rom. v. 12 he deduced that in Adam all sinned, not mystically, but literally, since the effect of his sin has by God's decree been made a contagion to the whole race. The fact of original sin may, therefore, be spoken of as a punishment for Adam's sin. Sin after baptism is worse, since it is not merely due to the contagion inherited from him, but is a repetition of his disobedience.

> I will weep for thee;
> For this revolt of thine, methinks, is like
> Another Fall of Man.[2]

The chief merit of Augustine is his emphasis on the Divine Grace. To him this Grace appeared, as it does to most who have any spiritual experience, as predestinating and irresistible. He looked back to Adam, and ascribed to him a perfection which he might easily have kept, since the Grace of God co-operated with him. But his Fall brought condemnation on all mankind; for we were all in Adam at that time, in the idea of God and in the seed of humanity; and

---

[1] 'On two fundamental points as to the nature of man Calvin's doctrine diverges considerably from that of St. Austin, who did not hold that man, though sinful, was totally depraved, and who was careful to maintain that men are fully responsible for their actions' (W. Cunningham, *St. Austin*, p. 86).
[2] *Henry V*, Act II., sc. ii., 140.

therefore his disordered and vitiated nature has been propagated in us. ' Thus by the wrong use of free will that series of calamities began which has led the human race in an unbroken chain of miseries from its depraved origin, as from a rotten root, to the ruin of the second death, which has no end, and from which those alone are excepted who are set free by the Grace of God.'[1] Grace now appears in a different form ; it is not only a Divine Presence which may be rejected ; it assumes the appearance of an irresistible power, dealing with a mass of corruption. Hence it is prevenient and predestinating, as well as irresistible ; and the number destined to full salvation is fixed and unchangeable.[2] There are degrees of happiness, as well as of punishment, in eternity. Those who are condemned are left to be judged according to their deserts ; but that meant eternal punishment. All the freedom and happiness which enter into the perfect state of Heaven must be a gift of Divine Grace ; and the same will which expresses itself in Grace to the saved must operate with equal authority in the deprivations of the lost. ' No one is delivered except by an undeserved mercy ; and no one is damned except through a deserved judgement.'[3]

To fully realize this was Augustine's idea of Perfection. But it is impossible to do so during this mortal life. Until the Divine Purpose has been completely revealed, there can be no assurance of salvation, and no full deliverance from the inner corruption. To many it will seem that Augustine has overlaid his central thought of the infinite goodness and love of God with that of predestinating grace and judgement.[4] Yet he never wavers in setting forth love as the end of man's communion with God. Faith and hope are only of use as they are joined with love. The aim of all the Divine messages, whether as precepts (*mandata*), or counsels (*consilia*), is to educe love. As love grows, it masters lust ; in the future state, when earthly passions have passed away, it will be all in all.[5] Aquinas quotes a saying of Augustine that the contemplation of God is promised us as being the goal of all our actions, and the everlasting perfection of our joys. Deeper

[1] *De Civ. Dei*, xiii. 14.
[2] 'Certus numerus electorum, neque augendus, neque minuendus' (*De Correp. et Gr.*, 39, c. 13).
[3] 'Nisi per indebitam misericordiam nemo liberatur, et nisi per debitum judicium nemo damnatur' (*Enchiridion*, 94-108).
[4] Harnack, v. 238n.　　[5] *Enchir.*, 114-20.

even than the pessimism which had come from a contemplation of the world's wickedness and misery is the confidence which he had learnt from Christ—that in the end he will find the Divine Purpose to be nothing else but love.

(3) *The City of God*

The ideal life is not purely one of unification through the mystical theism, nor purely one of reconciliation through the Divine Grace; it is also one of fellowship in the Redeemed Church. No grander conception has ever come before man's mind than that of the City of God. There have always been two cities or states; and both have been built on love, since hatred builds nothing. ' But these two states have been created by two different affections; the earthly by the love of self to the contempt of God, the heavenly by the love of God to the contempt of self.' When we follow the working out of this conception we find it neither so great nor so adequate as we had hoped. I think that his mother, for all the beauty of her character, exercised a narrowing influence. His conception both of the Catholic Church and of the Heavenly Jerusalem was never freed from the limitations which her piety and her fears imposed.[1]

The city which is being built by the love of God is a city of eternal peace, whose mystical name is Jerusalem; and there the discords of time will be resolved into the harmony of eternity.[2] In depicting the earthly Church as a copy of this, St. Augustine endeavoured to bring together certain conflicting views. From one aspect the Church consists of the elect, a fixed number known only to God; from another it consists of all who are holy and spiritual; from yet another, seeing that no one is perfectly holy and spiritual, its essential characteristic is that it is able to bring about reconciliation between God and man through the remission of sins. ' Per remissionem peccatorum stat ecclesia quae est in terris.'[3] From this some idea of a purgatorial fire inevitably arose. If there be the idea of a perfect community, to which many

---

[1] Cf. *Conf.*, ix. 13. 37.
[2] ' Nam et ipsius civitatis mysticum nomen, id est Hierusalem, quod et ante jam diximus visio pacis interpretatur.' *De Civ. Dei*, xix. 11 : De Beatitudine pacis aeternae, in qua sanctis finis est, *id est vera perfectio*.
[3] Harnack, v. 165*n*.

belong who are by no means perfect, it seems fitting that there should be some purifying discipline hereafter.

Augustine was careful to point out that this applies only to believers. The ungodly cannot enter the Kingdom of God unless there be given them a penitence leading to the remission of sins.[1] He condemned Origen's hope for the ultimate conversion of the Devil and his angels as an attempt to appear more merciful than God.[2] All punishments are not purgatorial. Nevertheless, his general view of the future state, as we might expect from his Platonism, was one of discipline and purgation. He was convinced that in the fires of Purgatory there were degrees of punishment which would be gradually mitigated, and finally altogether cease; and there might be mitigation even in the fires of Hell. 'It must not be denied that even the eternal fire itself, in accordance with the diversity of merits even of the wicked, would be to some milder, to others more severe, either because its force and ardour would vary according to the punishment which each had deserved, or because, while it continued to burn with equal fierceness, it would not be felt with equal pain.'[3]

The elect had set before them the hope of the Beatific Vision; but the Christian, as distinct from the Neo-Platonist, expected to enjoy it as a member of a society. Only by a few (Augustine practically said by no one) could the standard of attainment that was necessary for it be reached in this life. Hence it must be attained hereafter by purgatorial discipline. Two addenda were made of much significance: first, the fires of eternity are only purgatorial for those who have entered the *Societas Sacramentorum* during this life; second, since there is communion between the Church Here and the Church Beyond, the Church Here is able, by its prayers and offerings, and especially by the sacrifice of the Mass, to affect the state of those Beyond.

In discussing the eschatological teaching of the Second Period (from A.D. 254-730), Hagenbach makes this illuminating quotation from Schmidt: 'The belief in an uninterrupted endeavour after a higher degree of Perfection, which death itself cannot interrupt, degenerated into a belief in Purgatory.' No one did more to fix the mind of the Church in this direction than St. Augustine; nor was it all degeneration. Many of the ideas of Purgatory became very retrograde, so that it was not

[1] *Enchir.*, 69.   [2] *De Civ. Dei*, xxi. 17.   [3] *De Civ. Dei*, xxi. 16.

without reason that Bishop Latimer spoke of Purgatory Pick Purse. But some conception of Purgatory there must be for any perfecting of the whole Church of Christ. Even Augustine, however, never worked out the thought that there must be social relation if there is to be ethical probation and purgation. We find it necessary continually to guard against the idea that Death and Pain are essential to Perfection. The essentials are Faith and Hope and Love; and these come from God, and from the social relations in which He places us. Death and Pain are the accidents which He may use in perfecting.

3. DIONYSIUS THE AREOPAGITE

Before leaving what we may call the early Church, we must examine the writings of an unknown man, who wrote under the name of Dionysius the Areopagite, which have had extraordinary influence on the formulation of the Christian ideal. We need not too sternly condemn the fashion of using pseudonyms; but it must be admitted that a good deal of this writer's authority sprang from the belief that he belonged to the apostolic age. Erigena translated the principal works into Latin, and incorporated many of the ideas in his own treatise, *De Divisione Naturae*. Aquinas refers to him simply as Dionysius, always speaks of him with deference, and usually treats his opinion as decisive. When the authenticity of these writings came to be critically examined, it was soon obvious that they could not have come from the hand of St. Paul's convert. They are, in fact, dependent on the works of Proclus (b. A.D. 411), one of the last of the Neo-Platonists. As a result of this criticism their value greatly depreciated. In modern times interest has revived through the renewed study of Mysticism, which we may contemplate as part of the Way of Perfection.

It is matter for regret that Dionysius looked to Proclus rather than to the far nobler system of Plotinus; but possibly it was the Triads and the Pluralism which he learnt from Proclus which gave to his teaching such authority in the Middle Ages. There are two main reasons for the effectiveness of Dionysius: he set on a firm basis the ecclesiastical system, which was proving so attractive to many minds; and then, while supplying this firm philosophical basis, he justified philosophy, and gave scope for the boldest speculations, so that the intellectual activity of men found employment without breaking the ecclesiastical system.

(1) *The Knowledge of God*

There are two ways, he says, the affirmative and the negative, by which we may come to such knowledge of God as is possible for us. It must be understood that there is an ultimate Agnosticism. 'But this we must say—that it is not the purpose of our discourse to reveal the Super-Essential Being in its Super-Essential Nature, for this is unutterable, nor can we know It, or in any way express It, for It is beyond even the Unity; but only to celebrate the Emanation of the Absolute Divine Essence into the universe of things.'[1] Bearing this limitation in mind, we may learn to know truly about God since He is the source of all. The affirmative path (*via eminentiae*) consists in applying our ideas to God in the highest degree, and leads to the differentiated manifestations of the Godhead in the Trinity. The Super-Essential and Supra-Personal Godhead had within Itself the principles both of Unity and Plurality. These principles form, as it were, two streams, which emanate and ceaselessly revolve, but without leaving any mark until the time appointed for history to begin. Dionysius is no more able than the rest of us to explain how it was that history did begin. Yet, seeing that all has emanated from one source, and that what appears is a true type, the seen of the unseen, it follows that we may truly affirm of Him that which we perceive in His creation, only with the pre-eminence of full perfection.

It is, however, by the negative path (*via negationis*) that we attain to the deepest knowledge. 'The Supreme Godhead Itself, in one of the mystical visions whereby It was symbolically manifested, rebuked him who said, What is Thy name? and, as though bidding him not to seek by means of any name to acquire a knowledge of God, made the answer, Why seekest thou thus after My name, seeing It is secret?'[2] This teaching has profoundly affected Mysticism; the Divine Gloom is Light unapproachable. It did not, of course, originate with Dionysius, who himself refers to the *Elements of Divinity* by St.

[1] *De Div. Nom.*, v. 1 (Rolt's translation).   [2] *De Div. Nom.*, i. 6.

Hierotheus. 'The Deity is perfect in those things that are imperfect, as a source of Perfection; it is perfectionless in those that are perfect as transcending or anticipating their Perfection.'[1]

In considering the most important of all the Divine titles, that of the One, Dionysius says explicitly that the Creator of all things must be denominated as at once Perfect and Beyond Perfection, since in His simple Unity He must not be limited even by the idea of perfection, nor yet by that of personality. 'Moreover, the title Perfect means that It cannot be increased, being always perfect, and cannot be diminished, and that It contains all things beforehand in Itself, and overflows in one ceaseless, identical (because timeless), abundant, and inexhaustible supply, *whereby It perfects all perfect things, and fills them with Its own perfection.*'[2] To some it will seem that we are here in a purely philosophical altitude, without any religious significance. In his essay on Dionysius, Westcott says that these writings bear the impress of a particular age and school, and even of a particular man, not wholly of a Christian type. Yet Dionysius had a deep conception of the Trinity, and of Jesus as the eternal revelation of God. He recounts, for instance, how in the *Outlines of Divinity* (now lost) he had traced the conceptions which belong to the affirmative method, and especially that which shows 'how Jesus, being above all essence, has stooped to an essential state, in which all the truths of human nature meet.'[3] It was this clinging to the historic revelation in Christ which saved Dionysius from many of the errors of Basilides, and enabled him to present a theory of the way to the knowledge of God which the Church was able to accept. The practical gain was that it left a place for the exercise of the reason in the times of the greatest ecclesiastical intolerance.

(2) *The Way of Union with God*

The first step is taken when, like Abraham or Muhammad, we break away from the idea that the Godhead can be confined in any idol. In a way it is negative; we say, 'That is not God.' But this negative would have no meaning but for a positive conception that God is. Yet still a distinction exists between

[1] *De Div. Nom.*, ii. 9. [2] *Ibid.*, xiii. 1. [3] *Myst. Theol.* iii.

myself and God; and this distinction is the cause of the problem of evil. Dionysius is convinced that evil is a necessary result of creaturehood; the streams of potentiality, particular and universal, which eternally emanate from the Super-Essential Godhead, have ceased to find their perfect fulfilment therein, and have passed out into creation. These streams are good in themselves; and evil is naught, Non-Ens, simply the sign of failure to find satisfaction within the Godhead. Yet Dionysius is troubled by the thought that there must be some reality in evil. 'If evil is the destruction of things which have being, that depriveth it not of its own being. It itself still hath being, and giveth birth to its offspring. Yea, is not the destruction of one thing often the birth of another? And thus it will be found that evil maketh contribution unto the fullness of the world, and through its pressure saveth the universe from destruction.' This objection, which rises in his own mind, Dionysius answered by saying that evil *qua* evil causes no existence or birth. '*Qua* evil it only debases and destroys; but it taketh upon itself the form of birth and essence through the action of the Good. Thus evil is found to be a destructive force in itself, but a productive force through the action of the Good.'[1]

The overcoming of sin and the entering into communion is through a perception of the soul's identity with God. It begins with prayer: 'Hallowed be Thy Name, Thy Kingdom come, Thy will be done.' But this mental prayer, in which the renunciation of self is involved, passes into an ecstatic perception of God as the higher self. I live; but this new egoism has lost the lower selfishness, and become Christ-in-me, the hope of glory. This truly Scriptural conception, however, became in Dionysius obscured by the *via negativa* to which he was devoted. This is shown in the opening passage of the *Mystical Theology* dealing with the Divine gloom. 'By the unceasing and absolute renunciation of thyself and all things thou shalt in pureness cast all things aside, and be released from all, and so shalt be led upwards to the Ray of that Divine Darkness which exceedeth all existence (lit. the Super-Essential Ray of Divine Darkness).'

Here we see the strength and the weakness of the Areopagite. There is a true conception, not really Pantheistic or Agnostic,

[1] *De Div. Nom.*, iv. 20.

of the ineffableness of God, and a deep conviction that all is from Him. We seem to be drawing to ourselves a chain of light; but it is in truth shining upon us to our spiritual uplifting; just as, when from a ship we seize a rope fastened to a rock, we are not really drawing the rock to us, but ourselves and the ship to the rock.[1] The account in Exodus xix. and xx. of how Moses sanctified himself and the people, and how he heard the trumpets, and saw the many lights, and received in his soul the illumination of the Law, and then how he passed into the thick darkness where God was—this account Dionysius had always in mind. It seemed to him to speak of the triple way of purification, illumination, and final union with the darkness of the Unknown God. Nevertheless, his theology fails, not because it is not Divine enough, but because it is not human enough. It would not be right to say that Jesus is lost sight of; but the message of the Incarnation, with its sanctifying of the common life of men; of the Atonement, with its word of reconciliation to men who sin and suffer and die; and of the Resurrection, with its all but incredible hope for humanity; this evangel was never central to the teaching of Dionysius.

(3) *The Hierarchical Systems in Heaven and on Earth*

What gave interest to these writings and ensured their success was the doctrine concerning the hierarchies in Heaven and on earth. Here we have the warmer, more human touch, of which Dionysius felt the need all the more because of the effort which his soul was making to rise into the starry heights of Heaven. He speaks of three motions of the soul.[2] There is a circular movement, when it revolves round the Beautiful and the Good.[3] There is a straight movement, when it goes forward, in the case of the heavenly to help those beneath, in the case of men towards the outward world. But there is a spiral movement, which combines these; and for men that means that, while their nature circles round the Divine, they still use their reason in the activities of life. A place is thus found in the perfecting of the soul for fellowship, and for the order which is essential to fellowship.

The two writings, *De Coelesti Hierarchia* and *De Ecclesiastica*

---

[1] *De Div. Nom.*, iii. 1.   [2] *De Div. Nom.*, iv. 8.
[3] In Dante's Paradise the souls of the perfected all move with a circular motion.

Hierarchia, present the complement of the teaching in the *De Divinis Nominibus* and the *De Mystica Theologia*. All the hierarchies circle round the Divine Goodness; and it is through their desire for that blessedness that they possess their own being. The thrice three choirs of angels[1] are not original with Dionysius; but it was through him that the conception involved in them laid hold of the Mediaeval Church. Since the threefold grace of purification, enlightenment, and perfection flows through these orders, which are the evangelists or heralds of the Divine Silence, it is fitting that there should be orders in the earthly ministry. Uniformity and equality may be predicated of the Divine Goodness; but there may also be predicated diversity and orderliness.[2] Dionysius continued his triplets in the earthly hierarchy: (1) three sacraments—Baptism, the Eucharist, and Unction; (2) three orders—Deacons, Priests, Bishops; (3) *three orders denoting stages of spiritual progress*. The last three are connected with the sacraments and the ecclesiastical orders. First are those who have received baptism, and are being prepared by the deacon; then come those who are allowed to receive from the priest the sacred elements, and to share in that most glorious rite; highest of all are those who as monks have renounced the world, and who have received from the bishop the final perfecting which fits them for the unction of the Holy One.

By the time of St. Thomas Aquinas this theologoumenon had sunk deep into Christian thought. Over all and beyond all was the One; but from Him descended an infinite number of existences, whose glory filled Heaven and earth. Tier beyond tier they rose; and an eternal harmony bound them together. What was being done in the Church on earth was one end of a golden chain, whose other limit was beyond the thought of man or angel. To lay hold of that chain purity was needed, and illumination and union with the Divine. That could only be attained by contemplation, whereby we reach such deification as is in conformity with our nature.[3] When this was not accomplished for the Christian here, it would have to be hereafter. Dionysius himself says nothing about Purgatory; but it was from his teaching there sprung the congeries of ideas in regard to the hereafter which dominated the Church in the

---

[1] (1) Thrones, Cherubim, Seraphim; (2) Powers, Dominions, Mights; (3) Angels, Archangels, Principalities.
[2] *De Coel. Hier.*, vii. 4.   [3] *De Coel. Hier.*, i.

Middle Ages. The attainment of the end of our creation was considered as possible only for a few here upon earth. For most it was relegated to the future, i.e. it was divorced from reality. Obviously that deprives the quest of all ethical meaning. There may be—there probably are—purgatorial fires in eternity; but the deepest objection to any teaching of purgatory is when it involves the shirking of the ethical ideal as far as this life is concerned. Our greatest spiritual need of to-day is such an understanding of the mind of Christ that we may be able to proclaim the ethical reality of our personal life in eternity, and its correspondence with the present ecclesiastical order, without losing the conviction of the far-reaching importance of the decisions which we now make in the flesh.

PART IV
THE RESULTANT DIVERGENCES

CONTENTS OF PART IV

XII. THE IDEA OF ATTAINMENT UNDER THE SANCTION OF THE CHURCH

		PAGE
1.	BERNARD OF CLAIRVAUX	181
2.	THE MARKS OF THE FRANCISCAN REVIVAL	183
	(1) *Submission to Ecclesiastical Authority*	183
	(2) *Devotion to Christ*	184
	(3) *Poverty*	185
	(4) *Missionary Zeal*	186
3.	THOMAS AQUINAS	187
	(1) *The Active and the Contemplative Life*	190
	(2) *Superiority of the Contemplative Life*	191
	(3) *The Meaning of States of Life*	192
	(4) *The State of Perfection*	193
	(5) *The Episcopal State*	195
	(6) *The Religious State*	196
	(7) *Purgatory*	198
4.	THE CATHOLIC MYSTICS	199
	(1) *Their Attachment to Christ*	200
	(2) *Their Contribution to the Doctrine of the Trinity*	201
	(3) *Their Dependence on the Sacraments*	202

XIII. THE IDEA OF ATTAINMENT THROUGH OBEDIENCE TO THE WORD

1.	THE ATTITUDE OF JOHN WESLEY	206
2.	A CATENA OF METHODIST EXPERIENCES	211
	(1) *Jane Cooper*	211
	(2) *Hester Ann Rogers*	212
	(3) *William Grimshaw*	213
	(4) *John Laycock*	214
3.	THE METHODIST DOCTRINAL STATEMENTS	217
	(1) *Wesley's 'Plain Account of Christian Perfection'*	218
	(2) *John William Fletcher's 'Antinomianism' and 'Entire Sanctification'*	221
	(3) *R. Watson's 'Institutes' and W. B. Pope's 'Theology'*	223
4.	THE OBERLIN THEOLOGY	225

XIV. THE IDEA OF ATTAINMENT THROUGH THE WITNESS OF THE SPIRIT

1.	THE QUAKER MOVEMENT	230
2.	THE QUAKER TEACHING CONCERNING PERFECTION	233
	(1) *The Inward Light*	235
	(2) *The Long Pilgrimage*	237
	(3) *The Historic and the Inward Christ*	238
3.	THE VALUE OF THE QUAKER CONTRIBUTION	241
	(1) *Immediate Union with God*	242
	(2) *The True Glory of Humanity*	245

CHAPTER XII

THE IDEA OF ATTAINMENT UNDER THE SANCTION
OF THE CHURCH

IN chapter II. we saw reason to distinguish three sources, the Church, the Word, and the Spirit, from which all the doctrines of Christendom have been drawn. The course of our investigation has shown how widespread is the longing for a state of perfection. We have now to consider the divergences into well-marked varieties of religious experience, which have resulted from emphasis being laid on one or other of the sources. Within the area of the English-speaking world these varieties are clearly recognized in the conceptions of Evangelical Perfection which distinguish the Roman Catholic, the Methodist, and the Quaker. Some of these names were originally given in contempt. One may, however, be forgiven for using them, as being popular names, which plainly indicate those intended. It may suffice, therefore, if we trace the development of the idea on these three lines.

We turn first to those who lay stress on the Church as the source from which the idea has come, and as the means through which the idea is to be realized. For this study the Mediaeval Church makes an admirable base. While there have been developments in the Roman Catholic Church since, as for example in the doctrines of the Immaculate Conception and of Papal Infallibility, the way of perfection is still defined on the lines laid down by Aquinas. Probably such lines are inevitable for those for whom the authority of the Church is decisive.

1. BERNARD OF CLAIRVAUX

The Franciscan Revival was part of an extensive movement, behind which was the teaching of Gregory the Great (*d.* 604), and Bernard of Clairvaux (*d.* 1153). St. Bernard taught that we have union with God through knowing and loving Him. He strove to keep both prominent, the cognition and the will to love. The way of progress demands an earnest effort to rise to love for God. The New Testament rather speaks of the state which results from the love of God towards us.[1] But Bernard is thinking of love towards God, when he says that there are two arms of the soul whereby it lays hold of perfection, Contemplation which leads to Cognition, and Will which leads to Love.[2] The highest stage, pure love towards God, while the gift of the Divine Grace through Christ, entailed merit partly because of what the attainment meant in itself, and partly because it could only be attained by a choice which incurred earthly loss. In the *De Gratia et Libero Arbitrio* an effort is made to combine these ideas, so that, while we ascribe all to grace, we yet acknowledge merit in the free acceptance of that grace. This is the true following of Christ. In His case the surrender of His will to the Father's gave value to His atoning death.[3] It was considered that the apostles had walked in the same way: hence this following of Jesus was also called living the apostolic life. When men asked how it was to be done, the first answer was, by simple obedience, allowing the Church as the Inheritor of the grace of Christ to say exactly what the following of Him meant. The second answer was, by personal renunciation, the leaving of all to follow Christ. It would be quite a mistake to suppose that at any time the authority of the Church has superseded the desire of the individual for some personal act. The third answer said that the true following of the life of Christ culminated in a mystical union with God through Him. In working this out St. Bernard revealed his own spiritual insight. The lyric rapture of *Jesu dulcis memoria* denotes an experience in the true succession from Augustine. As Augustine used the language of the *Enneads*, so Bernard used the language of the *Confessions*; but each is the utterance of an immediate personal experience. In the *De Diligendo Deo* four stages are described. From the natural self-love, which is innate in all, the soul rises to the second stage of love towards God through reflection, the deep consciousness of its need. Then through gratitude and the contemplation of the Divine

---

[1] 1 John iv. 7–21, esp. 19 R.V.   [2] *Ep.*, 18. 2, Luthardt, i. 322.
[3] 'Non mors sed voluntas placuit sponte morientis' (*De Erroribus Abelardi*, viii. 21).

Goodness the soul becomes so purified that it learns to love God, not only for what He gives, but for Himself ; and thus to love also His works, and especially the souls of men. Here Bernard rises above the Neo-Platonic tradition by insisting on the contemplation of the Passion and Death of Christ. Beyond this there is still another, the stage of ecstasy, in which the soul forgets herself, forgets even the sister souls around, and turns wholly to God. To experience this emotion is indeed to partake of the Divine Nature. *Sic affici deificari est.*[1] This analysis is very characteristic of the Roman Catholic type of perfection. The love of God is the source and end of all attainment ; but a distinction is made between the first movement of grateful trust, and the final abandonment of self in the ocean of Divine Love. A place is left for brotherly love and for the service of humanity ; yet we may note that this came to be regarded as a stage, not always even a necessary stage, on the way to the divine rapture, *divina illa et deifica visio.*

2. THE MARKS OF THE FRANCISCAN REVIVAL

It was in a world whose ideals were set, and whose thinking was governed, as the Crusades bear witness, by St. Bernard, that Francis of Assisi heard the call. Bearing in mind the origin of the Franciscan Revival, Neo-Platonic, Augustinian, but immediately and dominantly Bernardine, we may mark off the following distinctive features. (1) It was in no sense a revolt against ecclesiastical discipline : indeed it resulted in greatly strengthening the authority of Rome. (2) At the same time it was marked by an endeavour to express devotion to Christ apart from ecclesiastical routine. (3) This devotion expressed itself towards God in poverty and mystical surrender. (4) Towards the world it expressed itself in missionary zeal.

(1) *Submission to Ecclesiastical Authority*

Distinctive of the Franciscan movement was the obedience exacted towards those in authority in the Church. I do not say that this was the most important mark ; but I have placed it first because it regulated the whole. For several years Francis opposed the advice of Rome that he should form one of

[1] *De Dil. Deo*, 10. 28, Luthardt i. 323.

the Regular Orders, for he was afraid that it would mean the loss of spirituality. Nevertheless, when the advice was given in the tone of a command, he never dreamed of resisting, as the Rules of A.D. 1221 and 1223 plainly show. 'All the brothers must be Catholics, and live and speak as Catholics. If any one, by his words or deeds, should sin against the Catholic Faith and Life, and not repent, let him be cast out of our Fraternity.'[1] Brother Leo was one of those most intimate with St. Francis; and we have no reason to doubt that the *Mirror of Perfection* is a faithful record.[2] The subject of c. lxxviii, is, How he wished his order to be always subject to the protection and correction of the Roman Church. In c. lxxxvii. is an account of the three sayings which were left to the friars. 'Namely, that in token of my memory and benediction and will, they should always love one another, as I have loved and always do love them; that they should always love and observe our Lady Poverty; and always remain faithful subjects to the prelates and clergy of holy Mother Church.' This description is typical of the spirit which controlled this revival of piety. The virtues on which St. Bernard laid most stress, *caritas et humilitas*, seemed naturally to issue in obedience and subjection to holy Mother Church. Some of these exhortations may have been added later, when that obedience was being strained and sometimes broken; but they are the natural outcome of Franciscan teaching.

(2) *Devotion to Christ*

I have laid weight on the fact that this revival, in its search for perfection, accepted as an axiom that the quest must be made within the pale of the Roman Church. But the driving force was the desire to express one's love to God and Christ in some personal, distinctive way, within the limits of the Church, but not as part of ecclesiastical routine. The letters of St. Francis are full of exhortations to show one's love to God, and they are full of doxologies because of His love. A prayer attributed to him portrays the abandon into which those who had tasted something of the Divine Love were led. 'Lord, I pray Thee, that the burning and delicious ardour of Thy love

[1] Rule xix. of the Friars Minor.
[2] Speculum Perfectionis, *circa* 1227, with later additions.

may detach my soul from all things which are under heaven, so that I may die for love of Thy love, O Thou who for love of my love hast deigned to die.' Revival always comes through some fresh glimpse of Divine Love, as manifested in Christ dying for us ; for this vision issues in a desire for union. The fascination of the Divine Presence prevails over its awefulness. Celano said of St. Francis : ' His whole philosophy, his whole desire as long as he lived, his sole wish was constantly to seek, among wise and simple, perfect and imperfect, the means to walk in the way of truth, and to become more perfect.'

(3) *Poverty*

The desire for ways of uttering love has found varied expression. Roman Catholic Ethics has never thought of the Counsels of Perfection as limited to the three well-known renunciations, but includes in that term any way by which the soul is able to give special proof of its love. Anything which goes beyond what is required partakes of the nature of a gift, and becomes meritorious in the sight of God. In the best teaching it is understood that the value of the renunciation depends on its being an expression of love, although the thesis of the Jansenists as to the necessity of love was rejected. In practice, however, the carrying out of the Counsels came to be limited to the three renunciations as regards God, and such counsels as loving one's enemy, and giving superfluous alms, enumerated by Ambrose and Aquinas, as regards one's neighbour. Looking backward we may call it ' the apostolical life,' if we think of the apostles as celibates, without property and without personal ambitions. Looking forward we may speak of it as ' the angelical life,' if we imagine the life beyond as free from those desires which lead to the lust of the flesh, the lust of the eyes, and the vainglory of life. In practice, moreover, emphasis has tended to rest on one or other of the three renunciations. In the Early Church it was on celibacy, as we note in the teaching of Ambrose ; in Aquinas the highest place was assigned to obedience.

The interest of the Franciscan Revival is largely due to the fact that for the first time the pre-eminence was given to Poverty. Francis not only accepted Poverty as a help to attain his goal, he came to love her for the joyous freedom which she gave. As he spoke of himself as the Lord's troubadour, so he called himself the wooer of the Lady Poverty. There is a simple and charming allegory by an unknown Franciscan in the thirteenth century, entitled the *Sacrum Commercium*, which describes the wooing. It begins, ' Among the cardinal and excelling virtues, which prepare a place and a mansion for God in the Soul of Man, and show a more excellent and a speedier way of approaching and attaining unto Him, Holy Poverty shines resplendent in her authority, and excels all others by her peculiar grace. *For she is the Foundation and Guardian of all the Virtues, and holds the Primacy among the Evangelical Counsels.'* This figure so touched men's imagination that Francis and Poverty became inseparably associated. Dante refers to it in the *Paradiso* ! [1]

> By these two lovers, in my speech diffuse,
> Thou Poverty and Francis now mayest know.

Some absurdities arose, as when the blessed Francis was represented as expressing jealousy that any one should be poorer than he was,[2] or when he rebuked a novice for desiring to have a Psalter for his own use.[3] But there is a great underlying idea which is indispensable for perfection, the idea of detachment. Whatever possessions one may have, whatever pleasures one may enjoy, including the possession of books and the pleasures of the intellect, are to be held and enjoyed with detachment. It is necessary, not merely to remind ourselves that they are fugitive, but to be ready at any time, and, without murmuring, to surrender them. The question may be put, how far a detachment which is purely within the will is sufficient, and whether the ordinary vicissitudes of life will furnish adequate occasion to test the reality of the detachment. While for most the changes and chances of this mortal life will afford sufficient test, the instance of the rich young ruler is proof that to some the call will come with the urgency of a special act of renunciation.

(4) *Missionary Zeal*

It might appear that such an ideal as that of the Minorites would exclude Missionary work. Francis himself hesitated as to whether he should preach or give himself up to a

---

[1] Canto xi. 11. 28–123.   [2] *Spec. Perf.* c. xvii.   [3] *Spec. Perf.* c. iv.

contemplative life. But the principle of the revival was a profound sense of the Divine Love; and this was in itself an energy which, apart even from conscious apprehension, led to evangelistic enterprise. Those rules which deal with Missionary work are designed to restrain and regulate the energy which was seeking vent in this way. But what was their Gospel? and to whom was it directed? Was it to the poor that they should be satisfied with their poverty, and indeed rejoice in it? or to the rich that they should abandon their wealth? Was it a Gospel for the world as it was, seeking to uplift, but content to accept the economic conditions of the age? or was it a Gospel of a new world, ushering in wholly new conditions? It may be said at once that St. Francis was the last man to trouble himself about these logical problems. The movement worked from within outwards, from those who had as minor friars left all to follow Christ, to those who were already monks, but had drifted from their first love; then to all the clergy; then to the laity; and finally to the outside world, including Saracens and other infidels. It was a great thought with a noble aim. Nevertheless, a nemesis came upon it, owing to the refusal to consider what the Gospel really was, and to the setting up of poverty as an end in itself. The love which poured itself out in acts of mercy brought a rich reward, and stimulated the whole Church. Such love can never be without blessing. But it needs to be supplemented by thought, even by the much decried learning, in order to declare to the world the true end of the evangelical counsels.

3. THOMAS AQUINAS

By St. Francis and his followers the ideal of a life of renunciation was carried out with a rigour which has never been surpassed. It meant, however, separation from the world's progress and from every effort to increase its amenities; and it led to intellectual poverty. The joyous freedom which came from renouncing earthly cares often turned to a morbid depression known as *accidie*, through the lack of any outlet for natural energy. This intellectual vacuity was filled for mediaeval life by St. Thomas Aquinas, a theologian who resembles Calvin in the sweep and range of his thought. Even the *Institutes* is not a more astonishing example of mental grasp of vast problems than the *Summa Theologica*. He studied under Albertus Magnus, from whom he learnt to appreciate the method of Aristotle. These two put together separately, but no doubt with mutual consultation, a systematized statement of the scholastic view of God and the world. The influence of Aquinas has been more lasting than his master's; and we may fairly say that no small part of that influence is due to the impression made by the serenity of his confidence in the authorities on which he relies.

(1) The Canon of Scripture had long been settled; and it is as true of him as it is of Calvin to say that he never consciously differs from passages within the canon.[1] But he was not hampered by the absence of specific scriptural teaching, and in that case was satisfied with other sanctions. Moreover, his exegesis does not go beyond that of his day. Thus, in the important discussion of the comparative excellence of the active and the contemplative life, much weight is attached, not only to the comparison between Martha and Mary, which is undoubtedly pertinent, but also to that between Leah and Rachel.[2] We never find Calvin descending to the puerility of some of the arguments drawn from the latter comparison.

(2) Aquinas accepted the authority of the Fathers; but he did not defer to them as unreservedly as to Scripture. If he puts a quotation from the Bible into the objector's mouth, he feels it necessary to show that the passage has not the meaning assigned; but when he so uses a quotation from the Fathers, he often passes on to his own statement without explicitly refuting it. The writers to whom he refers most are Jerome and Augustine, especially the latter. He also frequently consulted the Conferences of the Fathers, and the writings of Dionysius the Areopagite and Gregory the Great.

(3) Besides these he was guided in his whole method by Aristotle, whom he designates pre-eminently the Philosopher. It must be set to the credit of the Middle Ages that there was so much recognition of the worth of non-Christian thinking. The *Summa* seeks to unite the ideal of Aristotle, for whom the highest good consists in a life of sufficient leisure to devote oneself to intellectual activity and spiritual contemplation,

---

[1] Harnack, vi. 156*n*.
[2] The comparison between Leah and Rachel can be traced back to Augustine *Contra Faustum*, xxii. 52–8.

with the monastic ideal which had been revived with such energy by the Mendicant Friars.

(4) Aquinas vigorously maintained the place and authority of the Reason. In the first part of the *Summa* he upheld the thesis that the fact of the Divine Existence can be proved by the natural reason; and all through he based his theology on a belief that whatever may come by revelation will always be found to be in conformity with reason.

(5) I have endeavoured to do justice to the candour and the seriousness with which Aquinas grappled with the supreme problems; but it cannot be denied that he came to them with a mind biased towards the ecclesiastical dogmas of his day. Nor is this a vice; for an unbiased mind would be a monstrosity, incapable of progress. What emerges from a study of the *Summa* is the dominance in the thirteenth century of an eclectic theology, in which the ideal for man (*beatitudo*) was drawn from the monastic movement, from the Aristotelian philosophy, and from the hierarchical system. The whole bent of Aquinas from childhood (he was born in 1225) was towards the Church. After overcoming some resistance from his family he entered the Dominican Order, which had been founded in 1215. He had a natural tendency to accept the rulings of the hierarchy, to which he felt that so much was owing for the conservation of the truth. This explains why his theology, and in particular his formulation of the Christian ideal, has never been superseded in the Roman Church. In the *Summa* we have an exposition of that conception of perfection, in which the Church is the primary factor. The principle is stated in *Secunda Secundae*, Q. 1, A. 9 : ' Sed contra est quod Ecclesia universalis non potest errare, quia Spiritu Sancto gubernatur, qui est Spiritus veritatis : hoc enim promisit Dominus discipulis.' Here it is obvious that, while the Spirit and the Word are both appealed to, it is the Church which is decisive.

The sweep of St. Thomas's mind enabled him to survey the whole field, and to keep it before him. In reviewing those sections which deal specifically with our subject, I do not forget that they rest on a long process of reasoning, in which he has been striving to amalgamate with Catholic dogma the philosophy of Aristotle, together with Neo-Platonic elements added by the Arabians, Avicenna and Averrhoes. The questions which concern us are dealt with in *Pars Secunda Secundae*, QQ. 179–89. These eleven questions I have condensed under six heads, with a paragraph added in regard to Purgatory.

(1) *The Active and the Contemplative Life*

St. Thomas has a noble idea of what life means. It is not merely existence: a man lives in that in which he finds most delight, on which he is most intent, and in which he would desire to pass his time with his friends.[1] The Christian life may be rightly divided, according as men prefer action or contemplation. He is far too clear-sighted to suggest that life can be exactly divided, still less that men can be separated into two classes; but he argues that a ruling tendency may be apparent. Some may be so engaged in good works as to have little time for prayer, and none for meditation; others may be so engrossed in contemplation as to have no energy for active life. It must be understood that the active life covers the operation of the moral virtues; it is best described as consisting in our relation with other people. If we practise the moral virtues because of their inherent attraction, our exercise in them belongs exclusively to the active life; but if we look on them as necessary steps to contemplation, and practise them for the sake of the purification which they bring, so that at last we may see God, then it becomes part of the contemplative life. Similarly with Prayer and Teaching; these may be regarded as active or contemplative, according to the intention in them. If doctrinal instruction be given with the object of directing action, it belongs to the active life; if out of sheer love for and delight in the truths taught, to the contemplative. It is easier to remain in the active life, since that is more natural for us; but its scope is bounded by this present life. The contemplative life is one of delight (*delectatio*), even in this world; it consists purely in the contemplation of God, and not of any truth, such as in philosophy or science: nevertheless, since we come to the knowledge of God through His works,[2] the contemplation of the Divine effects also belongs to the higher life, inasmuch as man is guided thereby to the knowledge of God.[3] The exclusion of images

---
[1] *Nic. Eth.*, ix. 4, 9, 12.   [2] Rom. i. 20.   [3] Q. 180, A. 4.

is the determining note which distinguishes contemplation from meditation¹. It is not possible to attain to the vision of the Divine Being² in this life ; nor is it possible to remain long in the highest state. The highest is that which St. Paul had in rapture, which is to be thought of as midway between this mortal life and that which is to be.³

(2) *Superiority of the Contemplative Life*

The question of degree in merit is fully discussed by Aquinas ; and he agrees with Gregory that great are the merits of the active life, but greater still those of the contemplative. The active life, so far from hindering the contemplative, prepares for it, and continues with it, though it usually becomes more and more subservient. One who has been immersed in contemplation may be called to an active life, especially in the case of a prelate ; but even then he ought to continue to excel in contemplation, though he may have less leisure for it.

Behind this view lie certain ideas which leavened the thirteenth century, that great century whose praise Ruskin loved to sing. The aim which the earnest seeker should set before himself is the Beatific Vision,⁴ the essence of which is the knowledge of God ; and his highest bliss or beatitude is in the operation of that which is highest and best in him. The perfection of this operation depends on four things : (1) on its residing in the intellectual being himself, and being desired for its own sake, and not for something which it produces ; (2) on its being the operation of the highest faculty ; (3) on its object being the highest possible for the faculty concerned ; (4) on the beauty of its working, to the end that it should work perfectly, easily, and delightfully.⁵ The highest bliss is a life in which the intellect operates in ceaseless activity towards the highest object. This brings with it infinite delight, in one way the delight of exercise, because each individual delights in the operation which befits him, according to his own nature and habit, in another owing to the object, in so far as one

---

¹ Butler, *Western Mysticism*, p. 289.   ² ' Ad visionem divinae essentiae.'
³ ' Unde supremus gradus contemplationis praesentis vitae est, qualem habuit Paulus in raptu, secundum quem fuit medio modo se habens inter statum praesentis vitae et futurae.'
⁴ P. H. Wicksteed, *The Reactions between Dogma and Philosophy*, pp. 582–659.
⁵ ' Quarto, ex forma operationis, ut scilicet perfecte, faciliter et delectabiliter operetur ' (*Contra Gentiles*, i. 100, cit. Wicksteed, p. 616n).

contemplates that which one loves.¹ Professor T. C. Hall, therefore, is mistaken in saying, ' What Aristotle meant by the contemplative life was a life of ceaseless curiosity ; what Aquinas meant by it was a life of devotional submission.'² As a matter of fact Aquinas is thoroughly convinced of the need for the exercise of the intellect : his difficulty often is to show the place of the will. The origin of the higher life is in the desire, the appetite (*affectus*); and, since the end corresponds with the beginning, there is the delight of satisfied desire in the end. ' This is the ultimate perfection of the contemplative life, namely, that the Divine Truth be not only seen but loved.'³ It is true that he conceived of the highest stage as involving abstraction from all outward appearances; but in this he was only following Aristotle. Whatever knowledge may have been gained in the study of the creature is not lost, but may be taken up into the higher mood. We cannot forget that whatever learning survived the confused activities of the Middle Ages came through the monasteries; and it seems possible that in the future there may be an abstract thinking about God, in which the scientific progress of humanity shall be garnered.

(3) *The Meaning of States of Life*

According to Aquinas the status of a man consists entirely in his freedom or servitude, a fact which he illustrates from the civil law. In the spiritual realm there is a twofold servitude and a twofold freedom in regard to sin or to righteousness.⁴ The inception of the Christian life is in breaking away from free indulgence in sin ; then comes freedom from sin, but with an apprehension of justice as a bondage ; but at the highest that is swept away with the incoming of the Lord's Spirit, which is Love (*Charitas*). ' There are three states of the converted, the beginning, the middle, and the perfection.'⁵ This attempt to distinguish definite and well-marked stages of progress in Love was unfortunately followed by a quite unsuccessful endeavour to connect them with the offices discharged within the Church. St. Thomas has no difficulty in showing that the variety within the Church contributes to its perfection, activity, and beauty ; and in theory he makes

---

¹ Q. 180, A. 7.   ² *Hist. of Christian Ethics*, p. 318.
³ Q. 180, A. 7, r.o.1.   ⁴ Rom. vi. 20, 22.   ⁵ *Moral.*, xxiv., cit. Q. 183, A. 4.

a distinction between states, duties, and grades.¹ But it was a great calamity that the question of spiritual progress became associated with the different duties performed in the Church, and with the different ecclesiastical grades and orders. These last are necessary; they contribute to the beauty of the Church; but they must never be thought of as marking stages of spiritual growth. Now, whatever Aquinas may say, there is inevitable confusion when they are so closely and so unnecessarily associated. It is in my judgement his gravest error, and the cause of much misguidance in the practice of life. The root of it may be traced back to Dionysius, when he connected the hierarchical system with the ladder by which humanity rises to God. The fact that the Church owed a great debt to the hierarchy during the breaking up of the Empire induced many to accept the idea of Dionysius. Aquinas found it ready to hand, and wholly congruous to the thought of his time; but his vigorous defence of the setting apart of a state of perfection as part of the organization of the Church stereotyped a conception which is spiritually disastrous.

(4) *The State of Perfection*

The notion of a State of Perfection is very valuable. The idea is of a State in which the soul has entered on its maturity, and perceives the goal towards which it is striving, while it is yet conscious of considerable failure. Aquinas writes admirably on this theme.² Perfection consists in Charity, which is the bond of all the virtues; and it is concerned with the evangelical precepts even more than with the counsels; and it is attainable in this life. He distinguishes the absolute perfection, which belongs to God alone, and that in which the whole affective faculty of the lover turns only to God, which is only possible in our eternal home (*patria*), from what may be called a third perfection, in which the soul decisively puts away all that hinders its tending towards God. This last, which does not exclude the need for pardon for venial sins,³ is possible in this life.

These distinctions are useful. Most of those who object to a Doctrine of Perfection do so on the ground that the term

¹ Q. 183, A. 3.   ² Q. 184.
³ ' Si quis dixerit . . . hominem posse in tota vita peccata omnia venalia vitare, nisi ex speciali Dei privilegio, anathema sit ' (*Conc. Trid.*, sess. vi., can. 23).

should be predicated of God alone, or else only of the future life. It may be noted in passing that these objections will not hold together. If Perfection is only to be predicated of Deity, then it is just as inapplicable to us in the future life as in this.[1] Even in Heaven all will not have the same capacity : the *lumen gloriae* will not therefore shine before all with the same brightness. Yet it may be truly said that all are perfect, since the attainment which they have made has become natural to them through the Divine Indwelling. Similarly we may say that in this life the soul may reach that which is proper to the mortal state. Aquinas insists that it is not possible to anticipate the Beatific Vision, in this departing from the Neo-Platonic tradition. If to any it is given miraculously, it must be through some temporary alienation from the body, as in the case of Moses and Paul. This insistence gives all the more weight to his testimony that there is a perfection attainable here, which is natural to our mortal condition.

I have already referred to the grave error of connecting this state with certain duties and grades. In Q. 184, A. 5 one of the objections is that no class of men is specially assigned to the state of the proficient or of the beginners : therefore it would seem that neither should any class be assigned to the State of Perfection. Would that he had listened to this objection, which he states so fairly ! But the force of tradition was too strong. He discovered that there are two classes in the State of Perfection, i.e. prelates and religious. Here we perceive the influence of Dionysius. The quotations from him are decisive, e.g. in articles 5 and 6, ' Sed contra est quod Dionysius (*Eccl. Hier.*, v., cir. med.) attribuit perfectionem episcopis tanquam perfectoribus ; et (ibid., vi.) attribuit perfectionem religiosis, quos vocat monachos, id est Deo famulantes, tanquam perfectos.'

It must in justice be said that it was considered open to all to attain the highest apart from these orders ; and it was never denied that those who belonged to them might not only not be perfect themselves, but might even be finally damned. Dante, who carefully followed Aquinas, placed Pope Boniface VIII in the Inferno. But the effect was to dissociate the quest for perfection from the workaday world ; for men were content to leave it to those definitely set apart. Aquinas

[1] *Summa*, I., Q. 12, A. 4.

makes the best case he can. He dwells on the fact that for the State of Perfection it is necessary that those entering should have a sense that they have undertaken a perpetual obligation. The state must be so marked that it shall not be regarded simply as an advance in sanctification, but as a new stage in the Christian Way. Just as Baptism and Confirmation indicate earlier stages, with a solemnity which makes it hard to draw back, so the entrance on Perfection must be impressed with awe upon the mind. This is done when it is joined with the episcopal ordination, or with the solemn monastic vows.

(5) *The Episcopal State*

The episcopal office is the highest step in the ecclesiastical hierarchy.[1] St. Thomas has no doubt that the distinction between bishop and priest goes back to apostolic times, though he is well aware that in the New Testament *episkopos* and *presbuteros* are interchangeable. The difficulty which he has to face is how to grade the three classes, Bishops, Priests, and Religious, with some approximation to their spiritual worth.

The highest class is that of Bishops : they are manifestly superior to the parish priest, since it is by their direction that priests are ordained and appointed. Of the priest we may say that he has an office pertaining to perfection, rather than that he is actually in the state. The bishop is also higher than the religious for two reasons : he puts into action for the good of others the love which he has learnt in contemplation ; and he is the dispenser of perfection to others. St. Thomas does not, of course, mean that the bishop takes the place of the Holy Spirit, when he calls him the perfecter, but simply that it is through him that any one is able to take the vows of entrance into the State of Perfection. Because of this high position no one must seek after the episcopal office. It is lawful, and indeed praiseworthy, to desire to enter the religious state, because that involves no authority, and makes no claim, but is simply the utterance of an aim. On the other hand it is not lawful absolutely to refuse an appointment to the episcopate. A certain reluctance, a

[1] Q. 185.

murmured '*nolo episcopari*,' is perhaps fitting; but, once it is put forward as the injunction of a superior, it should be accepted for the sake of serving the Church.

On p. 189 I stated the reason why the theology of Aquinas still governs the doctrine of the Roman Catholic Church. Some developments, however, there have been. One, of great significance, has been the inclusion of the Priesthood within the State of Perfection, placing it between the Episcopal Order and the Religious, and thus bringing the Religious State into greater subjection to the Hierarchy. Bishop Bellord voices the modern Romanist view by saying that there are three classes, Bishops, Priests, and those who have made the Religious profession, in order of excellence. ' The Religious State is below the Priesthood in its functions, and does not demand the same degree of internal perfection, although its rules are more methodical and stringent.'[1]

(6) *The Religious State*

The objections to the use of the term, the Religious State, were recognized by Aquinas, and were set forth forcibly and candidly by him.[2] In reply he says that the term is used by a figure of speech known as antonomasia, whereby a name which may be predicated of many is reserved for that of which it may be predicated in the highest degree. The argument is that the predicate ' religious ' is so exactly applicable to those who have taken the vows of poverty, &c., that it may be used by itself to designate them. It must be remembered that St. Thomas uses ' religion ' in its highest connotation, as that by which we are bound to God, and by which we make an offering to Him. ' Wherefore, those are called religious antonomastically who give themselves up to the Divine service, as offering a holocaust to God.'

It is not necessary to concern ourselves with all the delicate questions of terminology with which he found himself confronted.[3] Behind all is a mistaken idea of religion, due, in the end, to a mistaken idea of God. He saw clearly the better way, which he states in the objections; but he was swayed by the prejudices of his day. Thus he was led to state the three great abnegations which are most pleasing to God, and to

[1] *Meditations on Christian Dogma*, ii. 251.   [2] Q. 186.   [3] QQ. 186-9.

UNDER THE SANCTION OF THE CHURCH

declare that they must come under a vow.[1] It was an easy transition to make religion consist in the keeping of these vows. In further discussion of the religious life he declared that a preliminary vow might be taken, and that children should be received into religion, quoting in support Matt. xix. 14.[2] This is one of the weakest points in the system. Browning satirizes it in *Fra Lippo Lippi*:

> Brief, they made a monk of me;
> I did renounce the world, its pride and greed,
> Palace, farm, villa, shop and banking-house,
> Trash, such as these poor devils of Medici
> Have given their heart to—all at eight years old.

It is true that vows before puberty were not binding in the eyes of the Church; but on a sensitive conscience they retained their hold. ' Si tamen voto vel juramento se adstrinxerint ad aliquid faciendum, obligantur quoad Deum, si habeant usum rationis ; sed non obligantur quoad Ecclesiam ante quattuordecim annos.' It will be noted that these vows meant the renunciation of things of which the child has had no experience, and which are necessary for the continuance of the race.

Seeing the innumerable difficulties which the identification of the Religious Life with the State of Perfection brought in, difficulties as apparent to Aquinas as to any modern critic, why does he so tenaciously cling to it ? The answer is that it enabled him to accept the common view of Christendom that the religious life was only truly lived by those who had taken the vows, and at the same time to weld together the hierarchical system and the monastic ideal. As a matter of fact the episcopacy was only included by a *tour de force*. Aquinas explicitly excluded all ecclesiastical prelates except bishops. But the inclusion of the episcopacy enabled him to knit the monastic ideal into the ecclesiastical system. We may compare the alliance which he made between the ecclesiastical tradition and the Aristotelian philosophy, of which Dr. P. H. Wicksteed says : ' He was urged to his task by his deep love of them both and his firm conviction that both were true. His love made him feel that they ought to be friends everywhere as they were in his own heart ; while his deep conviction of their truth taught him that in the deepest nature of things they actually

[1] Q. 186, A. 6. [2] Q. 189, A. 5.

O

were friends. But he loved the church tradition more deeply than he loved Aristotle, and his conviction of its truth stood on a different plane and reached a higher level of certainty.' Similar remarks apply to the alliance which he was seeking to consummate between the hierarchical system and the monastic ideal. In some ways the difficulty was less, as the alliance was already in being. But there was continual friction, and Aquinas set himself to explore some formula of concord, not without success. Yet here too the dominant partner was the ecclesiastical system. He urges the superiority of the episcopal state to the religious, and that not merely in authority, but in spiritual worth, *in genere perfectionis*, in the very region of spiritual attainment. Significant also is the fact that he makes obedience the chief of the vows.[1] St. Ambrose exalted continence, and St. Francis poverty, but to St. Thomas it was plain that obedience was the chief. He brings forward some sound arguments; but his real motive is that of maintaining ecclesiastical discipline. When he comes to the subject of future rewards, the episcopacy drops out of sight altogether. It has no significance for the perfection of eternity. But the gifts, the dowries, the fruits, and the aureoles of the blessed, especially the last two, are closely connected with the religious life, the state of perfection on earth.

(7) *Purgatory*

During this investigation it has become more and more evident that some conception of Purgatory[2] is bound up with the doctrine of perfection. Modern criticism of the Roman doctrine, if I follow the trend rightly, is from a different standpoint from that of the Reformers. The latter had no objection to the teaching that destiny was fixed at death: in fact they cut away those addenda by which the Roman Church had somewhat alleviated that tremendous statement. But modern thought criticizes the mediaeval doctrine because it does not go far enough. It is too mechanical; and there is no scope in it for the exercise of ethical choice, and for the social intercourse, which is essential to spiritual development. Aquinas dealt with the question of Purgatory in two

---

[1] *Summa, Secunda Secundae*, Q. 186, A. 8.
[2] Supplement to the *Summa*, QQ. 69–86 on the Last Things, QQ. 87–99 on Purgatory.

appendices compiled by Nicolai from the *Commentary on the Sentences*. The destiny of every soul is fixed at death, though there is a general judgement to come. He found some difficulty in explaining the word in Nahum i. 9 (LXX.) : ' God will not judge the same thing a second time.' But he was not shaken in his conclusion. Purgatory is only for the baptized. He does not specifically refer to the heathen ; but he carefully discusses the fate of unbaptized infants ; and he agrees with Augustine that their punishment, since it is only for original sin, is of the mildest. Though they can never attain to the union of glory, they are not utterly separated from God, but may rejoice in Him by their natural knowledge and love. Purgatory, which lies direct in the way to Heaven, is for those who have been baptized, and so washed from original sin, whose mortal sins have been forgiven in this life, but who have not yet attained perfection : it is even for those who may have been in the state of perfection, but have not yet attained. The fire of Purgatory is the same as the fire of Hell, and only differs in its effects. Indeed it is in proximity to Hell, and Aquinas discusses, though he rejects, the thought that some souls in Purgatory may not be aware whether they are damned or not. App. i. Q. 2, A. 4 is very important, ' Whether venial sin is expiated by the pains of Purgatory as regards the guilt.' The following sentence shows the position afterwards taken up by the Reformers : ' Some have asserted that no sin is remitted after this life as regards the guilt ; that if a man die with mortal sin he is damned and incapable of being forgiven ; and that it is not possible to die with a venial sin and without mortal sin, since the final grace washes the venial sin away.' In effect that means the attainment of perfection by an act of final grace in the hour of death. The arguments which St. Thomas used in refuting this proposition are quite conclusive ; but modern thought would extend his conclusions by asserting the full ethical opportunity of the future life.[1]

4. THE CATHOLIC MYSTICS

The practical and theological ideals exemplified in St. Francis and St. Thomas need to be supplemented by some reference to the mystical way. We must not indeed identify

[1] See article by C. W. Emmet in *Immortality* by B. H. Streeter and others.

the teaching of perfection with mysticism. It is true that the heart of mysticism is a yearning for union with the Immanent Deity. It is true also that the Evangelical Message contemplates attainment through union with the perfections of God. But the Evangelical Way is through Faith, Hope, and Charity, which are not mystical at all. If we follow the division of the saints into practical and contemplative, we might agree that the contemplatives are equivalent to the mystics. Von Hügel, for example, speaks of St. Catherine as a great, original, winning contemplative, while her disciple, Ettore Vernazza, he calls a massive practical saint. But this means that the mystical, contemplative life is only one out of many; or perhaps one had better say that, in any life which attains full reality, it is only part of the way.

(1) *Their Attachment to Christ*

Mysticism is not necessarily Christian, but when it is it looks back to Christ in His historic revelation of Himself, and turns towards Him in His spiritual indwelling. This is the mark of the Friends of God, Meister Eckhart, Tauler, and Suso, of Ruysbroek, Thomas à Kempis, and of such women as Teresa and the two Catherines of Siena and Genoa. Eckhart, for instance, says: 'We ought to be so conformed to the image of our Lord Jesus Christ as to be the reflection of all His works and of His Divine form.'[1] Again, von Hügel, while giving due proportion to the Neo-Platonic and Dionysiac influences on St. Catherine of Genoa, shows how truly Christian was the experience into which they were interwoven. Soon after her conversion she had a vision of the offering of the Blood of Christ; and her conversion developed so rapidly that the flame of full perfection soon broke out.[2] This appears to have been the only time when she had such a picture of the Passion, a fact which is not to be regretted. Mysticism is apt to express itself in symbols of Pain and Death and Erotism, which are not without danger. St. Catherine of Siena said that she was betrothed to Christ with a ring, which none could see but herself. The great Spanish Mystics, such as St. Teresa and St. Juan of the Cross, were distinguished by their devotion to the

[1] *After Supper in the Refectory.*
[2] Per la viva fiamma d'infocato amore il dolce Iddio inperse in quell' anima ... tutta la perfezione.

Person of Christ and to Him alone. Inge declares that this gives them a kinship with evangelical Christianity.[1] In some cases the Roman Church failed to differentiate those mystics who were inspired by Christ, and who had a true love for the Church, from those who were altogether non-Christian. As Meister Eckhart was charged with Pantheism, so Molinos was accused of Quietism before the Inquisition, and ended his days in prison. Pantheism and Quietism are always the chief rocks of Mysticism, only to be avoided by personal devotion to Christ. The teaching of which both the Roman Church and the Reformed Churches most strongly disapproved was that of the One Act, the teaching, that is to say, ' that the turning of the soul towards Reality, the merging of the will in God, which is the very heart of the Mystic life, was *One Act*, never to be repeated.'[2] The danger of such teaching was not only lassitude and ethical indifference, but that the soul might cease to feel any further need of Christ.

(2) *Their Contribution to the Doctrine of the Trinity*

Where these pitfalls have been avoided, the Mystics have been of service in interpreting the experiences of believers, and in vivifying the doctrines of the Faith. Rodriguez found much help from St. Catherine of Siena in explaining, for example, why the soul has to shut itself in a narrow place like a pearl in a shell,[3] and why there are periods of aridity in prayer, and desolations.[4] Light has been thrown by the Mystics on the doctrine of the Trinity. St. Francis de Sales magnified his call to the episcopate, and testified that during the ceremony of consecration God permitted him to be conscious of the working in his soul of the Three Persons of the Ever Blessed Trinity, and of the grace infused by them while the three consecrating bishops did their part.[5] This testimony is valuable. The origin of the doctrine was in the apostolic experience of the method of the evangelical revelation ; and the doctrine should be regarded, not as an intellectual subtlety, but as the inadequate expression of an ineffable experience. An illustration may be taken from *The Interior Castle* of St. Teresa, where the

[1] *Christian Mysticism*, p. 231n.   [2] Underhill, *Mysticism*, p. 389.
[3] *The Practice of Christian Perfection*, I. viii. 12.   [4] Ibid. 20-24.
[5] *The Spirit of St. Francis de Sales*, Part III., on Ecclesiastical Perfection and the Duties of the Ministry.

saint describes the soul's progress from one mansion to another. In the Seventh Mansion she says, ' By some mysterious manifestation of the truth the Three Persons of the Most Blessed Trinity reveal themselves, preceded by an illumination which shines on the spirit like a most dazzling cloud of light. The Three Persons are distinct from one another; a sublime knowledge is infused into the soul, imbuing it with a certainty of the truth, that the Three are of one substance, power, and knowledge, and are One God. Thus that which we hold as a doctrine of faith, the soul now, so to speak, understands by sight, though it beholds the Blessed Trinity neither by the eyes of the body nor of the soul, this being no imaginary vision. All the Three Persons here communicate Themselves to the soul, speak to it, and make it understand the words of our Lord in the Gospel, that He and the Father and the Holy Ghost will come and make their abode with the soul that loves Him and keeps His commandments.'

(3) *Their Dependence on the Sacraments*

The Mystics of whom we have been speaking were guilelessly Christian and Roman Catholic. Some of them were beatified, and some of them were imprisoned; but when the latter action was taken it was through lack of vision in the Church leaders. The mysticism which they practised was distinctively Christian; and they confessedly found the ecclesiastical forms of inestimable benefit. This was manifest in their attitude to Holy Communion. We might have surmised that those who professed to discover reality in detachment from the tangible would have been alienated from all forms; but we find on the contrary in this whole typical group a yearning for the sacramental symbolism. From her conversion St. Catherine of Genoa was a daily celebrant. ' When she saw the sacrament on the altar in the hands of the priest, she would say within herself: " Now swiftly, swiftly convey it to the heart, since it is the heart's true food." ' This was the saying of a woman of much independence, with more than a touch of obstinacy in her, one who availed herself little of that direction on which the Roman Church usually insists. If she celebrated so frequently, it was not through compulsion or even suggestion. St. Catherine of Siena often passed immediately from Communion into a state of ecstasy in which she lost all world consciousness. Some exquisite sayings are attributed to Eckhart in refuting the objections of one who shrank from partaking. ' If you wish to be rid of all imperfection, and at the same time to be endued with goodness and grace, to be led blissfully back into the Fountain-head, and to be brought home—then keep yourself in such a state as to be able worthily to receive the Blessed Sacrament. Then indeed you will be united to Him, and ennobled with His Body. Yes, your soul will be brought so close to God, that neither angels nor seraphim nor cherubim could distinguish or discover the difference, for where they touch God they touch the soul, and where they find the soul they find God.'

These instances are sufficient to show that the great Catholic Mystics found in the observance of Holy Communion spiritual elevation. Yet I think we may perceive some lack of that robust piety which characterized the Reformers, and which sprang from their conviction of personal responsibility for sin, and of personal redemption from sin. As the Gnostics changed the Cross into a barrier to fence off the Pleroma, so the Mystics tended to make the Sacrament a medium for spiritual experience without first realizing it as a symbol of redeeming grace.[1]

---

[1] Forsyth, *The Church and the Sacraments*, chap. xiv.

Chapter XIII

THE IDEA OF ATTAINMENT THROUGH OBEDIENCE TO THE WORD

The Reformers had no quarrel with the Church as to the doctrines of God and of Christ. The breach was ultimately due to a dispute as to the method by which the penitent believer could obtain the end of his salvation. No one perceived this more clearly than Ritschl.[1] It was the glory of the Reformation that it aimed at bringing the ideal life back into the common ways of men. The Church had reached a condition in which there was much need for cleansing and reforming; and this was mainly due to the fundamental error of separating the quest for Perfection from the work of the world. The Reformers taught that the only Perfection for which the Christian need strive was that of one who had been justified and reconciled in Christ, and whose life was marked by patience, humility, and prayer. If a man thus became conscious of his worth as a child of God, 'his life would become a unity, subordinate to, yet recognized in, God's final purpose.'[2] Besides this Godward aspect of Perfection, they insisted on such fidelity in a man's vocation as would give him freedom and lordship towards the world, which are essential marks of the higher life.[3] 'Christian Perfection is to have an earnest Fear towards God; and then to conceive a great Faith, and to trust for Christ's sake that God is reconciled; and to seek from God, and confidently to expect, help in doing all things in our calling; and all the time to do good works diligently in ordinary life, and to follow our calling. In these things is true Perfection, and the true honouring of God.'[4] The Reformers found the Church so imbued with the monastic ideal that it was unable to receive the new wine.

---
[1] Harnack, *History of Dogma*, vii. 192n.
[2] A. E. Garvie, *The Ritschlian Theology*, p. 357.   [3] Ibid., p. 349.
[4] *The Augsburg Confession*, 27, A.D. 1530, one of the chief Lutheran symbols.
'In his rebus vera perfectio et verus cultus Dei.'

Hence they turned to the Word, not in desperation or as a last resource, but because it was, in truth, their sanction and authority. The Word became identified in popular usage with the Bible; but the true thought is much deeper than that. The Word is the historic revelation of God in Christ; we know it primarily through the Bible, which thus becomes of inestimable worth; but the two should not be confused.

I take, therefore, as the second type, those who believe that they can attain their goal by trusting in a Word which has reached their inmost nature, convinced their reason, and gained their willing obedience, and which they believe to be the Word of God. And I take to illustrate this type that movement which is known as Methodism, because, more definitely than any other, it has endeavoured to retain and to realize the teaching of Perfection, while at the same time accepting whole-heartedly the Reformed contention that it must not be separated from the ordinary life of men.

There are likenesses between the Franciscan and the Methodist Revivals; but there is a wide difference in the sanctions on which they rely. St. Francis, while he received many impulses from the Word and was undoubtedly guided by the Spirit, looked up to the Church as his final authority, and never dreamed of transgressing its limits. In the Methodist Movement we are conscious of being in a different atmosphere.[1] John Wesley had a love for the Church deeper than many of his followers have realized. In a letter to his brother he wrote: ' I am at my wits' end with regard to two things—the Church and Christian Perfection. Unless both you and I stand in the gap *in good earnest*, the Methodists will drop them both.'[2] But when there was a conflict of authorities, the decision rested with the Word. At the first Conference of Methodists six clergymen and four lay preachers met at the Foundery.[3] The discussion was conducted by way of question and answer on the themes of Justification, Sanctification, and the relation of the Methodist movement to the Church. The belief was expressed that the design of God in raising up the preachers called Methodists was to reform the nation, and more particularly the Church, and to spread scriptural holiness through the land. The answers to the

---

[1] H. B. Workman, *The Place of Meth. in the Cath. Church*, chap. v.
[2] May 14, 1768, *Works*, xii. 125.   [3] June 25, 1744.

question whether they did not entail a schism in the Church are significant. ' Answer 1.—We are persuaded that the body of our hearers will, even after our death, remain in the Church, unless they be thrust out. 2.—We believe, notwithstanding, either that they will be thrust out, or that they will leaven the whole Church. 3.—We do, and will do, all that we can to prevent those consequences which are supposed likely to happen after our death. 4.—But we cannot with good conscience neglect the present opportunity of saving souls while we live, for fear of consequences which may possibly happen after we are dead.'[1]

These answers throw a flood of light on the attitude of the early Methodists. They saw the danger of a breach with the Church of England, and determined to use all their influence to avoid it. But they never regarded the fear of such an issue as being decisive in regulating their conduct. The last sermon which John Wesley preached before the University of Oxford, and which he undoubtedly considered of the nature of a manifesto, bore the title ' Scriptural Christianity.'[2] In both Romanists and Methodists we find an earnest search for holiness, which they defined in practically the same terms. But the authorities to which they appeal seem poles apart. If the Romanist feels that he has the sanction of the Church, he can always find some text to justify it ; if the Methodist believes that he has the sanction of the Bible, he is confident that he will be able to embody it in some Church organism.

Similarly, the Methodist deeply honoured the work of the Holy Spirit in bearing immediate witness to his soul of the truths which he had learnt in the Scripture. But he was not prepared to follow any advance beyond the historic Word. Therefore the whole movement, while extremely progressive in regard to Church organization, in regard to doctrine became ultra-conservative.

1. The Attitude of John Wesley

The Methodists were far from finding a doctrine of Perfection ready to hand, as Aquinas did. They were, of course, familiar with the prayer in preparation for Holy Communion. But the nearest approach to definite teaching was in the Religious

[1] J. S. Simon, *John Wesley and the Methodist Societies*, p. 212-13. [2] A.D. 1744.

Societies, which had been in existence since 1678, and which were, for the most part, associated with the Anglican Church. Dr. Simon has given a full description of these Societies, though he disagrees with Canon Overton's dictum that Wesley intended his Societies to be on the same lines. Overton proceeds : ' How it was that the Methodist Societies took a different course is a very interesting, and, to a Churchman, a very sad question.' I gather that Simon's position is that the separation was not only inevitable, but not to be deplored. Without such separation Methodism could not have accomplished what it has. At the same time, grave evils have ensued. The loss of so much of the specifically Methodist element from the Anglican Church meant that for generations those who with any definiteness sought after Perfection within that communion have tended to do so on Romanist lines. The evil effect within Methodism has been in the loss of Church consciousness, with the result that attainment has become too much a purely individual concern.

In the early spiritual development of John Wesley this Church consciousness was prominent, as is manifest from his relations with the Holy Club and the Fetter Lane Society. He was attracted, he tells us, by the genial and moderate asceticism of Clement of Alexandria ; and one of his first poems was composed after reading Clement—probably the seventh book of the *Stromateis*.

> Here from afar the finished Height
> Of Holiness is seen ;
> But oh, what heavy tracts of toil,
> What deserts lie between !

This influence remained to the end, though with diminished force. In a letter to his brother in 1772 he wrote : ' I often cry out, " Vitae me redde priori ! " Let me be again an Oxford Methodist ! I am often in doubt whether it would not be best for me to resume all my Oxford rules, great and small. I did then walk closely with God, and redeem the time. But what have I been doing these thirty years ? ' This strong ecclesiastical feeling, which is often associated with asceticism, appears plainly in his relations with other seekers. What made the Moravian influence so much more powerful with Wesley than the Quaker was that, in addition to the piety and assured faith which he admired in both, the former had an elaborate Church order and discipline. When, later, he broke with the Fetter Lane Society, he did so because he found a teaching gaining ground among them which may be summed up thus : ' If you wish to believe, be still ; and leave off what you call the means of grace, such as running to Church and sacrament.' Against this his whole nature rose in revolt. There has always been a mystical element in the section of Methodism which has retained the distinctive title of Wesleyan[1] ; but it has been kept in restraint by a sense of ecclesiastical order, and by devotion to the Scriptures. In a letter to his brother Samuel, John Wesley wrote : ' I think the rock on which I had nearest made shipwreck of the faith was the writings of the mystics : under which term I comprehend all, and only, those who slight any of the means of grace.'[2]

A further stage in Wesley's progress was reached through hearing Luther's preface to Romans, which describes the nature of justifying faith. In his account[3] the junction of scriptural authority with personal experience is quite typical of the Methodist way. ' I felt my heart strangely warmed. I felt I did trust in Christ, Christ alone, for salvation ; and an assurance was given me that He had taken away my sins, even mine, and saved me from the law of sin and death ; and then I testified to all there of what I now felt in my heart.' His whole nature had long been set towards God ; but it was in this experience that his soul swung to its rest. The simplicity, candour, and openness which marked him made him ready to receive fresh impressions all through his life. But this experience shows the rock on which he built. Some correspondence which he had with the notorious Dr. Dodd illustrates this.[4] ' I therein' (i.e. in the Sermon on Perfection) ' build on no authority, ancient or modern, but the Scripture. If this supports any doctrine, it will stand ; if not, the sooner it falls the better. . . . My father gave me, thirty years ago, to reverence the ancient Church, and our own. But I try every Church and every doctrine by the Bible. This is the word by which we are to be judged in that day.' This principle he carried through life. Thus, after an interview with Bohler,

---

[1] This is shown in some of Charles Wesley's hymns, e.g. ' Come, O thou Traveller unknown,' which is a mystical interpretation of Jacob's wrestling, and ' Thou Shepherd of Israel and mine.'
[2] A.D. 1736.   [3] 1738.   [4] 1756.

he says: 'I could not comprehend what he spoke of an *instantaneous work*, I could not understand how this faith should be given in a moment : how a man could at once be thus turned from darkness to light, from sin and misery to righteousness and joy in the Holy Ghost. I searched the Scriptures again touching this very thing, particularly the Acts of the Apostles ; but, to my utter astonishment, I found scarce any instances there of other than instantaneous conversions ; scarce any so slow as that of St. Paul, who was three days in the pangs of the new birth.' In spite of his own experience, in which assurance was long delayed, Wesley was so impressed by this reading of Scripture that it led him towards the conception of an instantaneous passage, not only into conversion, but into the state of Perfection. This interview with Bohler, on April 22, 1738, was undoubtedly formative of the experience on May 24, 1738, referred to on the preceding page. This experience should not be spoken of as conversion, but rather as the emergence into a sphere of conscious assurance of the love of God, and of communion with that love, which is what we mean by Perfection.

I find in all these earnest seekers a deep confidence in the love of God. Their sanctions—an infallible Church or an infallible Bible—often lead them astray. But even these have their authority, because they have come from the love of God. Behind the Methodist, as behind the Franciscan, Revival, there was a definite preaching of a way of Perfection ; but there was such preaching because of the overwhelming sense of the Divine love, which made the soul long for something more than being saved so as by fire. The best of John Wesley's hymns are translations, for he lacked his brother's gift of original verse ; but it is worth noting what hymns—German, French, and Spanish—he turned to for inspiration.

> O God, of good the unfathomed sea !
> Who would not give his heart to Thee ?
> O God, Thou bottomless abyss !
> Thee to perfection who can know ?
> Jesu, Thy boundless love to me
> No thought can reach, no tongue declare.
> O God, my God, my all Thou art !

These titles are sufficient to show the secret inspiration. In a letter to Coughlan in 1768 he wrote : ' You never learnt, either from my conversation, or preaching, or writings, that " holiness consisted in a glow of joy." I constantly told you quite the contrary: I told you it was love; the love of God and our neighbour; the image of God stamped on the heart; the life of God in the soul of man; the mind that was in Christ, enabling us to walk as Christ also walked.'

There were differences of opinion among the Methodists. Charles Wesley insisted on the gradualness of the transition to the higher state, and made the standard so high as to be unattainable, except through a long course of discipline. Against this John vehemently protested. Whitefield was definitely against the whole doctrine: 'That monstrous doctrine of sinless Perfection, for a while, turns some of its deluded votaries into temporary monsters.'[1] Fletcher practically agreed with John Wesley, though he objected to the term 'sinless,' and emphasized the growth within the state. One sharp difference between them proves that they had realized the difficulty in regard to those who have not attained in this life. John Wesley believed that for such, perfecting would be in the hour of death, following the common Calvinistic teaching in this respect. Fletcher poured not unmerited scorn on this idea of a Death-Purgatory.

But, on the whole, we may say that this doctrine became distinctive of Methodism. In the Methodist hymn-books, especially those connected with the Wesleys, there is a unique section, 'For Believers Seeking Full Redemption!' The hymns of Charles Wesley frequently refer to being perfected; and in them he is often carried beyond the cautious statements in his sermons.

> Anger and sloth, desire and pride,
> *This moment* be subdued!
> Be cast into the crimson tide
> Of my Redeemer's blood!

A touching letter written by John Wesley in his eighty-eighth year contains this paragraph: 'I am glad brother D—— has more light with regard to a full sanctification. This doctrine is the grand *depositum* which God has lodged with the people called Methodists; and for the sake of propagating this chiefly he appears to have raised us up.'[2] In a previous

[1] Tyerman: *Life of John Wesley*, ii. 562.   [2] *Works*, xiii. 9 (1790).

THROUGH OBEDIENCE TO THE WORD 211

letter he had urged the same correspondent not to put the attainment to some distant occasion. Repeatedly we find Wesley saying to his people, quite in the manner of Hebrews, that the reason for coldness and failure is that they have not pressed on to perfection. All this shows the reality of the doctrine, and the grip which it has on the Methodist mind.

2. A CATENA OF METHODIST EXPERIENCES

The type of piety displayed in the spiritual progress of John Wesley may be further illustrated from the experiences of some other Methodists. The following are some of its distinctive features: (1) It was always based on Scripture, often on some text conceived as peculiarly appropriate. (2) All progress was made by Faith, by which was meant, not merely assent to a proposition in Scripture, but an experimental apprehension within the soul. (3) This act of Faith, which is a true movement of the soul towards God, must also be conceived as taking place within a Society. No part of Christendom has laid more stress on fellowship than the Methodist. (4) While freedom is left for emotion, there is a rather unexpected suspicion of it. The outbursts of emotion in the Revival can easily be accounted for in an uneducated people suddenly confronted with a great hope. The remarkable fact is the steady way in which from the first the emotion was regulated and subdued.

(1) *Jane Cooper*

I purpose linking together a few examples of the distinctive Methodist type of piety, noting especially in what respects they assist us in the task of making a constructive statement of the way of attainment. Jane Cooper has been called Wesley's pattern saint. Her letters, which were published after her death, and a few references in Wesley's *Works*, enable us to appreciate the nature of her spiritual life. It is well described in the preface which Wesley wrote to her letters. ' All here is strong sterling sense, strictly agreeable to sound reason. Here are no extravagant flights, no mystic reveries, no unscriptural enthusiasm. The sentiments are all just and noble ; the result of a fine natural understanding, cultivated by conversation, thinking, reading, and true Christian experience. At the same time they show a heart as well improved as the understanding; truly devoted to God, and filled in a very uncommon degree with the entire fruit of His Spirit. . . . This strong, genuine sense is expressed in such a style as none would expect from a young servant maid: a style not only simple and artless in the highest degree, but likewise clear, lively, proper: every phrase, every word being so well chosen, yea, and so well placed, that it is not easy to mend it. And such an inexpressible sweetness runs through the whole as art would in vain strive to imitate.'[1]

This is a true delineation of the characteristics of the spiritual life of this saintly woman, and well expresses the Methodist ideal. It is obviously a life which is open to all, and which does not depend on any natural endowments, or on any favourable opportunities. The true conception of Perfection is that it ought to be, and may be, a common, ordinary experience. It should be the normal state of all healthy Christians. In a letter to Miss Loxdale in 1781 Wesley warns her against being too much impressed by the treatises of Madame Bourignon on *The Exterior and the Interior Life*. He warns her not to be too much attracted by what is strange, unusual, peculiar; and he concludes thus: 'I desire nothing, I will accept of nothing, but the common faith and common salvation; and I want you, my dear sister, to be just such a common Christian as Jenny Cooper was.'[2] This experience, it is to be noted also, was neither purely intellectual nor purely emotional. The mingling of sound understanding with deep feeling was largely due to the meetings for Christian fellowship, which are so essential and invaluable a part of Methodism.

(2) *Hester Ann Rogers*

While Methodism has always insisted that being made perfect in love ought to be the ordinary experience of all Christians, there has been, side by side with this, a mystical element; and Mysticism demands some psychical endowments which can never be described as ordinary. We have seen how the Wesleys shrank from the Mysticism which neglected the means of grace; but there is a true Mysticism, which may

[1] *Works*, xiv. 260.   [2] Ibid. xiii. 102.

prove of great service to faith. Wherever we find it among Methodists, it is always ballasted by Scripture and Theology. One of the most striking instances of the union of careful adherence to Scripture with mystical experience was that of Hester Ann Rogers. She had a very vivid assurance of communion with the Persons of the Trinity. Because this and similar experiences have been suggested by Scripture, by Theology, and by the witness of others, we must not deprive them of reality. The continued life of Jesus necessarily involves that our communion with the Son must be distinguished from that with the Father. If we remember that the Divinity of Jesus Christ was conceived as luminously in Wesleyan Theology as it was in Lutheran, we shall not be surprised to find a combination of the experience of being made perfect in love, with a mystical communion with the different Persons of the Trinity. Wesley at one time considered that this mystical communion was the highest stage; but he was soon convinced that it was not so, though it was usually associated with the attainment of full Perfection.[1]

(3) *William Grimshaw*

The two men to whose experiences I shall now advert show how fully the early Methodists had mapped out the State of Perfection. Wesley sets it forth with his usual lucidity in a letter to Miss Ritchie in 1778. ' The plerophory (or full assurance) of faith is such a Divine testimony that we are reconciled to God as excludes all doubt and fear concerning it. This refers only to what is present. The plerophory (or full assurance) of hope is a Divine testimony that we shall endure to the end; or, more directly, that we shall enjoy God in glory. This is by no means essential to, or inseparable from, perfect love. It is sometimes given to those that are not perfected in love, as it was to Mr. Grimshaw. And it is not given (at least, not for some time) to many that are perfected in love. I do not say you ought to pray for it, but I think you may, only with absolute resignation. In this, as in all things, His manner and His time are best.'[2]

William Grimshaw was a clergyman in Yorkshire. After a wild and reckless youth, he had entered the ministry without

[1] *Works*, xii. 335.
[2] Origen distinguished similarly the stages of Christian Perfection (in Rom. iv. 6).

P

any spiritual understanding. His conversion came through a terrifying conviction of sin. Hence his experience greatly differs from that, for instance, of Fletcher. 'He carries fire,' said Wesley, 'wherever he goes.' He had some remarkable psychoses, in one of which he fell into a trance while conducting Morning Prayers in Haworth Church.[1] During this trance he had a vision of the hands and feet of the Lord Jesus, with fresh blood streaming from them. This convinced him that he was accepted in Christ. A few years later,[2] in renewing with special solemnity his covenant with God, he referred to a wonderful manifestation of the Deity to him. Still later, in 1761, in an interview with Wesley, he stated that he firmly believed in, and daily prayed for, the Perfection of which Wesley had been preaching, ' namely the love of God and man producing all those fruits which are described in our Lord's Sermon upon the Mount.' It is plain, therefore, that Grimshaw did not conceive of the earlier experience as having in itself brought Perfection. To his nature, we should imagine, the assurance of salvation came easier than the charity which he saw clearly was the true end.

(4) *John Laycock*

I am able to bring forward a striking witness as to the development of Methodist teaching in the generation following Wesley. The author of *Methodist Heroes in the Great Haworth Round*, himself at the time a lay preacher in extreme old age, showed me a note-book left by his father, John Laycock, in a secret drawer. I spoke of the work on which I was engaged, and was allowed to make extracts. It is a document of much psychological value. It was written by a man of intelligence. He was no genius finding fresh and vivid ways of utterance; he was content to use the formulas current in his circle; but he used them with a clear understanding of what he wanted to say. This note-book was written to refresh his own memory. He may have thought of it as being helpful to his family afterwards; but he took care to keep it secret during his lifetime. All this sustains the statement, of which I have no doubt whatever, that here we have a humble, trustworthy, and intelligent endeavour to express a profound experience.

[1] In 1746. [2] In 1752.

THROUGH OBEDIENCE TO THE WORD

Feb. 20, 1823.—The Lord has been drawing my mind for several weeks past in an extraordinary manner to seek for establishment and settling in the grace of sanctification. This state neither exempts from trials nor temptations; of late they have been strong and subtle; but ' I hold Thee with a trembling hand, and will not let Thee go, till steadfastly by faith I stand, and all Thy Fullness know.' The full Assurance of Faith, and in particular of Hope, has been set before me as the very blessing I stand in need of; and such was the melting, humbling, and fervent spirit of my mind, with such a sweet drawing in prayer and desire as I never felt before, I feel I cannot rest till brought to experience the sealing influence of the Spirit, which I believe to be the same as that state mentioned by the apostle, viz. the full Assurance of Hope.

Feb. 27, *Thursday.*—This evening I was favoured to meet with a few friends who enjoy the above blessing, and who are living a lively, happy, holy life as the fruit thereof. We spent most of the time in prayer, and God was powerfully present. To describe what I felt is impossible. I nearly lost sight of all except that God and Christ and Heaven were revealed to me; and in answer to continued, agonizing prayer it was given to me then to say that the Lord had sealed me His to the day of eternal redemption, or given me the possession of the full Assurance of Hope. This was accompanied with such a sweet peace and serene state of mind, together with such an exulting in praise and glory to God, as nearly took away my sleep for a few nights. I could say in the poet's words more fitly than ever : ' My days are spent in doing good, my nights in prayer and praise.' Oh, the depth of the riches of the Divine goodness to unworthy me, to have the faith, or, as the apostles term, the *persuasion,* that I am established and sealed the Lord's for ever, and that no trial, difficulty, or temptation should move me fills me with joy unspeakable. Believing is quite easy; duty is pleasant; all is in the order of God (sin excepted); passages of Divine truth are applied with peculiar force and with sweet constraint. I am labouring in all things temporal as well as spiritual to do all to the glory of God.

March 4.—Blessed be God, though I have been weak in body through the agonizings in prayer and the peculiar joy imparted on the memorable night of Thursday last, I do find, on careful examination, that I was most consciously led by the Spirit; and such was the manner God was pleased to lead me—together with the scriptural ground which I find amply furnished in the sacred truth—that I hesitate not to say that the work is a real, genuine, experimental enjoyment of a high state of the full Sanctification and Assurance of Hope unto the end; leading me as a consequence to humility of soul, and a strong propensity to retirement both from the world and from unnecessary engagements in Church matters. Oh, what sweetness do I find in conversation with my God; and so strong do I find the ties of Divine Love that in such a frame I would wish to depart and be with Christ, which is far better; and still quite willing to wait or do all the will of my Lord.

At this time I was made acquainted with the possibility of receiving a higher enjoyment of distinct fellowship with God the Father. This I believe Mr. Fletcher, Mr. Wesley, Ann Cutler, Lady Maxwell, and D. Renty speak of. Also a few who I believe enjoy it of my particular acquaintance, whose conversation and prayers were made very instrumental in the Lord's hands of bringing me forward to its enjoyment. But though thus favoured I found but little satisfaction as to what I had to believe, and what the enjoyment of such a blessing would prove. I felt no scruples in my mind respecting the Trinity in Unity and the Personalities of the Godhead. However, my desires, my prayers, and my inquiry were that I might be scripturally right; and though I could assent to the respectable testimonies above mentioned, yet I could not exercise faith for its acceptance till I was directed to the 14th and 15th chapters of John; and from these chapters I was much encouraged to hope for the blessing: in every means of grace, both public and private, my prayer was for this manifestation; and such happy, holy mourning did I feel on many occasions as cannot be described.

After seeking in the above manner for about a fortnight, on Monday evening, March 17, I was favoured to meet two of my Christian friends, who both enjoyed what I sought; we besought the Lord Jesus to reveal the Love of the Father: the intercourse was sweetly open, and we continued wrestling a considerable time, during which at times I had much hope. Then again suggestions from the enemy that I should not receive the blessing then: however, I was assisted to believe, and for some moments incessantly to say, Lord, I do, I will believe; and thus engaged I waited the witness of the Spirit, which was shortly after blessedly imparted, so that I could cordially say, Glory be to the Father, Glory be to the Son, and to the Holy Ghost—— This was accompanied with such a deep, reverential awe of the Divine Majesty and Glory of God, such an adoring of Him, that on many occasions I found no power to use words in drawing nigh for prayer.

March 24.—Blessed be the Lord for the unspeakable riches of His grace to me the past week, such a week's enjoyment of Divine fellowship and sweetness in converse with the Blessed Trinity as is only known to faithful souls. Oh, what depths of love, and heights of both knowledge and experience do I see before me! And how surprised I am at my past though sincere profession coming so far short, as much below the standard of Christian privilege. How thankful I should be that my merits have not been weighed; but according to the rich mercy and faithfulness of my Saviour, through faith He hath blessed me in a most glorious manner. Praise the Lord, O my soul!

With this long citation (which I have copied exactly from the note-book shown me) I will conclude this selection of Methodist experiences. Its psychological value I find it hard to over-estimate. We may note the continual reference to Scripture; the seeker has no sort of confidence in his experience unless he is convinced that he is scripturally right. Faith is insisted on ; but it is a faith which is thought of as a spiritual movement. The believer, reaching out after God, meets definitely with Him. This experience is conditioned, and to some extent kept in bondage, both by the Sacred Writings, and by the dogmatic Theology of the Church, but by the former most decisively. Hence the distinctive Methodist experience has in our day been profoundly affected, and undoubtedly chilled, by the historico-critical method of Scripture study. In the experiences, however, which we have just glanced at, we are face to face with eternal reality. No criticism, either of the Scriptures or of dogmatic Theology, can do away with that. It is to our infinite loss if we neglect it. It seems to me possible that from the progress of our knowledge we shall return to this direct and immediate experience of God ; and we may hope that through knowledge will come purification, so that we may escape some of the dangers into which Methodist experience in the past has been liable to fall.

3. The Methodist Doctrinal Statements

There has always been a tendency in Methodism to undervalue the intellectual appeal. Wesley was so careful to declare that faith was not a mere intellectual assent ; and the appeal to the emotion, and still more to the will-to-believe proved so effective, that the place of the intellect was judged to be slight. Consequently, there has not been such contribution to theological advance as might have been expected from the mental energy evoked.

Methodist doctrine sprang from the Church of England, whose doctrinal standards have affinities with the Lutheran, the Calvinist, and the Romanist position ; but it was the Lutheran element which became dominant in Methodism.[1] The term Christian Perfection fell into disuse among the Reformers, and was all but crushed out of Evangelical Christianity, partly as a result of the protest against Rome, and partly through the disgust inspired by some fanatics. The effect of this was that Protestantism was inclined to lose the sense of exaltation so manifest, for example, in the Pauline

[1] ' It is certain that he [Luther] transformed, as no Christian had done since the age of the apostles, the ideal of religious Perfection ' (Harnack, *Hist. of Dogma*, vii. 192).

Epistles. Haering is but expressing the deeper Lutheran view when he contends that the phrase, so firmly embedded in the New Testament, should not by any means be given up. ' The term, so to speak, recognizes the duty of gratitude for God's work—how great it is, and how it ever demands more and more; and the duty of self-encouragement in the maintenance of the position we have attained in order to fresh advancement.'[1] It is the inevitable culmination of any doctrine of Assurance. The Lutheran Symbols rejected the proposition that good works are a hindrance to salvation; they rejected equally the proposition that they are essential. All progress is by faith; and both Assurance and Perfection (the terms are not synonymous) are attained by faith alone. These were the lines on which Methodism developed. I purpose considering now some of its standard statements.

(1) *Wesley's ' Plain Account of Christian Perfection '*

In the year 1765, being then sixty-two years old, John Wesley published his treatise, *A Plain Account of Christian Perfection as believed and taught by the Rev. Mr. John Wesley from the year 1725 to the year 1765*. The title is instructive. The *Plain Account* makes no attempt to formulate a doctrine. It resembles Newman's *Apologia* in the fact that a large part is taken up with showing that Wesley had held this doctrine from the beginning. It was important to prove that he had learnt it at Oxford. He instances the influence of Taylor's *Rules and Exercises of Holy Living and Dying*; of Thomas à Kempis's *Christian's Pattern*; and of Law's *Christian Perfection*, and *Serious Call*. His aim was to show that he had come by the old Church path. He refers to a sermon preached in 1733, in which he did not scruple to use the term Perfection as identical with true religion.

He proceeds to recall some of the declarations made in the Conferences which he had assembled. The conception in his own mind was so clear as to give consistency to his casual utterances. Thus the objection was put : ' But he does not come up to my idea of a perfect Christian.' To which the answer is : ' And perhaps no one ever did, or ever will. For your idea may go beyond, or at least beside, the scriptural

---

[1] *Ethics of the Christian Life*, p. 306. See pp. 281-2.

account. It may include more than the Bible includes therein ; or, however, something which that does not include. Scripture Perfection is pure love, filling the heart, and governing all the words and actions. If your idea includes anything more or anything else, it is not scriptural ; and then no wonder that a scripturally perfect Christian does not come up to it.' While Scripture was regarded as supreme, experience was also demanded. Thus, in reply to the question, ' What does it signify whether any have attained it or no, seeing so many Scriptures witness for it ? ' the answer was, ' If I were convinced that none in England had attained what has been so clearly and strongly preached by such a number of Preachers in so many places, and for so long a time, I should be clearly convinced that we had all mistaken the meaning of those Scriptures ; and, therefore, for the time to come, I too must teach that " sin will remain till death." ' For this reason Wesley paid the utmost attention to such experiences as that of Jane Cooper, which he recounts at length.

In later editions of the *Plain Account* Wesley added some thoughts which occurred to his mind in 1767, and which may be taken as summarizing his views.

(1) By Perfection I mean the humble, gentle, patient love of God and our neighbour, ruling our tempers, words, and actions. I do not include an impossibility of falling from it, either in part or in whole. Therefore I retract several expressions in our hymns, which partly express, partly imply, such an impossibility. And I do not contend for the term *sinless*, though I do not object to it.

(2) As to the manner. I believe this Perfection is always wrought in the soul by a simple act of faith ; consequently in an instant. But I believe a gradual work both preceding and following that instant.

(3) As to the time. I believe this instant generally is the instant of death, the moment before the soul leaves the body. But I believe it may ,be ten, twenty, or forty years before. I believe it is usually many years after justification ; but that it may be within five years or five months after it, I know no conclusive argument to the contrary. If it must be many years after justification, I would be glad to know how many. Pretium quotus arroget annus ? And how many days or months, or even years, can one allow to be between Perfection and Death ? How far from justification must it be ; and how near to death ?

This summary makes us understand why Wesley may be called the man of absolute judgements.[1] At the same time it

[1] By von Hügel in discussing Wesley's criticisms of St. Catherine.

affords a good example of his open-mindedness ; no man was ever more ready to acknowledge an error or to accept new light. It would be absurd to take these thoughts as meant to be final. There are some obvious criticisms. If Perfection is wrought by an act of faith, we must think of it as wrought consciously. But that awakening which we call consciousness is usually a very gradual process. The fact that Perfection comes through faith, so far from involving the conclusion that it is instantaneous, rather implies that it comes gradually, with the gradual awakening of the soul's faith to consciousness. What Wesley is really contending for is that there are distinct stages in Christian experience ; and that one who has reached the higher has crossed, as it were, a line which definitely marks him off from his past, lower experience. The crossing of this line must be at some particular moment ; but he confuses this Divine uplifting to a higher sphere with the operation of faith, by which the soul comes into consciousness that through the Divine Grace it has passed into the higher realm.

A further criticism may be made as to the time. Neither Wesley nor any one else has adduced any valid arguments for the belief that the moment of perfecting is usually the hour of death. It is, however, a widespread conviction.[1] It probably lies behind the prayer in the Litany : ' From sudden death, Good Lord deliver us.' Any belief widely diffused among Christians deserves attention, even if it be not apparently backed by Scripture or reason, unless we are able to perceive the cause for the error ; but in this case the cause is fairly obvious. On one side was an intense conviction of the deep-rooted power of sin ; on the other an intense reaction against the Roman Catholic doctrine of Purgatory. In order to enter Heaven the soul must be altogether cleansed from sin. If that were not accomplished in this life, and if we must not imagine any discipline beyond, it seems plain that the final purgation must be in the hour of death. Wesley broke away from the Puritanic idea in that he thought it possible that some (he hoped an increasing number under the full Gospel) would pass into the higher stage even in this life. But he agreed that for the majority (at any rate until the Church in general had received a great uplift) the hour of

---

[1] This view is expressed with the utmost power and pathos in Dr. Whyte's sermons on David, Mary Magdalene, and the woman with an issue of blood.

perfecting is the hour of death. This is the weak point in Wesley's teaching. It will be remembered that many were drawing analogies between Romanism and Methodism; and he recoiled from anything which seemed to approach the doctrine of Purgatory. In the sermons cxii. and cxxii.,[1] which deal with the conditions in Hades, he is unable to think of those who have been cast with Dives into the unhappy division ever crossing the Great Gulf; but he does imagine that for those on the other side there would be a perpetual ripening, a continual progress in holiness and happiness, till they were made ready for Heaven.

All Christians are indebted to Wesley for the seriousness with which he grappled with the problems of the soul's end. If the conventions of his age still bound him in some directions, especially in the conception of the life beyond, no man more nobly set forth the immediate aim of a soul which is conscious of an eternal destiny. It is an aim to be pursued in all humility, yet with much confidence. 'Five or six and thirty years ago. I much admired the character of a perfect Christian drawn by Clemens Alexandrinus. Five or six and twenty years ago, a thought came into my mind, of drawing such a character myself, only in a more scriptural manner, and mostly in the very words of Scripture. This I entitled *The Character of a Methodist*, believing that curiosity would incite more persons to read it, and also that some prejudice might be removed from candid men. But that none might imagine I intended a panegyric either on myself or on my friends, I guarded against this in the very title-page, saying, both in the name of myself and them, "Not as though I had already attained, either were already perfect."'[2] There is an end, which is clearly seen, and towards which one may press forward with confidence, seeing that it is anticipated by faith in the soul's union with God.

(2) *John William Fletcher's Works*

The Rev. J. W. Fletcher rendered great help to the Wesleys. His beautiful and attractive Christian character, the lucidity with which he was able to set forth spiritual ideas, and the transparent sincerity of his words, gave to his championship

---

[1] *Works*, vii. 247 and 327.   [2] *Works*, iii. 273, A.D. 1767.

a peculiar value. The full titles of the writings above named may be given, since they indicate the chief points which he was concerned to declare. They are, *The Last Check to Antinomianism, a Polemical Essay on the Twin Doctrines of Christian Imperfection and a Death Purgatory,* and *Entire Sanctification Attainable in this Life.* Fletcher takes occasion to show that the doctrine of Entire Sanctification is fully taught in the formularies of the Church of England; it may have slipped into the background, like the teaching as to Justification by Faith, but it is an integral part of the whole. But his strength is given to proving the scriptural foundation on which it rests. ' If ye would attain an evangelically sinless Perfection, let your full assent to the truth of that deep doctrine firmly stand upon the evangelical foundation of a precept and a promise. A precept without a promise would not sufficiently animate you; nor would a promise without a precept properly bind you; but a Divine precept and a Divine promise form an unshaken foundation.' This paragraph from the third part of the tract on Entire Sanctification shows how rightly Fletcher is counted among those whose ideal finds its decisive sanction in Scripture.

The perils of Perfectionism are spiritual pride and moral laxity; but we must not give up because of such hazards. ' Do not cast away the doctrine of an evangelically sinless holiness, but contend more for it with your heart than with your lips.' Fletcher often modifies the word ' sinless ' by the adverb ' evangelically ' to denote a state which is dependent on the perpetual and conscious reception of the blessings which have come through the Atonement. He agreed with Wesley that no perfection should be conceived of which did not need continually the atoning blood.

One cannot but be impressed with Fletcher's anxiety to be just to the earnest striving after Perfection among those Calvinists who most vehemently repudiated the term. He never allows the quest to degenerate into a contention as to words. He says of the Calvinists: ' They dissent from us because they confound the ante-evangelical law of innocence and the evangelical law of liberty—peccability and sin— Adamic and Christian Perfection; and because they do not consider that Christian Perfection, falling infinitely short of God's *absolute* perfection, admits of a daily *growth*.' It is better, he holds, to be a Calvinist, proclaiming the necessity of sin in this mortal life, than to be a Perfectionist, swollen by spiritual pride or careless of moral law. He agreed with Wesley that the actual process is instantaneous, though he was more careful in stating that the full recognition by the believer may be gradual. He uses a beautiful illustration from the incident of the disciples receiving Jesus into their boat. ' Just so we toil till our faith discovers Christ in the promise, and welcomes Him into our hearts ; and such is the effect of His presence, that immediately we arrive at the land of Perfection.' This arrival he appears to identify with the Pentecostal Blessing. On the day of Pentecost the apostles and early disciples obtained this blessing ; and many others were converted who soon afterwards entered into the higher experience.[1] Fletcher then faces the question, How many baptisms or effusions of the Holy Spirit are needed to complete the work ? The Friends used to say of men like Woolman that they had undergone many deep baptisms. But, if that is the normal experience of those who attain, there is little value in insisting on a moment of arrival at the fullness. *What Wesley and Fletcher were really concerned about was the possibility of attaining in this life a state in which the soul should be fully prepared for its eternal existence.*

(3) *Richard Watson and W. B. Pope*

Richard Watson's *Institutes* was for many years the standard text-book for Wesleyan ministers. Its interest for us lies in the proof which it affords how deep-rooted was the belief that attainment was possible in this life. The author argues against the view that the final stroke, which destroys our natural corruption, is *only* given at death. ' If this view can be refuted, then it must follow, unless a purgatory of some description be allowed after death, that the Entire Sanctification of believers at any time previous to their dissolution, and in the full sense of these evangelic promises, is attainable.' The arguments which he brings forward to support this conclusion are quite cogent so far as they go. ' (1) That we nowhere find the promise of entire sanctification restricted to the article of death,

[1] *Entire Sanctification*, Part III.

either expressly or in fair inference, from any passage of Holy Scripture. (2) That we nowhere find the circumstance of the soul's union with the body represented as a necessary obstacle to its entire sanctification.'[1] This argument shows how closely the Methodists followed the lines of John Wesley. They limited their argument to proving that it was possible to attain Entire Sanctification in this life while implicitly accepting the Calvinistic idea of sanctification in the moment of decease (*in articulo mortis*) for those who had not yet attained. But the silence of Scripture seems quite decisive against connecting the hour of death in any way with sanctification. The Methodist theologians, however, steadily limited their attention to the points marked above.

I wish to express my indebtedness to the article on Entire Sanctification in W. B. Pope's *Compendium of Christian Theology*.[2] This and the article by Dr. F. Platt in Hastings's *E. R. E.* are the two best summaries which I have seen of the historical development of the doctrine. The subject appears to be a by-path in most theological systems; and yet, to use a striking phrase of Dr. Pope's, it is 'the vanishing-point of every doctrine, exhortation, promise, and prophecy in the New Testament.' Pope connects the Methodist with the Arminian doctrine of Sanctification. The Methodists, however, emphasized it much more than the Remonstrants, associating it with perfect love even more than with complete obedience. It is the chief glory of Methodism to proclaim Entire Sanctification as the duty and privilege of all. The duty of definite witness to the consciousness of spiritual victory was also urged. Methodist doctrine has always been vehemently opposed to Antinomianism. The effect cannot be better expressed than in Dr. Pope's words: 'While asserting that the eternal law of morals is abolished as a condition of acceptance, it holds, more strongly than the old Arminians, that it is still the rule of life. But it maintains that this has become the LAW OF CHRIST, and that the falling short of the highest standard of obedience is not reckoned as sin to him who is filled with love, and never violates the royal law. *As faith is reckoned for righteousness, so love is reckoned for obedience.*' The sentence italicized admirably epitomizes the Methodist view of the whole way of salvation.

[1] *Institutes*, iii. 198.   [2] *Compendium*, VI. iv. 4.

4. THE OBERLIN THEOLOGY

What is known as the Oberlin Theology is of much value for our subject. It was a modification of New England Theology by Dr. Mahan and Dr. Charles Grandison Finney. These men were both evangelists and theologians; and it may be noted as characteristic of the teaching of Perfection that it is frequently accompanied by Revival. I purpose studying this distinctive contribution to theology in Finney's *Lectures on Systematic Theology*, first published in 1846 and recently reissued. Finney went to Oberlin in 1835, where he continued as teacher of theology, pastor, and college president until his death in 1875. During this period he still kept up his revival meetings in the Eastern States until 1860.

The Oberlin Theology sprang from a Calvinistic soil; for New England thought at that time was governed by the teaching of Jonathan Edwards. In Finney's mind there was a strong reaction against this, due to the practical results of his revival work. He retained, indeed, a good deal of the Calvinistic outlook; but he felt the need for proclaiming an immediate and free and full salvation. He wished at the same time to give no opening to what he calls Perfectionism, a term which he applies to the Antinomian forms of the doctrine. In reply to those who urged that danger he said: 'It seems to me that one fact will set aside this objection. It is well known that the Wesleyan Methodists have, as a denomination, from the earliest period of their history, maintained this doctrine in all its length and breadth. Now, if such is the tendency of the doctrine, it is passing strange that this tendency has never developed itself in that denomination. So far as I can learn, the Methodists have been in a great measure, if not entirely, exempt from the errors held by modern Perfectionists. Perfectionists as a body, and, I believe, with very few exceptions, have arisen out of those denominations that deny the doctrine of Entire Sanctification in this life.'[1] It was this contact with Methodism during his evangelistic campaigns, both in America and England, which confirmed Finney in unfolding the distinctive Oberlin teaching.

The starting-point is in the idea of *ability*. Edwards, following Locke, had educed a theory of philosophical necessity,

[1] *Lectures on Systematic Theology*, xl. 455.

226   THE IDEA OF ATTAINMENT

which enfolded the whole rational universe. Man, even fallen man, has a natural ability to do what is right before God, but it is a moral impossibility that he should do so. There is, however, a gracious ability, which is bestowed upon the elect as a consequence of the Atonement. According to Edwards, volition is identical with sensibility; and moral inability consists in the absence of any inclination towards, or sense of, that which is good. There is in the natural man no motive sufficiently strong to lead to a right choice. To this Finney staunchly demurred. His legal training revolted against the idea of a law which it was impossible to observe; and his work as an evangelist made him feel that he must appeal to a conscious power of choice. At the same time he never lost sight of the fact that men do not come to Christ apart from the gracious influence of the Holy Spirit. The question in dispute is this: ' Is the fact that they never do so use them (i.e. their natural powers in the manner that God requires) without a gracious Divine influence, to be ascribed to absolute inability, or to the fact that, from the beginning, they universally and voluntarily consecrate their powers to the gratification of self, and that therefore they will not, unless they are divinely persuaded, by the influence of the Holy Spirit, in any case turn and consecrate their powers to the service of God?'[1] It was because he adopted the latter answer that Finney's Theology took on its Methodist tinge.

The first eight lectures are devoted to the subject of moral government and moral obligation. After discussing various theories, he says: ' Lastly, I come to the consideration of the practical bearings of what I regard as the true theory of moral obligation, namely, that the intrinsic nature and value of the highest well-being of God and of the universe is the sole foundation of moral obligation.'[2] Finney insists on the unity of moral action in opposition to the common idea of a mixed character of moral action, which leads men to imagine that there is something acceptable in a sinful life. The Church has greatly erred in supposing that a state of present sinlessness is rare and practically impossible. The obedience which God demands is entire—' a full and perfect discharge of our entire duty, of all existing obligations to God, and all other beings. It is perfect obedience to the moral law.' But this

[1] *Lectures on Systematic Theology*, xxxii; 342,   [2] Ibid., viii. 93.

should be regarded, not as impossible, but as normal for the Christian. Virtue is love, a spirit of benevolence, a desire for the happiness of God and of the universe. When a man, in the unity of his moral activity, turns with his whole nature to God in love, he is fulfilling every requirement of the law, and is therefore perfectly holy. Referring to the text, ' Thou shalt love the Lord thy God,' &c., he says : ' Here then it is plain, that all the law demands, is the exercise of whatever strength we have, in the service of God. Now, as Entire Sanctification consists in perfect obedience to the law of God, and as the law requires nothing more than the right use of whatever strength we have, it is, of course, for ever settled, that a state of Entire Sanctification is attainable in this life, on the ground of natural ability.'[1]

With all this, Finney lays much weight on man's natural depravity, and on the need for Atonement.[2] The corruption of the race through Adam's sin was not questioned in any form of New England Theology. Finney's exposition shows deep spiritual insight. God, he says, made the Atonement for His own sake, and in His own interest. ' God Himself was greatly benefited by the Atonement : in other words, His happiness has in a great measure resulted from its contemplation, execution, and results.'[3] The Atonement has also been a supreme benefit to the whole universe ; for it was an act, not of retributive, but of public justice ; and it has therefore exhibited to all rational creatures the merciful disposition of God. ' The Atonement is infinitely the most illustrious exhibition of mercy ever made in the universe. The mere pardon of sin, as an act of sovereign mercy, could not have been compared, had it been possible, with the merciful disposition displayed in the Atonement itself.'[4] This exhibition of God's love condemns selfishness, which is the sign of moral depravity. Sin does not reside in the constitution of man, with its natural appetites, passions, and propensities ; but in the yielding of the will to the selfish gratification of those propensities. Holiness consists in turning from sin to the law of God, as that law finds its highest expression in the Atonement.

It is a possible, it ought to be a common, experience for

[1] *Lectures on Systematic Theology*, xxxvii. 407. [2] Ibid., xxii.–xxvi.
[3] Ibid., xxvi. 275. [4] Ibid, xxvi, 279.

the Christian to render perfect obedience to God's will. It is true that obedience is not as yet what it would have been if sin had not entered into the world; for we have not the capacity for love which we should have had but for sin. But our obedience may be perfect, since its perfection depends, not on capacity or constitution, but on will. There must be some relaxation of the moral law, since its original demand was made on man as created in God's image; and man in his fallen condition cannot respond to such a demand. But it is just that such relaxation should be made if man offers whole-heartedly the best that he can. The value of the Atonement is that it removes the obstacle to pardon, inasmuch as it vindicates the moral law, and reveals the holiness of God's love. If a man offers, with his whole will, obedience in his present position, and according to his present powers, that is all that is required; and such obedience constitutes present perfection. But it is not denied, it is indeed implied in this teaching, that he may have larger opportunities, and greater capacity for love and understanding of its meaning, in the future.

The main objection to this theology is that it becomes too atomistic. The perfect obedience is, after all, only the perfection of the moment; and I think Dr. Finney does not adequately recognize the way in which character becomes impressed on the soul. This may explain why in *Lectures* xliii.–li. on Election, the Divine Purposes, and the Perseverance of Saints, he swings so much to the Calvinistic view. It would take us too far from our subject to discuss this; but it appears an attempt to adjust and rectify some of the positions into which his logic was leading him.

This theology differs from the typical Methodist form in the emphasis which it lays on obedience rather than on love.[1] But it has close resemblance in the fact that it presses home the possibility of attainment as immediately before us. Finney quotes with approval the saying that perfection in all things should be the unceasing and steady aim of every Christian. But he pours contempt on setting forth an aim, and in the same breath declaring that it can never, in the nature of things, be realized. ' I never shall forget the effect produced on my mind by reading, when a young convert, in the diary of David

---

[1] Contrast Dr. Pope's standpoint as presented on p. 271.

Brainerd, that he never expected to make any considerable attainments in holiness in this life.'[1] The discouraging effect of such a view, both on one's own efforts and on one's judgement as to the righteousness of the Divine demands, is manifest. The merit of the Oberlin Theology is in the fact that it so clearly and definitely and with such logical power sets forth conscious attainment as both possible and normal in this life for all believers.

[1] *Lect. on Syst. Theol.*, xxxvii. 422.

Chapter XIV

THE IDEA OF ATTAINMENT THROUGH THE WITNESS OF THE SPIRIT

1. The Quaker Movement

Of the three ways in which God has revealed Himself in Christ, the Church and the Word and the Spirit, it may be contended that the Spirit is primary : it is He who sanctifies the Church and inspires the Word. But in our consciousness the order is reversed. We first discern the Church, an organized body ; then we hear the Word speaking to our intelligence ; lastly we become aware of the Spirit, in whom Christ immediately witnesses to our souls. No better instance of attainment through the witness of the Spirit can be found than that which is known as Quakerism. Its historians are amply justified in declaring that its roots are in the beginning of Christianity. When we speak of the emergence of Quakerism in the seventeenth, and of Methodism in the eighteenth, century, we are speaking of particular organisms, in which ideas, which go back to the first centuries, have found notable expression.

We may pause to pay a tribute to the witness of Quakerism. The name was first given in derision, like that of Methodist. In his *Apology*, Proposition xi. 8, Barclay speaks of the inward travail, when the light is striving to break through the darkness, so that the body is greatly shaken, and there are many groans, sighs, and tears, as in the pangs of birth. 'From this the name of Quakers, i.e. Tremblers, was first reproachfully cast upon us ; which though it be none of our choosing, yet in this respect we are not ashamed of it.' The Society which drew together as the result of the movement which originated with George Fox took to itself the name of Friends. It is a name which lends itself to many interpretations—The Friends of Truth, The Friends of God, or of Humanity ; but it lacks distinctiveness. It is often best to use a name given in derision and make it honourable, rather than to select another which has nothing against it except that it has no peculiar significance. And certainly, if purity of life, earnestness of purpose, spiritual insight, and steadfast integrity under all extremes of fortune, have any honour among men, then the name of Quaker is one from which all reproach has been wiped away.

During the seventeenth century groups gathered together who called themselves Seekers. They found no satisfaction in any of the Churches, Episcopalian, Presbyterian, or Independent. It was from them that most of the Quakers came, and that their peculiar characteristics were derived. They were convinced that there was much yet to be revealed; and they were accustomed to waiting in silence, because they were also convinced that the revelation would not come through the upward movement of the human spirit, but through a Divine communication.[1] There is a likeness between this and that earlier movement of the fourteenth and fifteenth centuries, known as the Society of the Friends of God, which developed in the valley of the Rhine, and later in Flanders, with which are associated the great names of Eckhart, Tauler, Suso, and Ruysbroeck, and from which came that beautiful mystical treatise, the *Theologia Germanica*. The spiritual need to which Quakerism answered was also essentially the same as that which led to Quietism. Molinos, Madame Guyon, and Fénelon show the same longing for the restfulness of full attainment.

> Silent spirit dwell with me,
> I myself would silent be.

All this goes back to very old and persistent ideas, and has connexions with the Gnostic worship of Bythos and Sige. The danger is of relapsing into mere passivity, and of conceiving that the end can be attained by One Act. Fénelon, indeed, always protested that the true Orison of Quiet was no mere idleness and lethargy; and all wise mystics have been careful to declare that it is in reality a state of intense activity. Von Hügel bids us mark how Aquinas took over Aristotle's conception of *energeia* to express the activity of God: ' His very peace and stillness coming from the

[1] E. Grubb, *What is Quakerism?* p. 26.

brimming fullness of His infinite life.' Hence union with Him means being caught up into the intense activity of the central fire. We must avoid the error of supposing that in such a state God supplants man, an error which arises from the mistaken interpretation, through psychological and theological presuppositions, of a true spiritual phenomenon. From some of the Quietistic aberrations Quakerism has been entirely free. There has been no fanaticism in any real sense of the word, and certainly no disregard of morality. There has been some contempt for learning, and also for secular forms of government; but this has been largely counterbalanced by energy in business and in social reform. E. B. Emmott is justified in quoting a saying of Hannah Whitall Smith: ' Because they believed themselves to be the friends of God, they realized that they must be in the truest sense the friends of all the creatures He had created.'[1] The gravest defects of the Society have come from its contempt for historical and institutional forms of religion.

It is instructive to note how the society retains the impress of its founder. Macaulay's brilliant description of George Fox does no kind of justice to the real power of the man.[2] He was a man of high principle and spiritual insight, with a great kindness for his fellows; but the little help which he had received from learning led him altogether to despise it; and at the same time some mental instability induced a fixed antagonism to government and organization. He had neither historic knowledge nor what may be called the historic sense. It seemed to him that he had gained all that was needed by immediate revelation, and that there was no need for any historic continuity in order to guarantee its truth. The ancient Church buildings have spoken to many of the labour and sacrifice of past generations, given freely and not without blood, in order to retain their faith. The ancient Church ritual has been an incalculable boon to many in its eloquent testimony to the long and unbroken sequence of believers who have lifted up their voices in worship. Fox's understanding was not strong enough to enable him to enter into this fellowship. The fact that he calls churches ' steeplehouses ' is sufficient proof of this. If we turn to the Franciscan and the Methodist movements we find that in the one case

---

[1] *The Story of Quakerism*, p. 174.   [2] *Hist. of England*, chap. xvii.

it evolved wholly within the pale of the historic Church, in the other, while there was a great breach, yet it was one deeply deplored, strenuously opposed, and only accepted finally with the utmost reluctance. But the Quakers had from the beginning tenets which were incompatible with any historic, organized Church. I find in many Quaker writings to-day an acknowledgement of consequent loss.[1] This must be borne in mind in estimating the value of their noble and progressive contribution to the Doctrine of Perfection.

2. THE QUAKER TEACHING CONCERNING PERFECTION

Although the common people classed the Quaker with the Puritan, they were really poles asunder, the former being from one aspect more nearly related to the Romanist.[2] The Quaker conceived—as the Romanist had done, and as the Methodist did in the next century, but as the Puritan never did—that there was a way by which one entered into a relation with the Eternal which might rightly be called Perfection. Fox describes in a classic passage his search for light, and how vain were all his questionings. 'When all my hopes in them and in all men were gone, so that I had nothing outwardly to help me, nor could I tell what to do ; then, O! then, I heard a voice which said, " There is one, even Christ Jesus, that can speak to thy condition " ; and when I heard it my heart did leap for joy.'[3] While there is this earnest searching for light, there is little of that sense of guilt which gives such tragic significance to Bunyan's *Grace Abounding to the Chief of Sinners*. From the age of eleven Fox declared that he had lived in pureness and righteousness. 'The troubles to which he refers in his Autobiography, so far as they were more than physiological, were concerned with the evil condition of the world quite as much as with the sins and dangers of his own

---

[1] 'It would now, I think, be very generally admitted that primitive Quakerism opposed too rigidly the spontaneous to the reasoned and ordered, the inward to the outward, and that it made too little of tradition and education. The weaknesses of Quakerism lay, and to some extent still lie, in the tendency to distrust the intellect, to suspect the outward, and to neglect the historical' (H. G. Wood, *Quakerism and the Future of the Church*, p. 70).

[2] A character in one of Anthony Hope's books appears as a nun, and later as a Quaker. '"All in the same line," said her manager, with a fine indifference to the smaller theological distinctions.' That witty comment comes shrewdly near the mark.

[3] *Journal*, Bicentenary Edition, p. 11.

soul.'[1] To the Quaker the way of Perfection is simply that of obedience to the Voice within. He goes back to the Stoic conception of the reasonableness of the universe, and of himself as a part of the City of God. This truth had only to be received to bring into the perfect way. Hence he was little troubled by some of the things which have greatly dismayed his fellow pilgrims. Grave distress must arise when the Catholic finds that the Church, to whose Counsels of Perfection he has striven to give obedience, is by no means infallible. Say what we will, the Methodist cannot help feeling disheartened when he discovers that the Book, on which he has sought to mould his experience, is no infallible guide. From this trouble and dismay the Quaker is free. He has given no allegiance to any organization, whose buildings, whose ritual, and whose ministry link his age to the Early Church. He pays far more attention to the Book than he does to the Church; but he does not regard even the Book as primary.[2] When we contrast his view with the Methodist's, we note a broad difference. The Methodist has no confidence in any witness within, unless he can confirm it from the Word: the Quaker does not feel bound by any Scripture, unless it is in accord with the immediate revelation of the Spirit to his own soul. Even in such matters as non-resistance, the refusal to take oaths, &c., the true basis is not a literal interpretation of the sayings of Jesus, but a conviction that war and the taking of oaths are contrary to the mind of the Christ within. The appeal to the literal words in the Sermon on the Mount is in fact an appeal *ad hominem*, quite legitimate, and such as Jesus Himself used in argument with the Pharisees, but not to be considered a final statement.

And yet, while the Friends have gained a certain liberty as the result of their rejection of either the Church or Word as the ultimate authority, they have come into bondage in other ways. It seemed that nothing could be freer than their central principle: 'Where the Spirit of the Lord is, there is liberty.' But this very freedom became a source of bondage; for it was too individualistic. They found no difficulty in declaring that perfection was to be won by obeying the Inward Light. But such attainment, while quite real

---

[1] J. B. Pratt, *The Religious Consciousness*, p. 155.
[2] Barclay's *Apology*, Proposition iii.

and of much value, has this defect, that it has no outward bond, by which those who attain are held together. We find that the Quaker has to turn to the Church and to the Scripture in order to obtain utterance. If the buildings were taken away, if all ritual and ceremony were swept aside, if the records of the past were obliterated, we should discover that the hours of silence were very blank.

(1) *The Inward Light*

For a clear exposition of the doctrine of the Inward Light we may refer to Barclay's Second, Fifth, and Sixth Propositions, in which is manifest the mind of a master in spiritual things. He appeals to the Word, especially to those Scriptures which deal with the revelation in the Son, such as Matt. xi. 27, which he rightly perceives to be crucial. He also quotes from the Fathers, as in this very relevant citation from Augustine: 'It is the inward master that teacheth, it is Christ that teacheth, it is inspiration that teacheth: where this inspiration is wanting, it is vain that words from without are beaten in.'[1] Illustration and argument are added from the Cambridge Platonist, John Smith. Our survey ought not to pass over that group, Henry More, Ralph Cudworth, Benjamin Whichcote, and John Morris[2]; and we are grateful to Barclay for reminding us of the nobility of their conception of the mode of Divine revelation. With consummate power he concludes thus: 'That which any one firmly believes, as the ground and foundation of his hope in God, and life eternal, is the formal object of his faith. But the inward and immediate revelation of God's Spirit, speaking in and unto the saints, was by them believed as the ground and foundation of their hope in God, and life eternal. Therefore these inward and immediate revelations were the formal object of their faith.' He proceeds to prove that such revelations still continue. Many were willing to admit that there had been such in the past, but argued that they must have ceased now, owing to the absence of the portents which confirmed them. This objection appears to have been one of the strongest against which he had to contend. In the next century the

---

[1] Tract. Ep. Jn. iii.
[2] Inge, *Christian Mysticism*: chapter on Nature-Mysticism and Symbolism.

Methodists were attacked by Bishop Warburton because they claimed equal privileges in the Holy Spirit with the apostles. Against the temper which would relegate all personal, immediate communion with God to a remote past, the Quaker and the Methodist made a much-needed and effective protest. The modern mind has such a sense of continuity that it is rather inclined to discredit records which presuppose an entirely different spiritual environment. Our problem is not to justify the children of God to-day in claiming equal rights with those of two thousand years ago, but to explain records which appear to assign to a bygone age superior privileges.

Barclay then proves that the Spirit presents the truth to the mind, and that this immediate presentation of Divine truth is something beyond the mere apprehension of a written record. It is not the result of a logical conclusion, for reason cannot deal with the highest. He further shows that the Papist bases his confidence in the Church and in tradition on the fact that the Church is led by the infallible Spirit; and that the Protestant, when asked why he makes the Scriptures his rule, has no other reply than this, that in them the mind of God was inwardly, immediately, and objectively revealed by the Spirit of God; all this leads to the conclusion as to the supreme value of the inward, immediate, objective revelation, still continued to the people of God.

It would be most unjust to suggest that the Quakers ignore Christ: all the light comes from Him. But there seems no real place for anything which may be spoken of as Atonement in their system. They are divided by a great gulf from the Puritan experience which issued in so profound a sense of sin. The progress of the soul to Perfection, in their view, is by spiritual illumination, through the opening of the soul to admit the light, rather than by the complete transformation of an evil mind into a good. On the other hand, they were very clear as to the universality of redemption. They were saved from the error of the Calvinists, who limited it to the elect, and from that of the Remonstrants, who added to the saving effect of ' that Divine and evangelical principle of light and love, wherewith Christ hath enlightened every man that comes into the world,' the absolute necessity of an outward knowledge of it. The Friends perceived that this limitation did in effect constitute an election, and that of a most arbitrary kind. One result of the Quaker attitude was the broad-minded way in which they accepted the testimony of heathen writers.[1] This gave great offence; and in one tract Quakerism was denounced as the Pathway to Paganism. But the whole of their conception of the way of Perfection would fall to pieces if it were not joined with the idea of universal light. It is suggestive that the early Friends believed that their message had only to be proclaimed to be successful.

(2) *The Long Pilgrimage*

The title for this section is taken from one of the Swarthmore Lectures, a series named from the home of Margaret Fox, the centre of early Quakerism. It is a felicitous description of human progress in the light of the Christian Hope. It also suggests something of the disillusionment which came to the Society when the early radiance had passed into the light of common day. To say that Quakerism has had to traverse a great disappointment is not to condemn its message, or to doubt its ultimate victory. All great movements have had to undergo the same testing of their faith. But the frustration of their first hopes was peculiarly bitter to the Friends, just because their appeal was so democratic and universal. If the democracy itself repudiated the claim, the basis of their faith seemed to be shaken. The history of the Society circles round the effort to re-affirm the primary message, with those modifications which have come through contact with the world's democracy.

The idea of a pilgrimage appeals to the Quaker's sense of the brotherhood of humanity through the Light within, while it allows scope for spiritual movement. The doctrine of the Light has had to face two questions. If there is a Light which lighteth every man, what place is there for collective progress? If the Light is given, like the light of day, what need is there for struggle and effort? The Quaker answers these questions by conceiving of the history of humanity as a pilgrimage, in which no hostile tribes have to be overcome, and in which there is no occasion for erecting any edifices. But this is so obviously not a full account of human progress that he was almost

[1] Thus Elisha Bates, in *The Doctrines of Friends* (1825), quotes from many pagan writers, and this especially from Plutarch: ' It is a law . . . dwelling in the mind always . . ., which never permits the soul to be destitute of an *interior* guide.'

compelled to limit the pilgrimage to a select band. The teaching of Elias Hicks, who became the leader of the dominant party in the Great Separation in America, is instructive. ' The doctrine of the " Light " carried Elias Hicks unconsciously to the very verge of a doctrine of election. He tends to take the decisions of life away from the rational will and to centre them instead in this mysterious principle, so that even belief or faith, as St. Augustine would say, is not a thing to be settled by reason—it comes, if it comes at all, as a gift of Grace. . . . The Light acts best, as the Quietists maintained, when the man himself is still and reason is quiescent.'[1] The true spiritual history of mankind is enshrined in the progress of those in whom the Inward Light has become more and more dominant. The Fall depicts an historical event; but it is a Fall which consists ' in turning away from the inward spiritual guide, in trusting the outward senses and outward passions, and especially in following the desire " to know good and evil " without the instruction of the Light within.'[2] There is, therefore, no racial corruption, and as an almost inevitable corollary, no racial attainment, and no racial progress. All that is required is the awakening of the individual soul, in order that Christ may shine upon it.

The above must not be taken as a summary of the whole Quaker position, though it clearly represents that of a strong party. On the other hand, there are many who are welcoming the light of modern thought, and many also who are turning to the organized Churches to search out ways of fellowship, not only in social service, but in religious worship. As a result there has been much earnest study of psychology, especially of mass psychology, which has borne fruit in the movement known as Copec. The lengthening out of the Pilgrimage, which has proved so bitter a disappointment to the Society of Friends, has not been without compensation. The first message has been enriched and deepened and freed from the censoriousness which defaced it.

(3) *The Historic and the Inward Christ*

The keenest controversy within the Society of Friends itself was in regard to Christ ; and the main reason for the opposition

[1] Rufus M. Jones, *Later Periods of Quakerism*, p. 447. [2] Ibid., p. 452.

of men like Baxter and Bunyan was due to the fact that they considered that the continued humanity of Christ was denied. The early Friends moved, consciously or unconsciously, on the lines of the Fourth Gospel, though without the interest shown by the evangelist in the details of the historic life. There is much to be said for their contention that the term ' The Word of God ' should be applied to Christ rather than to the Scriptures. But when they spoke of Christ they tended to lose touch with the record of His life in the flesh. Barclay indeed, who was a very careful theologian, declared emphatically : ' By this we do not at all intend to equal ourselves to that holy man, the Lord Jesus Christ, who was born of the virgin Mary, in whom all the fullness of the Godhead dwelt bodily, so neither do we destroy the reality of His present existence, as some have falsely calumniated us.'[1] His teaching is that the Inward Light comes to us mediately ' through that seed, grace, and word of God, wherewith we say every one is enlightened.' Yet in a way it may be said to come immediately, since it is only mediated through the witness of an Inward Christ. Barclay is not clear on this point, owing to confused ideas of personality. In *The Historic and the Inward Christ*[2] E. Grubb gives a full criticism of the defective ideas of the early Quakers as to what constitutes personality. This is a defect which has vitiated all their thought, and prevented them from realizing the worth of ' creaturely activity ' in personal life and endeavour. To speak of the Inward Christ as the Seed became one of the formulas of Quakerism. It takes us back to the *Logos Spermatikos* of Stoicism, which Justin translated into Christian terminology. In Justin the term is equivalent to the Holy Spirit. Quakerism worked on the same lines. Grubb affirms that they never intended to separate the light in their souls, which they called the Light of the Inward Christ, from the life and character of Jesus on earth ; but he acknowledges that their Christology did in effect tend to such a separation. He quotes a passage from James Nayler, which he says every Quaker would accept : ' This Seed all shall know, which is beloved of the Father, and heir of the everlasting Kingdom, who strives not by violence, but entreats ; who seeks not revenge, but endures all contradictions against himself, to the end he may obtain mercy for all from the Father, and hath

[1] *Apol.* vi. 13.   [2] pp. 48-53.

power to subdue all things by overcoming. So this seek in yourselves and all men, and in it seek one another as brethren. This is that which is perfect, and is never to be done away, neither can it be overcome by the world; wrath cannot enter it, pride cannot enter it; it strives for nothing but to live its own life.'

The mysticism which underlies this teaching is not necessarily anti-evangelical. We may properly apply the attribute 'evangelical' to all who believe in Christ. But there is a technical sense in which we assign the term to those who lay special stress on the proclamation of the Evangel, as it is set forth in the Bible, especially in the New Testament. Now the Quaker mysticism is prone to become quietistic. At one time there was a danger that the meetings would become altogether vacuous, without intellectual distinction or missionary purpose. The impact of Methodism, which was essentially, even in the technical sense, evangelical, proved a great blessing to Quakerism. Dr. Rufus Jones sums up three well-defined tendencies, which shaped themselves in the Society in the half-century between 1775 and 1825. 'There appears under way (1) a clearly marked tendency to mould and formulate Quaker thought in the direction of evangelical doctrine. There is at the same time in evidence (2) a strong set of current in the direction of an excessive reaffirmation and reinterpretation of the principle of inward light as the sole and sufficient basis of religion, and this in a somewhat anti-evangelical direction. Finally (3) there is a tendency, though much more limited, to conform to the world, and to accept the conclusions which rationalists and deists, in the name of " enlightenment," were pressing upon the attention of thoughtful men and women everywhere.'[1]

An examination of these currents, which still continue, will show that they are due to the varying conception of the relation between the Historic and the Inward Christ. Where, largely under the influence of Methodism, the evangelical note prevails, it results in a return to the presentation of the historical Christ.[2] It is marked by fervent missionary zeal, and by a deep sense of the value of human personality, and of human co-operation in the evangelization of the world. It is weak through the feebleness of its desire for progressive knowledge

---

[1] Rufus M. Jones, *Later Periods*, p. 275.   [2] Ibid. Intro. p. xiii.

under the guidance of the Inward Christ. (2) and (3) are the specifically Quaker tendencies. In both there is the conviction of fresh, continued revelation from God, direct and immediate through the Inward Christ, and by no means dependent on that which was once given through Jesus of Nazareth. In (2) the revelation comes in the stillness of the soul, which is seeking to put aside all desire and thought, in order that it may receive the message in quiescence. In (3) there is insistence on the vigorous co-operation of the intellect. It reverts to the Stoic conception of the union of man's reason with that of the universe.

3. THE VALUE OF THE QUAKER CONTRIBUTION

We are now in a position to estimate the special Quaker contribution to the doctrine of Evangelical Perfection. We may still turn to Barclay for a summary. The Eighth Proposition deals with this subject. It considers the state of those who have not resisted the light, but admitted it; who have not hardened their heart against the holy Seed, but allowed it to enter in, so as to produce a holy, pure, and spiritual birth. ' In whom this pure and holy birth is fully brought forth, the body of death and sin comes to be crucified and removed, and their hearts united and subjected to the truth ; so as not to obey any suggestions or temptations of the evil one, but to be free from actual sinning and transgressing of the law of God, and in that respect perfect : yet doth this perfection still admit of a growth ; and there remaineth always in some part a possibility of sinning, where the mind doth not most diligently and watchfully attend to the Lord.' It must be borne in mind that this movement was quite as much a revolt against Puritan teaching as against Anglican or Romanist. Barclay explicitly repudiated the statement of the *Westminster Larger Catechism* that it is impossible for any man, even the best, to be free from sin in this life ; and that the very best actions of the saints, their prayers, their worships, are impure and polluted. There is a remarkable likeness between Quaker and Methodist doctrine in this matter ; and it is worth noting how closely both associate the subject with that of Perseverance.[1] There is a good reason for that. If we venture to

---
[1] See Elisha Bates, *The Doctrines of Friends*, chap. vi.

assert that it is possible to enter on a state which may be called Perfection, it must be with a double measure of humility and in fear and trembling. The Puritan is able to speak of unconditional perseverance, precisely because he denies the possibility of attaining assurance in this life. The Quaker agrees with the Methodist as to the removal, not only of actual, but also of original sin, and I think speaks with more confidence and decision on the matter. Both also look forward, but somewhat dimly and uncertainly, to attaining even in this life a state from which there can be no falling away. Wesley calls this the full Assurance of Hope. In the Ninth Proposition Barclay deals with the question of Perseverance and the Possibility of Falling from Grace ; and he concludes that, while there is a possibility of making shipwreck of faith, even after having tasted the heavenly gift, yet a stability in the truth may be secured from which there can be no total apostasy. ' We also see that some of old and of late have attained a certain assurance, some time before they departed, that they should inherit eternal life, and have accordingly died in that good hope, of and concerning whom the Spirit of God testified that they are saved. Wherefore we also see such a state is attainable in this life, from which there is not a falling away: for seeing the Spirit of God did so testify, it was not possible that they should perish, concerning whom he who cannot lie thus bare witness.'

I will now specify the main Quaker contributions to this doctrine, not as suggesting that they are peculiar to Quakerism, but pointing out how they find fresh life in the tenets of that body.

1. *Immediate Union with God*

The first great contribution of Quakerism is this : that it is possible to attain to that union with God which is the essence of Perfection *immediately*. In our common speech we use the adverb in a temporal sense ; but it may be employed in a slightly technical sense to denote the absence of any mediation. The old Anchorites, in seeking the perfect way, made their escape from the ceremonies of the Church, and mostly abandoned any study of the Bible. Similarly, the Quakers protested against any person or any form being interposed between the soul and God. It is well known that from the moral dangers into which many sects professing such doctrines have fallen, the Friends have been happily and honourably free. This is due to the fact that their teaching of immediacy has been linked with a conception of attainment by way of Stillness.[1] Quakerism is closely associated with Quietism; and Quietism must not be considered as a sporadic type of religion, a capricious sport, springing up from time to time, but rather as a permanent constituent in the fullness of the Catholic Church. In the seventeenth century and the early part of the eighteenth it almost seemed as though it might become the principal factor in Church life. This was shown, not only by the spread of Quakerism, but by the cultivation of silent prayer in the movement which centres round the names of Molinos, Madame Guyon, and Fénelon. Molinos taught that there were two stages in the soul's expansion—meditation and contemplation. In the higher stage the soul puts away what the Quakers called creaturely activity, and God becomes all in all. ' Molinos insisted, in the very words which Madame de Chantal had already used, that *God will have all things done by the operation of His own activity, and that therefore the quieter I keep the better all things succeed.*'[2] Madame Guyon and Fénelon were truly saints; and though moral charges were brought against Molinos, there seems to have been little ground for them. The point which I am suggesting is that this Quietism proved a safeguard from many of the moral dangers connected with the idea of immediate attainment.[3]

There are sayings of Jesus, about the leaven which a woman hid in three measures of meal, and about the treasure which a man hid in the field, which have a bearing on this subject. Without question some deep reason exists for hiding the leaven and the treasure within the soul.[4] Elizabeth hid herself when she found that the Lord's promise was being fulfilled; and the Friends have a saying about travailing with the Seed which is very pertinent. There is a purifying influence in stillness. The Old Testament prophets were imbued with the belief that what was needed to revive religion was a quiet waiting upon God, whose breath sweeps through the soul.[5] The pantheist,

---

[1] See Steven, *The Psychology of the Christian Soul*, p. 45, ' The Value of Quiet.'
[2] Rufus M. Jones, *Later Periods of Quakerism*, p. 45.   [3] Ibid. p. 968.
[4] Wordsworth gives the poet's reason in his reply to the expostulation of his friend Matthew, q.v.
[5] Ezek. xxxvii.

the prophet, the poet, and the Quaker would not agree as to how they should denominate the Power that sweeps through them in the time of waiting ; but they would all consent to its beneficent, purgatorial effect. And they would be right. From the corruption that is in the world the hour of stillness is very cleansing. This is the explanation of the fact, to which Dean Inge calls attention, that the Quakers, almost alone among the sects which have ostentatiously despised form and order, have escaped the imputation of licentiousness.[1]

If this be so, it sets a seal upon their specific contribution to the doctrine, and still more to the practice of Perfection. One notes a growing conviction to this effect among earnest seekers. The idea is not merely of silent worship, but of silent worship *together*. Besides the hours of solitude, the Church is seeking for hours of silent fellowship. The same intuition, which shrinks from the morbid and dangerous conditions of the mediums employed in Spiritualism, is turning to the saner methods of Quakerism. We want, indeed, to avoid the error of making Silence an end instead of a means, and of glorifying it as though it were better than Speech. The Gnostics worshipped the Silence of Eternity ; but the true object of Christian adoration is not the Silence but the Word of God. But we may learn the lesson of Quietism, without being betrayed into its vagaries. When Quakerism became affected by Evangelicalism, as it did especially in America, it was found necessary to learn the use of organization and form and order. It was possible to receive a personal blessing by sitting still ; but missionary work demanded energetic co-operation. The Friends have never been averse to organized effort in philanthropy and in social reform : they have had to learn the value of it in evangelism. It is well, however, that the whole Church should remember the debt owed to those, of whom we have taken the Friends as a striking example, who have made us see that, in attaining communion with God, there is a place for silent meditation and contemplation, unmediated and purely receptive. The hour of quiet waiting, the passivity of utter peace in preparation for the light and witness of the Inward Christ is needed to-day. ' It is worth almost any struggle and sacrifice and trial of patience to preserve the opportunity, the chance for these free breathing times of the

[1] *Christian Mysticism*, p. 259.

soul; these healing, refreshing hushes, when, even though the fire may not seem to fall on our prepared altar, we at least get a breath of celestial currents, and have hints of realities beyond the din and noise of earth and time. So to reconstruct the type of meeting, in the interests of practical efficiency, that this central feature of worship should be lost, would be a calamity both to Friends and to the world, now seriously in need of a demonstration of the value of worshipful hushes.'[1]

(2) *The True Glory of Humanity*

The second great contribution of Quakerism consists in teaching us that union with God becomes full and perfect in proportion to the intensity of our humanity. This was the idea which Fox strove confusedly to express. He wanted to show that the Lord spoke to him, and dwelt in him, because of his humanity, and not because of any gift or order bestowed upon him. If by priesthood you mean the right of access to God, that right was his by virtue of his humanity, and not through any endowment or ordinance. This conviction brought him into antagonism with the Predestinarianism of the Calvinist as well as with the Sacerdotalism of the Catholic. His soul rose up in remonstrance against any taking away of the key of the knowledge of God, and preventing those who would from entering in. On the whole this is the noblest remonstrance that man can make. He is not protesting because he is shut out from the possession of material wealth; nor yet because his opportunities of self-development are limited, like ' the rude forefathers of the hamlet,' of whom Gray sings. His protest is against any bar to the free and immediate communion of his soul with God. Behind it is a deep conviction that, if such communion be granted, all other wrongs will be righted in time.

While we may use the word ' protest,' we must not think of the idea as mainly negative.[2] A layman does not denote one who has failed to gain the privileges of the priesthood; he is one who belongs to the People; he is within the covenant; he has obtained the right of immediate access; and he exercises his rights as part of the whole, and in submission to the

---

[1] Rufus M. Jones, *Later Periods of Quakerism*, p. 990.
[2] Moberly, *Ministerial Priesthood*, chap. iii.

interests of the whole. The reason for accentuating this point is that it is possible so to dwell on the protest as to lose sight of the positive aim. There *are* distinctions in human life. The distinction of sex goes deep, though it does not plumb the depth of humanity. The distinction of orders within the Church is quite a real one, though it does not curtail the full priesthood, and the right of access, even to the privilege of perfect communion, possessed by each believer.

The purpose of the distinctions seems to be to bring out the glory of the whole, and to enable it to realize its fullness. The spiritual value of sex is in the way it enables man, through the very separation, to understand more fully the meaning of humanity. The little child makes no separation; but with growth the distinction becomes prominent, until sometimes it appears to be the very mark of man or woman. Yet we find that love, to be love, must transcend it, and pierce to the humanity beneath.

> Many loved your beauty and your grace;
> But one man loved the pilgrim soul in you.

Where there is no recognition of sex we do not find the full flavour of humanity; but true lovers never rest until they discover, with a shock of surprise, the human soul, like to their own, within. Similarly, where no distinction of orders is made within the Church, we get a tame and monotonous simplicity. The proper office of the ministerial priesthood is to reveal to the whole people, and continually to remind them of, the glorious opportunities of the common priesthood. Again and again, when the ministry through spiritual lassitude neglects to set forth the treasures of the kingdom of heaven, or through spiritual pride claims an exclusive right to those treasures, it is necessary for the Laity, the whole People under the Covenant, to register a stern protest. But the supreme need is that the spiritual privileges, which are ours in Christ, should be realized by a redeemed humanity.

Quakerism surprised a great truth when it discerned that man had the potentiality of entering into communion with God in all His Fullness, by the very fact that he was man, and in proportion to the intensity of his humanity. It faltered and failed, because it did not follow out its own intuition. It put aside so much that belonged to the true glory of humanity.

The lines on which Wordsworth moved in art were similar to those on which Quakerism moved in religion. There is in each lack of colour. The Quaker is so afraid of symbolism that he refuses any outward sacrament : he is so anxious that there should be no hireling or sacerdotal ministry that he turns away even from that leadership without which there can be no adequate missionary enterprise.

In the Review and Forecast at the end of his book on the *Later Periods of Quakerism*, Dr. Rufus Jones probes the question of the future of Quakerism, and even asks whether it has any future at all. Writing as one who belongs to an entirely different type of Christian endeavour, I feel how much would be lost if the witness of the Friends were obliterated. The conception of a Way of Perfection, in which the true glory of humanity is realized, and which is open to all by virtue of their humanity, must be retained. Others have proclaimed this ; but none more directly and vehemently than the Friends. Curiously enough the human interest, which is indigenous in Quakerism, has found an outlet in non-religious ways : the Friend allows free play to the humanism, which he has learnt from religion, in every sphere except that which is definitely religious. There is, of course, a ministry in the Society, of which John Woolman was a noble example. It was expected that there should be a call to it ; and it was conceived as entirely prophetic. Its nearest likeness is with those who are called local preachers in Methodism. But the Quaker regarded such a ministry as essentially itinerant, its main object being to seek for ' opportunities ' of eliciting the best in any family or group, or in assisting those in whom the soul was stirring towards the higher life. This is the only distinction, and it is a very slight one, made within the Society. Yet it is apparent that all human progress has been marked by increased complexity of organization ; nor can we see any reason why religion should be exempt from this law. All the Lord's people are potentially prophets and priests ; but there may be a ministry specifically called to take the lead in either capacity. *But no office, whether of prophet or of priest, must be confused with the attainment of Evangelical Perfection.* The teaching of the Friends in this matter is particularly clear and definite ; and **it has** been splendidly exemplified in their witness, and in their **services** for humanity. It has, therefore, an abiding worth.

PART V
CONSTRUCTIVE

CONTENTS OF PART V

XV. A SUMMARY OF CONCLUSIONS

	PAGE
1. THE BASIS OF THE DOCTRINE	251
(1) *The Wide Extent of the Quest for Perfection*	251
(2) *The Inalienable Place of the Quest in the Christian Gospel*	252
2. THE PERMANENT GAIN FROM THE TEACHING OF THE PAST	255
(1) *Christian Perfection to be Defined as Perfection in Love*	255
(2) *The Marks of Perfection considered as a State of Life*	257
(3) *The Essential Place of the Church*	262
(4) *The Continual Need for the Word*	264
(5) *The Abiding Presence of the Spirit*	266
3. A MODERN FORMULATION OF THE DOCTRINE	268
(1) *Perfection and the Individual*	269
(a) *A Present Experience through Faith and Hope*	269
(b) *Consummation of this Experience in Eternity*	271
(c) *The Demand for a Re-statement of the Doctrine of the Future Life*	273
(2) *Perfection and Society*	275
(a) *Social Reform and Progress*	275
(b) *The League of Nations*	276
(c) *The Reunion of Christendom*	277
(3) *Perfection and Christian Preaching*	279
(a) *Perfection not an Esoteric Doctrine*	279
(b) *The Importance of Terminology*	281
(c) *Need for an End or Aim in Personal Experience*	283
(d) *Need for an End or Aim as a Motive for Missionary Endeavour*	284

Chapter XV

A SUMMARY OF CONCLUSIONS

1. The Basis of the Doctrine

No doctrine in Theology can be judged apart from its effect on character and destiny. If it is to stand, it must be so human that it will appeal to mankind everywhere, yet it must be so Divine that it may be recognized as conveying a message from above. The foregoing investigation has proved (1) that the desire for a state of perfect attainment is extremely widespread, and (2) that such attainment is an inalienable part of the Gospel revealed in Christ. The doctrine of Evangelical Perfection, therefore, stands on a firm foundation; for it is the application of the doctrine of the Perfections of God, as revealed in His creative and redemptive work, to the necessities of the spirit of man. In this closing chapter the conclusions to which the historical survey has led will be set forth; but before that is done it will be well to note how firm is the basis on which they rest. We shall then be in a position to judge how far these conclusions sustain the thesis enunciated at the beginning,[1] and how far they prepare the way for a modern formulation of the doctrine.

(1) *The Wide Extent of the Quest for Perfection*

The eighth chapter was devoted to an examination of the movements outside Christianity which have affected the evangelical conception. It did not attempt to do more than refer to those systems of thought, whose effects on the earlier and more plastic years of Christian theology can be directly traced. But even that cursory survey made it plain how widespread was the longing for a higher state, and how earnest was the

[1] p. 6.

search for the way to it. Our knowledge of the Way has been permanently enriched by the spiritual discoveries associated with the names of Plato and Aristotle, of the Neo-Platonists and the Stoics, and with the many diverse movements which came flooding in from the East.

To say that the desire for Perfection is universal seems at first to be an exaggeration. Even among those who are closely connected with the Christian Church it appears to be confined to a small minority. On the other hand, we note that, wherever a certain standard of spiritual knowledge is reached, the mind inevitably seeks for a state of rest for the soul in union with God. By some it is dismissed as incompatible with the business of life; by some it is relegated to a future existence; by many it is left to the few who have the leisure and the vocation for it. But at any rate it is recognized, when religion has reached a certain stage, that there is a goal, towards which all who feel the cogency of the religious arguments must press, either Here or Hereafter. This is the sense in which we may speak of the Quest for Perfection as universal.

Such a sense, however, is sufficient for our argument. If this doctrine is to be firmly grounded, it must go down to the roots of human nature. But that is not the same as saying that it must be found wherever humanity exists. For in some of the lower forms it may not yet have come into consciousness; and in some of the higher it may have emerged, only to be dismissed from the mind, either temporarily or altogether. It is enough to show that *it emerges normally at a certain stage of human development.* The implications of such a fact are a question for psychology. From the religious standpoint we may say that, if in the evolution of man there emerges normally and regularly a desire for the perfect rest which comes from union with God, that desire must be an essential part of human nature.

(2) *The Inalienable Place of the Quest in the Christian Gospel*

In order to establish any doctrine, it is necessary to show, not only that it is human, but also that it is Divine. If the doctrine of the Quest for Perfection is to have a recognized place in Christian Theology, it must be because it forms an

A SUMMARY OF CONCLUSIONS

inalienable part of the revelation in Christ. In Buddhism and Neo-Platonism we receive an impression of the intensity and the urgency of the soul's yearning for God. On the other hand, the idea of a Divine Revelation is distinctly stated in many religions. But it is Christianity which has welded the two together, for in Christianity it is impossible to separate the upward movement of the human soul and the communication of the Father's love. Our attention, therefore, while it must have regard to the world-wide movement, must be concentrated on the particular form which it has assumed in Christianity.

Christian Perfection was defined by Ritschl as the subjective certainty of Reconciliation. Such a certainty, while relying on the witness of the Spirit within, is confirmed by a study of the Scripture, and of the history of Christian thought and experience. The definition given in the first chapter may be taken as a concise statement of the thesis which this essay is written to maintain; and in it care was taken to show the dependence of the State of Perfection on the Atonement. The phrase ' the Blood of Christ,'[1] with all its historic associations, and with its perpetual remembrance in the celebration of Holy Communion, was used as a succinct expression of that dependence. The phrase covers the life of Christ on earth in its full humanity and its surrender on the Cross; but it also leads us to think of that life as still continuing, as the source of cleansing,[2] the means of access to the Father,[3] and the sign of the New Covenant between humanity and God.[4]

The discussion in the fifth chapter as to the sense in which we should speak of the Perfection of Christ made it plain that such Perfection must refer, not only to the completeness of His life upon earth, and to His full attainment of glory in Heaven, but also to the power which proceeds from Him, by which His followers attain to likeness with Himself.[5] This dynamic may be spoken of as the Inward Christ, in differentiation from the Historic Christ.[6] The Inward Christ, however, cannot be distinguished from the Holy Spirit[7]; and the latter name is preferable, in so far as it presents to our mind the idea

---

[1] p. 7.   [2] Heb. ix. 14; 1 John i. 7.   [3] Eph. ii. 13.
[4] Heb. xii. 24.   [5] pp. 72 ff.   [6] pp. 238 ff.
[7] See Mackintosh, *The Person of Christ*, pp. 57 ff., on the correlation by St. Paul of Christ and the Spirit as they are manifested in experience.

of an activity which proceeds from the Father and the Son. It is remarkable how often the proficiency of the Christian is associated with a progressive apprehension of the distinctions within the Trinity. The reason is that such proficiency depends on an ever-deepening consciousness of the Atonement in Christ. The terminology, no doubt, varies. In some forms of spiritual attainment, which are truly Christian, the terms Trinity and Atonement are excluded, or at any rate regarded with suspicion. But it will be found that, where the attainment has the evangelical mark upon it, it depends on the revelation of the Father's love in Christ for sinful men, which is sealed in the soul by a Spiritual Presence; and for the expression of that supreme fact no better terms have yet been found than those of Trinity and Atonement. Many illustrations of this statement might be given. Roman Catholic and Methodist saints alike find here a basis for their faith. We may refer to the experiences of St. Francis de Sales and St. Teresa,[1] and of the early Methodist saints, whose experiences I have linked together in a brief chain.[2] The Friends make less use of the historic terminology; but their conception of the Inward Light rests on the same base.[3] The thought of the Trinity broadly distinguishes the Christian endeavour from Plotinus's flight to the Alone. It has swept away the idea of the Lonely God, and has unutterably enhanced our conception of the life of eternity. ' We read the great words: " Father, glorify Thou Me with Thine own self with the glory which I had with Thee before the world was "; and, as their solemn and elusive wonder lingers on the soul, we feel again how noble and subduing is that vision of the One God which beholds Him as never alone, but always the Father towards whom the Son has ever been looking in the Spirit of eternal love.'[4] The religious value of the idea of the Trinity is in enriching and eternizing our view of the love of God with which we have come into communion. The whole message of the Gospel finds its consummation in such a communion based on the great evangelical assumptions. The Quest, therefore, for such a communion, and the doctrine as to the way of attaining it, form an inalienable part of the Christian Gospel.

[1] pp. 201 f. [2] p. 213. [3] p. 235.
[4] Mackintosh, *The Person of Christ*, p. 526.

2. The Permanent Gain from the Teaching of the Past

The tracing of the idea of Perfection through its development in the Scripture and in the history of the Church has involved no little labour. It might be thought that the same results could be attained intuitively by an immediate spiritual perception. Our psychological studies, however, are teaching us that many even of those beliefs which we consider purely intuitive have come as the result of the experience of the past. Often we are amazed to find how little beliefs, which we have considered quite elementary, have emerged, where that experience has been lacking. Moreover, belief, by its very nature, has an element of uncertainty in it; and anything which can buttress it has a real value. The beliefs set forth in this section are so strongly supported by Scripture and Church History, especially in the experience of the saints, that we may fairly adjudge them to be assured gains from the teaching of the past. They are not mere truisms, for they have been reached through prolonged effort, and amid many doubts and questionings.

(1) *Christian Perfection to be Defined as Perfection in Love*

The New Testament discloses many ways along which the pilgrim may travel to his goal. In strict accuracy of statement Love ought not to be included among these. The dictum quoted from Dr. Platt's article,[1] that the closer definition of Perfection in the New Testament is always in terms of love, is amply justified. The other ways are to be regarded as means for realizing or for manifesting love. As the rainbow reveals the colours which make up the sun's spectrum, so the Divine Word shows that there are many tints which blend together in the pure light which we call love or charity. When St. Paul exalts Faith, or when St. James praises the fulfilling of the Law, it must be understood that Faith and the Law find their whole meaning in the Love of God, towards which they are leading. It was a right feeling, however, although it may have been carried to excess, which led the Jew to emphasize the law against using lightly or carelessly the Divine Name. Similarly, the deepest and truest natures are careful in using, even in human

---
[1] *E. R. E.*, ix. 729a; see p. 86.

relations, that word which we have learnt to think of as the supreme predicate for God. It should not be employed without a sense of wonder and awe. But no other word can take its place; and it remains as the final and best description of attainment.

This great thought, the outcome of the Evangel in the New Testament, is confirmed in Church History. Thus, in his letter to the Corinthians, Clement of Rome declared that ' by love all the elect of God have been made perfect.'[1] This simple and lucid phrase contains in germ the whole message. Nor do we find any deviation from it through the long pilgrimage of the Christian Church. Aspects of the truth are sometimes overstated in such a way as to lead to a neglect of the central thought; and sometimes the homage which is paid to it is only with the lips. But it may be asserted, without fear of contradiction, that, whenever any question has arisen, the Christian conscience has unhesitatingly affirmed that Love and Love only, is the true equivalent of Perfection. A striking illustration is afforded by a conversation which William Grimshaw had with John Wesley in 1761.[2] The gist of it was that he acknowledged the truth of what Wesley had just been preaching in the Churchyard as to the manner of full attainment. This perfection he was himself striving towards; and, though he had received in his soul the full assurance of Faith, and even of the Hope of eternal salvation, he knew well that he had not attained until he had been made perfect in Charity. When we remember the place which the Methodists assigned to Faith in the scheme of salvation, this tribute carries great force with it. If we turn to a Roman Catholic theologian such as Bishop Bellord we find the same testimony. ' Out of the many requirements for perfection, Divine Charity is the chief constituent. The love of God is the condition of all virtuous action, it leads to all virtues, and is the summary of them all.'[3] Illustrations might be multiplied indefinitely. They demonstrate that the Christian conscience has never wavered in its conception of the goal, at which man finds the prize of the upward calling of God in Christ Jesus.

Modern apologists are anxious to do full justice to the excellence of much of the teaching found outside Christianity.

[1] *Ad Cor.*, c. 50; see p. 129.   [2] p. 214.
[3] *Meditations on Christian Dogma*, ii. 247.

A SUMMARY OF CONCLUSIONS 257

They are confident that the originality of the evangelical message will not be impugned thereby. It is manifest, for instance, that the final and authoritative statement of Perfection as love towards God and one's neighbour was drawn from the old Jewish law. And even outside Judaism many admirable conceptions of the way may be found. Thus in the *Phaedrus* Socrates began by decrying love as a sign of madness, weakness, and instability; but his diamon warned him that he had erred in so doing; and the myth which follows denotes his penitence and recantation. For the vision of That-which-is, Love, purified and disciplined, is essential.[1] Yet, while we gratefully acknowledge so much noble and true teaching throughout the world, it may fairly be said that Christianity alone has set Charity in its right place. In the teaching of Gautama, of Plato, or of Plotinus, Love is a means rather than an end. It is an energy which may be used to cleanse the soul from the materialism to which selfishness naturally tends. But, in the teaching which the Church has learnt from Christ and His apostles, Love is the supreme attribute of God Himself, and is therefore the fulfilment of every movement which turns towards Him.

(2) *The Marks of Perfection considered as a State of Life*

We have seen that St. Thomas Aquinas assigns an important part of the *Summa* to the discussion of the *States of Life*,[2] in which he makes a distinction among the converted between the beginning, the middle, and the perfect. It is a useful distinction, if we avoid the error—which mars so much of his work—of connecting these states with ecclesiastical orders.[3] By a state we denote a spiritual condition which has been gained and made secure. It is not possible to be too definite in this matter. How far any state may be termed secure and permanent has been a matter for endless controversy. It may be hoped that, in addition to Scripture, modern psychology may shed light on this momentous question. Whatever possibility of lapse there may be, it may be confidently asserted that we do attain fixed spiritual conditions, in which the soul finds rest and security. The transition from one state to another may come through violent convulsion,

[1] p. 5.   [2] II. ii., QQ. 183-9.   [3] p. 193.

or by an imperceptible progress. The essential fact is that we pass into a new sphere, which may even be called a new creation. The word 'state' in itself designates something fixed and steadfast—not for eternity, but as compared with the more transient moods of the soul. It ought to be of assistance if we can perceive and recognize the various states through which the soul normally passes in its upward movement, and in which it finds rest and refection.

The use of the words 'State of Perfection' rather than Perfection has this additional advantage—that it enables us to think of a condition which is not final, *ne plus ultra*, but which is rich with the most gracious possibilities of further advance. Many objections to the term 'perfect' we have to disregard; for they would apply to any claim to spiritual progress. But the term may be validly objected to if it be taken to imply the reaching of a goal, beyond which there can be no development, nor any further ethical choice. The phrase 'State of Perfection' precludes that error; those who enter into that state come into a wide stretch of country, a land of far distances.

The marks of the state, so far as one is able to gather from those who have entered in, are Freedom, Joy, Expansion, and Lordship. The question of *the Freedom of the soul* has exercised all who have considered the meaning of progress. Several of Plato's myths, notably that of Er in the *Republic*, are intended to reconcile the idea of the soul's freedom with that of Necessity.[1] With this we may contrast Freud's statement that Free Will has been exploded by the scientific treatment of mental processes. It would be nearer the truth to say that Freedom, so far from being a heritage from the past, is something to be won in the upward movement of the soul. The idea of a state is intimately connected with that of freedom and of servitude. The higher state may be rightly spoken of as a State of Freedom. 'Where the Spirit of the Lord is, *there* is liberty.'[2] There is a joyful sense of deliverance from the bondage of sin, and even from the burden of the world, in so far as that burden oppresses the soul. It is true that the state may also be described as a State of Servitude; we know how gladly the apostles called themselves bond-servants of God and of the Lord Jesus Christ. But the

[1] p. 100.   [2] 2 Cor. iii. 17.

servitude has nothing degrading or oppressive in it. It is the thought of Freedom which stands out in the experience of those who have entered into this state, and which seems to them most distinctively to mark it.

The *note of joy* should also be emphasized. Even a casual study of the New Testament produces a sense of gladness and victory; and this impression is only confirmed by a deeper study.[1] Wherever the good tidings of great joy are proclaimed, they increase the beatitude of humanity. This is especially the mark of the higher state, in which the soul's freedom from sin and the world, and its bondage towards God, are more clearly recognized. Both the freedom and the servitude are a cause for gladness. Freedom by itself is too negative to have much meaning; it is because this freedom opens the door for a higher loyalty and service that it is so great a boon. Of the Fathers, no one more clearly delineated the way of full attainment than Clement of Alexandria; and no one laid greater stress on the freedom and joy into which the soul entered in the higher life.[2]

The proposition that this state is one both of freedom and of servitude may be supplemented by the statement that it is marked both by joy and sorrow. St. Paul, with his love of paradox, expressed this in the phrase, 'as sorrowful, yet always rejoicing.' An erroneous impression would be conveyed if we were to overlook the sadness which accompanies all progress. There is a type of conversion and of saintship in which this sorrow is very prominent and very persistent. Well-known examples are those of Bunyan and David Brainerd.[3] Professor J. B. Pratt, in his book on *The Religious Consciousness*, a psychological study which I have found most helpful, speaks of this type as the Bunyan-Brainerd type, so well is it expressed in their experiences. This sadness often prevails where there is a specific denial of the possibility of attainment in this present life. Under the gracious influence of his mother's presence Augustine experienced a foretaste of heavenly bliss; and he perceived that, if that could have been prolonged, he would have entered into fellowship with the joy of the Lord; but he was convinced that such experiences only come, if they come at all, as

---

[1] See article on 'Joy' in *H. D. C.*, i. 903*a*.   [2] pp. 145 et seq.
[3] See p. 228 for an instance of the discouraging effect of Brainerd's pessimism.

momentary flashes in this present life.[1] The result may be seen in the gloom which rested on his theology, and which has so gravely and so detrimentally affected the Church. This pessimism in regard to the possibilities of human life in this world is due to outside influences—in the case of Augustine the influence of Plotinus. The evangelical message, while it bids us enter into fellowship with the sufferings of Christ, does so with the assurance that thus we shall enter also into the joy that was set before Him. 'In sola cruce est perfecta laetitia,' said St. Francis. The fullness of joy even for the Master is to be realized in eternity; but already the assurance of it brings gladness into the soul.

The idea suggested in the mark of *Expansion* is that of continual and, indeed, eternal progress. Spiritual Perfection in its very nature cannot be static. 'Build thee more stately mansions, O my soul!' The joy which comes to those who have discovered the glorious sense of freedom which is the inheritance of God's children is greatly due to the wide views which appear before them as the mark of that glory.[2] These wide views bring with them a sense of awe and fear. 'Thou shalt see and be lightened, and thine heart shall tremble and be enlarged.'[3] But even this fear passes away with the intensifying of the knowledge of God's love, for perfect love casteth out fear.

The paradoxes in the marks of Freedom and of Joy are continued in this one of Expansion. It is an axiom of the saints that in order to accomplish anything in the spiritual realm limitation is necessary. This has affinities with the objection so often found in Greek philosophy to operate with the idea of infinity. Aristotle, for example, lauded moderation because he saw clearly that the confining of one's aim within a compassable area made for intellectual lucidity and for effectiveness. The saints urged the same limitation in the interests of spiritual efficacy. 'St. Catherine of Siena, in a dialogue which she composed on Christian Perfection, says that among other things which her Beloved taught her one was that she ought to shut herself up in the Divine will, as in a most secure retreat, and live there as a pearl in the shell, or a bee in the hive, without ever coming forth. That in the beginning perhaps she would find the place very narrow, but

---

[1] p. 166.   [2] Rom. viii. 21.   [3] Isa. lx. 5.

afterwards it would be larger ; and without once coming forth she might walk there as in the habitations of the blessed, and obtain in a short time what, out of that retirement, she would not be able to compass in a long term of years.'[1]

In this we are guided by the example of our Master. The terms used to describe the Incarnation denote emptying, limiting, and impoverishing. This limitation was for the sake of the benefits which Christ was thus enabled to bring to humanity, and also for the sake of the glory which came to Him through it. Many strong expressions are used in the New Testament to show the perfecting which resulted from the limitations and the sufferings of His earthly life. From this it is a just argument to say that His followers also are benefiting through the patient endurance of the bonds of mortality. There comes as the result an expansion of the spirit which would not have been possible if men had not, through the things which are seen and which have the limitations inherent in all that is visible, learnt to perceive the things that are unseen and eternal. ' For our light affliction, which is for the moment, worketh for us more and more exceedingly an eternal weight of glory.'[2]

A mark of this state, which arises from the preceding, may be described as that of *Lordship*. In the parables of the Talents and the Pounds the reward of the faithful servant is to enter into the joy of his Lord, and himself to have the joy of authority and dominion. The name which Jesus chose for Himself was that of the Son of Man ; but the name which the Church gave to Him pre-eminently was that of the Lord. Even in the days of His flesh the Son of Man had authority ; but after His glorification He becomes Lord of all. He has the keys of Death and of Hades. He has this authority as Son of Man, for it is in human form that the seer beholds Him with the emblems of supernal dominion in His hands. This prevalence He shares with His own. ' All things are yours ; for ye are Christ's, and Christ is God's.'[3] Lordship comes through knowledge, for those who have attained it are stewards of the mysteries of God. But since this knowledge is the knowledge of God, and since the inspiration for advance in

---

[1] Rodriguez : *The Practice of Christian Perfection*, I. viii. 12.
[2] 2 Cor. iv. 17.   [3] 1 Cor. iii. 21-3.

it is in the love which He has poured forth, it may be even more rightly said that Lordship comes through love. It was one of the first things which people noted of Christ, that He spoke with authority; and, whether they understood it or not, it was the love which filled Him which gave Him such power. 'It would seem that although the knowledge of God is the primary and essential element in the consummate state of blessedness, yet the derivative joy, that is the expression of love, gives it a higher perfection. And this is, in fact, the meaning of expressions that often occur in Aquinas, such as that the love of God is *altior* or *eminentior* than the knowledge of Him; or that, whereas beatitude consists *essentialiter* in the *visio Dei*, it consists *formaliter* in the *amor Dei*, where *formaliter* is used in the special sense of perfecting or adorning.'[1] We may say, therefore, of the disciples what we say of the Master—that their rule takes its authority from the love which fills their soul.

(3) *The Essential Place of the Church*

The New Testament teaching as to attainment depends on a belief in the full revelation of the love of God in Christ Jesus; but it assumes that the apprehension of that love will lead to fellowship with other believers. This theme runs through the First Epistle of St. John. If the spirit of hatred is in any one's heart, he cannot be walking in the Light, nor can he know the meaning of Divine Love. That Divine Love is the source of all blessing; but the deduction drawn from that fact is not so much that we should love Him in return as that we should believe in His love, and, as a necessary conclusion, love one another. This, as I tried to show in chapter VII on the Perfecting of the Church, is the sum of New Testament teaching. From the historical investigation we are able to judge whether the experience of the ages has ratified that conclusion, or added anything to it.

The survey of Church History discloses the fact that there is among earnest seekers after Perfection a longing for fellowship, together with much distrust of organization. The desire for fellowship is, of course, one of the elementary instincts of humanity; and progress only develops it. In Plato's idea of judgement the doom of the wicked soul is that all

---

[1] Wicksteed, *Reactions between Dogma and Philosophy*, p. 614.

A SUMMARY OF CONCLUSIONS

shun it, and it wanders about in helplessness.[1] It is the mark of virtue that it draws men together in the concord of a state founded on justice and goodwill.[2] This thought was carried forward by St. Augustine in his conception of the City of God.[3] Even earthly states must be founded on love, for hatred can accomplish nothing constructive. The love of the world is fundamentally selfish; and its constructive work cannot be permanent. But the love of God is building a city which is eternal. The higher the development of the soul, the more it turns to fellowship, and the association involved in fellowship.

Nevertheless, it is remarkable how much shrinking there is from organization. This is obvious, not only in such later movements as Quakerism, but in early ones such as Monachism. The flight of the monks into the desert was a breach with ecclesiastical organization under the impulse of a desire for Perfection. The aversion to anything like formalism or externalism is often coupled with a yearning for solitude.

Two considerations, however, have modified this proclivity to lonely meditation. One is that the individual rediscovers, under the influence of communion with the love of God, his need for fellowship with the souls of others. The consequent necessity for an organized society, whose members have many and varied functions, in order that individuals may *find* themselves in the true sense of the word, cannot seriously be questioned. ' As society implies persons regarding themselves and others as persons, so also the realization of human personality means its realization in a society; and, although this realization would seem to imply a difference of functions in the different members of society, it would imply in all the fulfilment of the idea of humanity, i.e. *devotion to the perfection of man.*'[4] This axiom, which has become a commonplace of philosophy, was intuitively perceived and joyfully accepted under the influence of Divine Grace. The headship of Christ involves membership in a Body, in which those who have many functions may work together in harmony and love.

The other consideration which has modified the propensity to retirement is the sense of the priestly work to which the elect are called. In Dan. vii. 27 the Kingdom of the Son of

---
[1] *Phaedo*, 108.   [2] pp. 101 f.   [3] pp. 170 ff.
[4] Green, *Prolegomena to Ethics*, III. ii., §§ 190–1 summarized.

Man is that of the elect of Israel, the saints of the Most High, with the idea inherent in it that they are to act as priests for humanity, for the uplift of all nations. That was a conception well established, and one with which the writer of Daniel, with his kindly attitude towards the nations, altogether sympathized. In the Christian use of the phrase 'the Kingdom of the Son of Man,' it was associated with the person of Christ, and the humanity of the Kingdom was emphasized. Again and again in Christian revival earnest spirits have broken away from the particularism implied in the idea of the Church in order to renew personal relations with God, or to widen the extent of Gospel grace. Many, therefore, speak of the Church as an intermediate method, with no meaning for the life beyond this world, and with very little for the future of religious life on this globe. Nevertheless, the need for the Church as a mediator between the individual and humanity, and between humanity and God, does not grow less. It is a ladder by which the individual rises to a conception of a humanity for whose evangelization he is responsible; while at the same time it preserves, as no other institution has ever done, the abiding value of the individual in himself. This mediatorial work enables the Church to exercise a priestly ministry towards God on behalf both of the individual and of humanity. It is, in effect, the Body by means of which the work of Christ in Heaven becomes efficacious in the world. The eternal value of the Church is bound up with the eternal value of the historic revelation in Jesus Christ. The work of the Church is the carrying on of that which Jesus began both to do and to teach. The perfecting of the Church consists in the filling of it with the Spirit, so that it becomes a perfect instrument to fulfil the mind of the eternal Son of God. This does not mean the literal carrying out of His injunctions as they have been transmitted to us; but it does mean that from the sources open to us, of which the Gospels occupy the first place, we should endeavour to be 'filled with the knowledge of His will in all spiritual wisdom and understanding.'[1]

(4) *The Continual Need for the Word*

The close of the preceding paragraph shows the connexion between the place filled by the Church and by the Word in

[1] Col. i. 9.

A SUMMARY OF CONCLUSIONS

spiritual attainment. Both have been tested by time, as only time can test; and both have proved their worth for the development of the soul. The permanent value of the Scriptures for spiritual experience is one of the assured results of history. If we seek for a reason for the pre-eminence of the Bible, we find that it is bound up with the primacy of the Christian evangel; and that evangel, if rightly understood, retains its primacy because of its universality, for it takes up all lesser revelations into its own glory. One of the burning questions in the early Church was, What should be done with the Old Testament?[1] The Church decided to retain it, but to retain it with the new content which had come through the Gospel. The leaders of the Church were influenced by the example of their Lord, and still more by the success which attended their efforts to find Him everywhere in it, and to relate all of it to Him. In doing this they were treading the path which He Himself had trod. Moreover, they discovered, in treading it, that they were finding the way of their own attainment. The Law and the Prophets and the Psalms, being related to Christ and suffused with His Spirit, became to them endlessly instructive for their own progress. Such a method is thoroughly sound and right, and is indeed employed, consciously or unconsciously, by all those who find in the Old Testament a true help in attaining further proficiency. ' The whole stream and drift of the Old Testament moves straight to the Cross of Christ. The whole New Testament is nothing but a portrait of Christ. Let a man seek the true course of his own life in the Word, and inevitably it will land him at the Cross, to seek mercy, as a perishing sinner, in the Saviour's wounds; and let him, starting afresh from this point of departure, seek his true course still farther, and inevitably what he will see will be, rising upon him in the distance, astonishing and enchaining him, but drawing him ever on, *the image of Perfection in the man Christ Jesus.*'[2]

This statement may be abundantly illustrated from the experience of the saints. No one can ignore or neglect the Scriptures without loss in the depth and content of the spiritual life. The method of search, however, has varied even among

---
[1] Harnack, *Hist. of Dogma*, Vol. I., Intro. chap. ii., pp. 41 ff.
[2] Stalker, *Imago Christi*, chap. viii., p. 164.

the most earnest seekers ; and so has the view taken of the source of scriptural authority. No candid inquirer can fail to see in the Bible some things which go contrary to his reason, and some which offend his moral sense. Various methods have been used to overcome these difficulties. The allegorical method, systematized by Origen, had an extraordinary vogue ; nor is it without validity still ; for some parts of the Bible are obviously allegorical, and from other parts many true thoughts may be learnt by the exercise of the fancy and the imagination. The method of the Reformers may be fairly described as accepting those large tracts of the Bible which they found fruitful in blessing, and putting aside the rest as inexplicable by our reason. This method had some justification. It has been repeatedly found that when the Bible has been condemned it has been on hasty and ill-considered grounds. But the historico-critical method far surpasses either of these. We cannot accept fanciful deductions as having any cogency in argument ; nor can we agree that a Word which is written in human language should be taken outside the province of human reason. It remains for us to face the question how we may utilize the results of criticism for the sanctification of the soul. If our argument is sound, then we ought to expect under the critical method a higher form of attainment. Nor are we without hope in looking for that. The type of spiritual life under the Reformers was higher than that under the monastic system ; and it was so largely because it was based on a more reasonable interpretation of Scripture, which brought it more into accord with the common life of men. It cannot, however, be denied that the Reformed type has had some grave defects ; and these may be traced to a failure to discern the evolutionary process in Scripture. They were due to the hardening into dogma of conceptions which were in process of evolution, some of which are developing still. The historico-critical method, which far more truly expounds the teaching of the Bible, ought to issue in lives of greater patience, gentleness, and truth, if our view of the place of the written Word in the scheme of sanctification be correct.

(5) *The Abiding Presence of the Spirit*

The discussion as to the main divergences in regard to the doctrine of Perfection led to the conclusion that the differences

A SUMMARY OF CONCLUSIONS

were not so much about the character of the state as about the ways of attainment, and the authorities which sanctioned them. There is, indeed, one great distinction between those who relegate the whole matter to the life beyond, and those who accept it as pertaining to our present condition. Among the latter there are three main types, which have been already fully discussed. It would be unjust to suggest that any of these deny the validity of all the authorities to which Christians in general appeal. The Roman Catholic and the Methodist would certainly vehemently proclaim their loyalty to the doctrine of the Holy Spirit. But among both these great bodies, which number between them the majority of those professing to be followers of Christ, there has been a marked reluctance to accept *the idea of a continued revelation*. It has been left to groups, of which the Montanists may be taken as the first representatives, to speak of a dispensation of the Paraclete, in which there shall be advance in the knowledge of God, even beyond that which has come through the historic revelation in Christ. In all these bodies there has been some weakness, which has prevented them from establishing themselves. They have had too much of the character of groups, drawn together and coagulated for a time, but not having the generic bond which makes a Church. Nevertheless, they have borne witness to a truth which has been in danger of being lost ; and their perpetual resurgence is a proof that they have a message.

The Quakers may be taken as a noble example, one which has had more power of continuance than is usual in this type. The fact that their influence has been out of all proportion to their numbers is a testimony to the place which they have filled. It is possible that the concentration on their message, which resulted in practical isolation from the historical continuity of the Church, was unavoidable. The human mind finds it hard to grasp more than one aspect of the truth. Will it ever be possible to see the truth as a whole, and to bring to that vision the energy which is shown by those who have been convinced of the infallibility of a part ?

When we speak of the abiding Presence of the Holy Spirit, and of His continuous work, we associate that Presence with Christ as the eternal Son of God. The Spirit guides men into all truth by delivering from the lower self, and bringing into the light of the higher, which is imaged in Christ. 'There is no higher creation of God than a spirit that is made in His own image, and in that spirit there is nothing higher than the knowledge and the love of God. But what, as we have already seen, the knowledge and the love of God mean, is the giving up of all thoughts and feelings that belong to me as a mere individual self, and the identification of my thought and being with that which is above me, yet in me—the Universal or Absolute Self which is not mine or yours, but in which all intelligent beings alike find the realization and the perfection of their nature.'[1]

This Spirit is the Spirit of Christ, and bears always the marks of His experience; but we are not fully honouring the Spirit if we confine His power of guiding into all truth within limits governed by the record of our Lord's life upon earth. Methodists, for example, have strongly urged and insisted upon the witness of the Spirit in confirming the soul's acceptance of pardon, of adoption, and, in the higher stages, of the full assurance of faith and hope. But they have hesitated to take any further step through fear of Antinomian excess. Yet it is surely probable that through all these centuries the Spirit of Christ will not have rested content with simply confirming what has been already promised. As a matter of fact, much progress has been made, but without a full understanding of what is implied in the steps that have been taken. The value of such progressive knowledge of God is becoming more and more evident. We may reckon among the assured gains of the past the firm belief that all advance in the higher life depends on the abiding Presence of the Holy Spirit. This Presence leads men forward in a long pilgrimage towards a goal not yet fully discerned, and continually brings fresh knowledge; yet, being the Spirit of Christ, it keeps them close to the revelation which came through Him, and is a strong guard against lawlessness.

3. A MODERN FORMULATION OF THE DOCTRINE

In the phrase 'a modern formulation' the intention in using the adjective is to assert that the statement of the doctrine here set forth is, in the judgement of the writer, in accordance with the main tendencies of modern theology. It is a

[1] J. Caird, *Intro. to the Phil. of Rel.*, chap. viii., p. 244.

A SUMMARY OF CONCLUSIONS

formulation which owes everything to the past; and yet it is one which could scarcely have been put together except in our day. In the attempt to formulate the doctrine, I have looked at it from three standpoints. (1) The Doctrine of Perfection has an import for the individual in his personal relations with the Unseen Father. (2) It has also a significance for the social ideal, both as that ideal concerns the fellowship of believers and as it concerns the Kingdom of Heaven in this world. (3) And, further, it carries with it a definite challenge to evangelization.

(1) *Perfection and the Individual*

(a) *A Present Experience through Faith and Hope*

In seeking to expound the message which this doctrine has for the individual, one must insist on its immediate application to his present condition. If he can in any way perceive it, then he may already apprehend it by faith, and in a true sense enter into the possession of it. This is the reason for the place which faith and hope occupy in the Christian scheme; and it is through the failure to recognize this that so many have relegated attainment to an unknown future. In his brochure on *Christian Perfection* Dr. Forsyth says that there are three ways by which men have sought to arrive at the goal, of which two are wrong and the third is right; but that all three are right compared with the notion that we are to wait for Perfection 'till some indefinite time in the infinite future.' Of these three he says: 'The first idea is Pietist; the second is Popish; the third is Protestant, Apostolic, Christian.'[1] These divisions practically correspond with those which I have denominated the main divergences. I have concentrated attention on typical forms in which these ideas have expressed themselves. The Pietist idea found a noble utterance in Quakerism. The Popish idea of Perfection may be conveniently and fairly adequately studied in the Franciscan Revival and in the teaching of Aquinas. The Protestant idea found vigorous expression in the doctrine and example of Luther; and Methodism, which is largely the product of Lutheranism, may be taken as typical of it.

[1] Forsyth, *Christian Perfection*, chap. ii., p. 54. This second chapter, on ' Sanctity and Faith,' is particularly stimulating to thought.

A SUMMARY OF CONCLUSIONS

Dr. Forsyth conceives of the first and second ideas—those which he calls Pietistic and Popish—as right in so far as they regard Perfection as a present possession, but as wholly wrong in the method by which they seek to ' possess their possessions.' It is Protestantism which with a strong hand has put them right; and it has done so by returning to the apostolic, Christian doctrine of the New Testament, the doctrine that our full salvation comes by faith. The viewpoint of this thesis somewhat dissents from that. It regards faith as substantially underlying every movement towards attainment. Any way which professes a present perfection must be, logically and inevitably, a way of faith. This faith enters into the whole spiritual life. It finds in the universe sources of knowledge, and it feels the need for personal exertion; but knowledge and works can never be rivals of faith; for whatever knowledge may have been gained, or whatever work may have been accomplished, faith still remains as indispensable as ever. 'We may well admit that we do not rightly know in what Perfection consists. It is something which we feel towards along the lines of our own highest experiences; and our idea is, to the end, something approximative—a hint, a suggestion, a bare outline.'[1] We are able to give a name—Love or Charity—to that which constitutes Perfection, which is something more than a name, because we know a good deal about it; but we agree that we can by no means fill in its meaning; and the identification of it with that objective reality which we call God must be by faith. 'No subjective experience, however momentous and significant it may be for the person who has it, can settle for everybody else the question: Is there in the universe a God who is personal and all-loving? No empirical experience of any sort can ever answer that question, and to the end of the world men will still be called upon to walk by *faith*, to make their venture in the light of what ought to be true, and in the light of what seems to them to be true, and to live by that faith.'[2] Such a faith presses on to the satisfaction of the imperative demand which the spiritual life makes upon us. Without faith there would be no exploration; but unless faith is able to find some satisfaction to its hunger and thirst it is worse than useless. In the evolution of all living organisms

---
[1] Pringle-Pattison, *The Idea of God*, p. 248.
[2] Rufus M. Jones, *Studies in Mystical Religion*, Intro., p. xxix.

there has been, from the beginning, what Professor James Ward calls 'a sort of unscientific trustfulness,' which seems to be engrained in them, and which is the cause of all their progress. The same law holds true in the evolution of spiritual life, up to its highest forms. There is a hunger and thirst after righteousness which we *trust* will be filled.

Faith, therefore, is especially associated with any form of spiritual attainment. But any satisfactory definition of religion must include, not only belief in a Power above oneself, which gives stability and rest to the soul, but also some expression of that belief in acts of worship and service. In order to know what acts are pleasing to that Power, the soul naturally turns to certain authorities for direction and sanction. It is here that the main divergences have arisen. I have found much spiritual help from all earnest seekers who have trusted in God. I would, however, agree with Dr. Forsyth that the Protestant idea of the way of Perfection is more truly evangelical and apostolic than either the Roman Catholic or the Quaker. The Protestant idea, the great names in the development of which are Luther and Wesley, rests more definitely and explicitly on Faith in God. The Roman Catholic dreads the world, and the Quaker dreads organization, as though God would be overpowered by them. And we must confess that the world draws away from God, and that organization has a deadening effect on the soul. Yet without the world and without organization we can do nothing. We cannot, therefore, believe that organized activity is to be avoided in the higher life of the soul. The Great Faith, which has never been lost, but which it is the glory of Luther and Wesley to have proclaimed with such force before all men, is this—that the Love of God is able to keep the soul in perfect peace in the midst of the world's work, and in the organized community of the Church.

(b) *Consummation of this Experience in Eternity*

Those writers who most vehemently assert the pertinence of the teaching of Perfection to this present life do so with the proviso that in its fullness it can only be applied to the life that is to be. This is the meaning of the distinction made between the full assurance of faith and the full assurance of hope.¹ 'All things are yours,' says the apostle, 'things present, and *things to come.*'² We refuse to be drawn into any comparison between the Christian graces, unless it be to assert with St. Paul, the pre-eminence of Charity. But it may surely be said that Hope is the most distinctive feature of the Christian message.³ For this there is a good reason, namely, the experiences connected with the Resurrection. With Christianity a flood of new conceptions came in ; and, even when old conceptions were taken up, they were transfigured with the new light. But this was not due to any great outburst of intellectual energy or to contact with outside minds. All who have left us any account of the beginnings of Christianity are agreed that it came through the sight of a Perfect Life on earth, and the hope kindled by the glimpse of a Perfect Life beyond. And they are right. We need not hesitate to acknowledge the indebtedness of Christianity to many conceptions which arose quite outside it. All these do not account for the great hope which arose, and which has remained so distinctive a feature of the Gospel.

The full assurance of hope is a confidence, engendered by the Resurrection and by the Presence of the Love of God, that it will be well with the soul in eternity. Such confidence is not purely a logical conclusion, although reason plays a large part in it. The Resurrection provides a reason for believing in the Divine care for the soul, even after this mortal life is ended. But such a reason depends on the credibility of outside witnesses. It cannot convince the soul unless united with the Presence of the Divine Love. It appears that even the eye-witnesses were dependent on that Presence for the full assurance of hope. Repeated protest has been made against the transference of Perfection to a future life ; but that protest is consistent with a belief in its consummation in the eternal life. There are limitations in this mortal life which affect the apprehension of Perfection. There may be limitations in the future life ; it is probable that there will be in the life immediately beyond the grave. But they are transcended in the eternal life.⁴ This eternal life is a present possession, which may be perceived by faith even now ; and in the full assurance of that we enter into the state of Perfection. It is possible,

¹ p. 213.   ² 1 Cor. iii. 22.   ³ Inge, *Personal Religion*, chap. iv.
⁴ Von Hügel, *Eternal Life*, esp. chap. xiii.

A SUMMARY OF CONCLUSIONS

even in this world, to have an apprehension of eternal life which shall go beyond the perception by faith ; but such an apprehension is always dim and transient. In the spiritual progress which lies Beyond, the eternal life will become more and more dominant and conscious, until the soul is filled unto all the fullness of God.[1]

(c) The Demand for a Re-statement of the Doctrine of the Future Life

The argument so far has led to the conclusion that, while Perfection may be truly said to be attained here, it must be consummated in eternity. This greatly enforces the demand, which is being urged from many sides, for a re-statement of our doctrine, as members of the Christian Church, of the future life. Some of the conceptions which are emerging may be referred to briefly.

(1) There must be a possibility of attainment beyond the grave for those who have not entered into rest here. But such attainment can only come through an ethical choice, for the Perfection of Love is more concerned with that than even with intellectual knowledge or mystical rapture. Hence it follows that death cannot be conceived as ending the period of probation. ' It may be said in general that Protestant theology has tended to make too much of death. There is no warrant in Holy Scripture for the assumption that death is an absolute dividing-line between one state and another ; still less that on one side of the line all is preparation, and on the other all recompense or penalty.'[2] This quotation from a conservative theologian is a sign how widespread is the conviction that our conception of life beyond the grave must include purgatorial discipline and eternal progress. This conception, it should be noted, contravenes the Roman Catholic doctrine of Purgatory quite as much as the general idea of the Reformers of a Death-Purgatory. The Romanist doctrine is quite definite that destiny for eternity is fixed at death, and that Purgatory is simply a period of expiation. Against this, modern thought is proclaiming, with increasing decisiveness, that the future life, if it is to have reality, must be one of free, ethical choice.

(2) The purification of the soul, its purgatorial discipline in

[1] Eph. iii. 19.   [2] J. E. C. Welldon, *The Hope of Immortality*, chap. vi., p. 303.

eternity, and its entrance on ever-deepening communion with the love of God, will come through its relations with other souls. We must not of course, think of the relations of earth as transferred to the future. The intimacies of marriage, for instance, will be abrogated. But as we have learnt here to know and love God through His creations, so there our progress will be through relationships, more beautiful and perfect, with other creature souls. The poets have in this matter shown the way to the theologians. Thus in the farewell scene in the *Idylls of the King*, Arthur clings to the hope that somewhere ' hereafter, in the world where all are pure,' Guinevere, purified and redeemed, will leap to his side and claim him as her own. ' Leave me that, I charge thee, my last hope.' No one has more persistently dwelt on the perfecting of the soul in the life beyond than Robert Browning. In ' Any Wife to Any Husband ' he pictures the wife as dying, and pleading with her husband. There has been no stain on their marriage, for she has always felt sure of his love and truth. But she fears that after she has left him he will turn aside. Somewhere in eternity they will meet because of that soul union by which she is immortally his bride. ' Chance cannot change that love, nor time impair.' He will come to her, she is sure, with the crown of many achievements upon his head ; but deep down in her heart there is the dread that, through the temporary separation which death is making between them, there will be the stain of impurity on his brow. She knows well that she will forgive ; but she pleads that there may be no need for it.

> Only, why should it be with stain at all ?
> Why must I, 'twixt the leaves of coronal,
> Put any kiss of pardon on thy brow ?

It seems a light purgatory, a kiss of pardon; but it is purgatory all the same. The sin which breaks Arthur's heart, the dread of which lies so heavy on the dying wife in Browning's poem, this sin is a sin against both God and man. The purgatorial fire, both in this world and in that which is to come, which burns it away, must be both Divine and human. It must be Divine, because it is essentially the revelation of the holiness of eternal love ; but it must also be human, because of the human anguish which sin has brought.

(2) *Perfection and Society*

(a) *Social Reform and Progress*

Many will object to this whole discussion on the ground that it leads us away from the social needs of our day. It greatly concerns us to be able to answer that objection. The effect of pure asceticism on the social order is carefully examined by Dr. O. Hardman in a recent book on *The Ideals of Asceticism*, especially in the seventh chapter. He finds that fasting, almsgiving, and prayer are always necessary in the quest for Perfection to which the Christian is committed, which ends in the complete discharge of the law of love. But he shows that such discipline is also of material service to the social order, partly as a protest, and partly as an example. When the ascetic ideal has leavened the world, ' the ills of society will begin to be done away, true progress will begin to be made, and the Kingdom of God will come apace.'[1] That is the best answer which can be given from Dr. Hardman's standpoint, which approximates to that of St. Bernard and St. Francis.

But, when all is said, such a standpoint does regard the progress of the soul and of the Church as having no direct relation to the progress of the world. The position taken by Luther, and later by Wesley, in their description of the Goal, was a revolt against this view. They perceived that the world was justified in its condemnation of an attitude which withdrew those who ought to be leaders from the interests of common human life. This appears to me the right line on which to reply to this objection. The path of spiritual attainment ought not to be separated from that in which humanity as a whole is moving forward. It is necessary sometimes to protest against the errors of humanity in shaping its ideals; and asceticism—or, to use a better word, temperance—is always needed. But the progress of humanity in increasing the amenities of life, and in seeking to extend those amenities as widely as possible, ought to receive the approval and support of those who feel the call to the higher life.

It must be said at once that this is not a lowering of the

[1] *The Ideals of Asceticism*, p. 221.

ideal in order to bring it into conformity with the world. Wisdom is justified of all her children. The uncompromising protest of John the Baptizer arrested the attention of men, startled their conscience, and prepared the way for the Divine Advent. But the witness of the Son of Man to the presence of the Kingdom of Heaven in the common life of men was even greater and truer. It is a great thing to say, 'I have such faith in God that I will cut myself off from the pleasures and even the comforts of life; and I will leave it to Him to give me what reward He will for the loss of these things.' We may well honour those who have so trusted in God to recompense them. But it is a still greater thing to say, 'I can trust in God to keep me amid all the throb and movement of this progressive world.' 'Among them that are born of women there hath not arisen a greater than John the Baptist; yet he that is but little in the Kingdom of Heaven is greater than he.'

In some such way one might reply to those who contend that the cultivation of the higher life is incompatible with interest in human affairs, in scientific progress, and in social reform. It seems probable that, with the increase of spiritual knowledge, we shall go even beyond the lines laid down by Luther and Wesley in claiming the multifarious kingdoms of the world. The quest for Perfection is needed in order to give unity and meaning and persistence to the world's progress. There are many who are striving earnestly to discover the secrets of Nature, and many who are striving honestly for the betterment of humanity, but who can give no rationale for their endeavours. And this is fraught with grave danger. For reason must assert itself; and where there is a deep, underlying pessimism and atheism there can be no strong guarantee of persistence. There is a renewing of effort which is only possible for those who wait upon the Lord.

(b) *The League of Nations*

The modern statement of the Doctrine of Perfection, in so far as the conclusions drawn from the previous investigation are correct, declares that the Love of God is sufficient to overcome the deadening effects of organization, as it is strong enough to transform to its own use the material blessings of the world. An excellent illustration of this is found in the League of Nations, in which the idealism of humanity has expressed itself in our days most plainly. Nevertheless, objection has been taken to it by some who have been among the strongest advocates of peace, on the ground of its organization. The Love of God, they say, and the reason which is at the heart of the universe, ought to be allowed to work freely, and without the use of any kind of force, in the souls of men. It seems certain, however, that it will be through the League of Nations or some similar organization—we trust in our time, but assuredly in some future generation—that the world's peace will be established. Nor does such a view dishonour God; on the contrary, it pays the highest tribute to His love in conceiving it as capable of transfusing a worldwide organization.

The teaching of Perfection is needed in order to give reason and persistence to the quest for peace. If we are to follow after peace steadily and without wavering, we must have a noble idea of it. Peace is not merely the absence of strife and danger, nor is it simply the enjoyment of Epicurean ease and pleasure. I have tried to show that the modern view of the ideal does not ignore the question of material comfort and prosperity. But if by peace we think only, or even primarily, of material prosperity, we are setting up an ideal which can never form any lasting inspiration. The teaching of Perfection sets before the individual an ideal of unbroken communion with the love of God. That ideal is the only one which can supply a worthy motive for undisturbed tranquillity. The knowledge of God will need to be amplified by the scientific study of Nature, and by the history of humanity. But it is that knowledge alone which will be able to satisfy the craving of the spirit of man during the thousand years of peace.

(c) *The Reunion of Christendom*

The desire for reunion throughout Christendom is manifesting itself in many ways, notably in the drawing together of separate denominations. It is probable that this partial reunion is all that we shall see accomplished in our generation; but it is a sign that is full of hope, the promise and the presage of the Church that is to come. It may be that the fulfilment

T

will come sooner than we dream. It is being hastened by some of those phenomena in modern life which cause so much foreboding. One of the signs of our time has been the overthrow of the infallibility of the various authorities, to which the earnest seeker after Perfection has been wont to appeal for sanction and assurance. But from the distress which this overthrow has caused one good thing has come, namely, the desire for union. So long as the seeker had a sanction, whether of Church or of Bible or of the witness of the Spirit in his own soul, which he judged to be infallible, he felt little need for union with others who followed other authorities. The experience of the past has often been that opposition to union has come from the most earnest, from those who, under one particular sanction, have found rest for their souls, and who felt no further need. The soul-shaking, which has come through the abandonment of the infallibilities, has led to a deepened sense of dependence on the Eternal Love. Moreover, this dependence on the Divine Love leads to a greater yearning for human love. In the course of his inquiry as to the meaning of Beatitude, Aquinas says that the Perfection of Love is essential to beatitude with respect to the Love of God, but not with respect to the love of one's neighbour. ' If there were but one soul alone to enjoy God, it would be blessed even though it were without a single creature whom it could love.'[1] Such a saying appears to do honour to God, and to His power to supply every need; but it is based on a misapprehension; for we have no conception of the enjoyment of the Divine Love except through the creature.

Under the influence of this motive there has been in our time a movement towards Church Union. In many ways the most hopeful method of approach is from the standpoint of the quest for perfect communion. It is from that quest that the desire for Union springs, and it is that quest which gives intensity and persistence to the desire. Moreover, the pure Christian tradition that Charity is the end of the quest has retained its hold on the minds of men, in spite of the aberrations which have from time to time arisen.

The idea of Perfection can never be satisfied with anything less than a full reunion; and we must continue to explore every

[1] *Summa*, I-II., Q. 4, A. 8.

channel through which there is any hope of reaching it. The idea contains the potentiality of reunion within itself; and it is through the idea that reunion will be accomplished. By faith we already discern that, when the Union is accomplished, its glory will be the greater for the variety that is in it. Diversity is, indeed, essential for the mediatorial and priestly work which the Church exercises towards the individual and towards humanity. It enables the Church to deal with the multiplicity of human character. If such diversity were only linked with the unity of the Spirit, the Church would be perfectly adapted for its office.[1] This problem of unification the individual has to face in his own life. The richer and fuller his experience, the more difficult it is to unify it. Yet he realizes that through that rich and full experience he enters into a unitive life, which is higher and better than would have been possible without. The same problem confronts the Church. As it is being worked out on so much vaster a scale, it is far more difficult to solve. But it is fundamentally the same problem; and the individual solution points the way to the ecclesiastical. 'O God of unchangeable power and eternal light, look favourably on Thy whole Church, that wonderful and sacred mystery; and by the tranquil operation of Thy perpetual Providence carry out the work of man's salvation; and let the whole world feel and see that things which were cast down are being raised up, and things which had grown old are being made new, and all things are returning to Perfection through Him from whom they took their origin, even Jesus Christ our Lord. Amen.'

(3) *Perfection and Christian Preaching*

(a) *Perfection not an Esoteric Doctrine*

An esoteric doctrine is one which is carefully preserved for those in the inner circle; and it may be said at once that there are no such doctrines in Christianity. All who have ears

---

[1] 'The vision which rises before us is that of a Church, genuinely Catholic, loyal to all Truth, and gathering into its fellowship " all who profess and call themselves Christians," within whose visible unity all the treasures of faith and order, bequeathed as a heritage by the past to the present, shall be possessed in common, and made serviceable to the whole Body of Christ. Within this unity Christian Communions now separated from one another would retain much that has long been distinctive in their methods of worship and service. It is through a rich diversity of life and devotion that the unity of the whole fellowship will be fulfilled' (*Lambeth Appeal*, pp. 27 f.).

may hear. The obstacle which the evangelist most frequently meets is rather this—that so many who have ears refuse to hear. It is through the need for overcoming this obstacle that reserve and restraint are inculcated in proclaiming the full Gospel.[1] The message may be met with indifference, with ridicule, or with direct opposition. The proclamation of the message in parabolic form, with reserve and restraint, is intended to provoke curiosity, and to safeguard it from the opprobrium of the world. Thus the Didache, in enforcing the prohibition against unbaptized persons attending the Eucharist, refers to our Lord's words, 'Give not that which is holy to the dogs.'[2] It is difficult, no doubt, to get the right mean; and much harm has been done through the misuse of the *Disciplina Arcani*. The whole Gnostic teaching was filled with the idea of Reserve, of a Fence which guarded the Pleroma, and which kept the unspiritual from understanding Divine Truth. Our best guide is a careful study of the practice of the Master, from which we may learn at any rate that this reserve should never be employed through cowardice or through contempt; and we must look to His Spirit to direct us on each particular occasion.

With this proviso, the Doctrine of Perfection ought to take its place among those which in their union constitute the full Evangel. Its neglect has been one of the main causes of weakness and failure. This was clearly foreseen by the apostles, and stated by them with uncompromising plainness. Failure to reach maturity in the spiritual life has often been due to the absence of instruction and culture; and this failure has had the disastrous result of bringing in the idea of a double morality, which is a foreign intrusion into the Gospel message. The true doctrine speaks of a natural and normal development which all Christians ought to expect and pray for. Where this is not taught by those who are leaders in the Church, the soul experiences a sense of disappointment, which may induce it to turn to those who will lead it astray. Foolish and hurtful notions of Perfection spring up in the soil where the wholesome teaching of the full Gospel has been omitted. The Church ought earnestly to strive to formulate a message in which the state of Perfection shall be set forth as the definite aim of all who have entered on the Christian way.

[1] See p. 142.   Didache 9.

(b) *The Importance of Terminology*

In order to make our Gospel acceptable, and to guard against misconceptions, it is important to find the best words to express the idea. A quotation from Archbishop Trench may bring this home. ' The Christian shall be " perfect," yet not in the sense in which some of the sects preach the Doctrine of Perfection, who, as soon as their words are looked into, are found either to mean nothing which they could not have expressed by a word less liable to misunderstanding, or to mean something which no man in this life shall attain, and which he who affirms he has attained is deceiving himself, or others, or both. The faithful man shall be " perfect," that is, aiming by the Grace of God to be fully furnished and firmly established in the knowledge and practice of the things of God ; not a babe in Christ to the end, " not always employed in the elements and infant propositions and practices of religion, but doing noble actions, well skilled in the deepest mysteries of faith and holiness." '[1]

This quotation has been given at some length because it expresses so clearly the objections to a Doctrine of Perfection which are felt by many. Yet, when we consider the abundant use of the word in the New Testament, and the fact that the idea runs through the whole of it, we are not prepared to acquiesce in the suppression of the term. The Gospel from the beginning made for itself a distinctive vocabulary. It took over old words and invested them with a fresh significance. The translation into another language, such as English, and the changes which take place in any living language, involve a continual readjustment of our vocabulary. But we shall be unwise if we jettison lightly any of the phrases which embody ideas that are native to Christian experience. And, after all, what better translation than ' perfect ' can be found ? Trench himself does not suggest one. ' Entirely sanctified ' has been put forward as a synonym. It appears, however, quite as objectionable, so far as any claim to holiness is concerned, and it does not bring out the idea in *teleios*. It must be remembered that we are speaking as among Christians. The world naturally resents any profession of religion and any

[1] *Synonyms of the New Testament*, xxii., p. 76. The closing phrase is a quotation from Jeremy Taylor's *Doctrine and Practice of Repentance*, i. 3. 40–56.

claim to holiness. But the true spirit of Christianity rejects the idea of spiritual proficiency as a privilege to be grasped at,[1] for its attention is absorbed in the contemplation of the Divine Love. Yet, without making any claim, the Christian is prepared to testify to the blessed experiences which come through communion with that Love. If that appears like boastfulness, it is a boasting which cannot be avoided. What the mature Christian is seeking for is some term which shall bear witness to the fact that he is assured that he has passed out of his nonage, and that he has arrived at a stage of firm confidence that the Divine purposes of love will be fulfilled in him, to his own eternal welfare, and through him to the blessing of many others.

The difficulty which we are facing is no new one. It is found in the Sermon on the Mount, where Jesus bids His disciples make no ostentation of their righteousness, and yet let their light shine before men. It is apparent in Phil. iii. 8–16, in which St. Paul, writing to Christians, puts aside any thought that he is claiming any superiority, while yet he is anxious to bear witness to the unity which his life has attained as the result of the goal which he is now able to perceive as the prize of his upward calling. John Wesley said that he prefixed the text, 'Not as though I had already attained,' to his *Character of a Methodist* lest it should be thought that he was making any pretension either for himself or for Methodists as a whole. All advance must be marked by humility and a conviction that the whole work is from above.

Some suggestions may be put forward to help in meeting a difficulty which every one feels. One is to speak, even among those who are like-minded, not so much of being perfect as of *entering into the state of Perfection*. It is a well-marked state, though its boundaries are purely spiritual. If we can get rid of the error which connects this state with an ecclesiastical order, we shall find the conception valuable. The words 'attain' and 'attainment' are also useful. I have, indeed, hesitated as to whether it would not be wise to employ the word 'attainment' in the title instead of 'perfection'; but the latter term is more common in Scripture, and has

---

[1] Phil. ii. 6. The spirit which led to Christ's humiliation should be reflected in His disciples.

taken much deeper root in the Christian tradition. The former term, however, I have found very serviceable in expressing the central idea.

(c) *Need for an End or Aim in Personal Experience*

Ever since I have been able to understand the argument in Green's *Prolegomena to Ethics* I have realized how cogent is the proof of the worth of the moral ideal. The line of thought is that there is always an ideal present, as a standard of ultimate good, before any one who really tries to go beyond the claims of conventional morality. ' That standard is an ideal of a perfect life for himself and other men, as attainable for him only through them, for them only through him ; a life that shall be perfect, in the sense of being the fulfilment of all that the human spirit in him and them has the real capacity or vocation of becoming, and which (as is implied in its being such a fulfiment) *shall rest on the will to be perfect.*'[1] This sentence finely expresses the basis in thought on which this whole discussion rests. All that is needed is to add to it the Christian manifestation of the Ideal. The Platonic and Aristotelian conceptions of virtue provided an intellectual medium through which the idea of universal good as realized in society might be uttered. The spread of the Roman Empire, to which no bourne was apparent, visualized this idea. Then the advent of Christ brought before men an exposition of the Ideal ; and His Gospel in all its fullness, including His Session in glory and His spiritual Presence in the Church, gave to the Ideal a value for eternity. The state of Perfection, of which we have been speaking, consists not so much in the attainment of the goal as in the vision of what the goal is. That vision has come through the life of Christ on earth, and is continued through His perpetual spiritual Presence. By the disciples the ideal is to be apprehended by faith under the conditions of earth ; but the ideal contains within itself a strong assurance of hope that the body of our humiliation will be conformed to the body of His Glory. Faith in the ideal, and hope arising from it, are needed in order to give meaning and unity to the spiritual efforts of our life.

[1] *Prolegomena to Ethics*, IV. iv. 375.

(d) Need for an End or Aim as a Motive for Missionary Endeavour

The history of the Church furnishes overwhelming proof that those who have arrived at the state of Perfection feel a strong impulse towards Missionary Endeavour. This impulse has had to overcome a tendency towards solitude and meditation on the Divine Love. In the practical outcome there has been much variety, owing to the diversity of dispositions and ability. Some are more prone to an active, energetic life; others to a quiet, reflective one. This variety may obscure the fact that in *all* there is a desire for contemplation, and in *all* there is a longing for Missionary Endeavour. The last term is used in its widest sense. It simply expresses the fact that Love necessarily desires to communicate itself. Missionary revivals invariably sprung from earnest effort to enter into communion with the love of God.

One effect of the teaching of Perfection ought to be to afford a basis for evangelical zeal. There was intense force in the old appeal from Missionary platforms to fly to the rescue of millions, who were rushing into eternity, to be for ever lost. The Christian conscience, when it awoke to all the implications of that statement, found it incredible. Yet deep down it is conscious that there is urgency; the King's business requires haste. The teaching of Perfection brings home the conviction that there is real loss for all, in any country, who have failed to obtain the fullness of communion possible in this life; and there is a loss which we cannot calculate, but which we know must be very great, for all those who have passed beyond without the support which comes from the knowledge of the love of God in Christ Jesus. The Spirit which proceeds from the Father and the Son is the Comforter, who sustains, not only in this life, but in the new conditions which lie beyond. The teaching of Perfection has almost always been accompanied by evangelical fervour, just because the love which is kindled in the soul makes it feel how irreparable is the privation of those who have not received the good news.

Here the present investigation must conclude. We have seen, in the course of it, that among the most earnest seekers and finders divergences have arisen; but we have noted that they have arisen, not about the central fact of the communication of the Divine Love in Jesus Christ, and of our communion with that love through His eternal sacrifice ; but about the methods by which we may overcome the natural disabilities of our present life. From this there springs up a strong confidence that it will be possible to express in words, and to realize in outward appearance, that unity of the Spirit which is the bond of peace. And those who have already attained unification and harmony in their own spiritual life through the indwelling of the Divine Love are the earnest of the unification and harmony of the whole redeemed Church in the Kingdom of the Son.

APPENDIX

WESTERN MYSTICISM

The views to which I have been led in seeking to substantiate the thesis enunciated in the definition of Christian Perfection appear to me to be strongly confirmed by a book on *Western Mysticism* by Abbot Butler, a Benedictine of Downside. In this book attention is drawn to a persistent form of Christian endeavour which the writer associates with the names of SS. Augustine, Gregory, and Bernard. Butler discerns in the teaching of these three doctors a clearly marked type of Mysticism. 'It may be described as pre-Dionysian, pre-scholastic, non-philosophical; unaccompanied by psycho-physical concomitants, whether rapture or trance, or any quasi-hypnotic symptoms; without imaginative visions, auditions, or revelations; and without thought of the Devil. It is a Mysticism purely and solely religious, objective and empirical; being merely, on the practical side, the endeavour of the soul to mount to God in prayer and seek union with Him and surrender itself wholly to His love; and on the theoretical side, just the endeavour to describe the first-hand experience of the personal relations between the soul and God in contemplation and union. And it is a Mysticism far removed from any kind of Quietism: though images and phantasmata and sense-perceptions are shut out from the imagination and memory, and the processes of reasoning silenced, and the faculties of the mind quieted, and words cease and language fails; all this produces not a blank, but makes room for the soul itself to actuate and energize with a highly wrought activity and intense concentration on God.'[1]

The term 'Western Mysticism' must not be taken as equivalent to Mysticism in the West: it is a convenient term to denote a form of spiritual endeavour which is particularly well illustrated by certain Western leaders. I consider that Dom Butler makes out a good case for this clearly marked type. He is, of course, aware that the predicate 'non-philosophical' applies more evidently to Gregory and Bernard than to Augustine. He tries to show that Augustine's Mysticism is in reality experimental rather than philosophical. In Augustine's case, however, his experience and his philosophy acted and reacted upon each other; and in many instances the experience was subsequent to, and dependent on, the philosophy. But, taking it all round, one may say that this is an extremely valuable differentiation; and it has points of contact with the Protestant ideal, as recovered by Luther and Wesley, which give it the utmost significance.

[1] *Western Mysticism*, p. 187.

Perhaps this may be illustrated from the methods employed in the textual criticism of the New Testament. There the aim of scholars is to classify the main types of texts which have arisen, to judge between them, and, by careful examination and comparison, discover a text which shall most nearly approximate to the original. Some MSS. are of greater value than others ; some types of text are superior in fidelity to the original. But no scholar would accept any type of text, even in the best MSS., as incapable of improvement by comparison with others. Something similar is being witnessed in our endeavour to recover the ideal of Communion with the Father as affirmed by our Lord. But in this search we are able to criticize and to correct the type into which we have come by inheritance by reference to the records of His Life, and by the direction of His Spirit. To the present writer the type which has been called Western Mysticism, especially as it has been revised and brought into closer touch with the Master's teaching in the forms of Lutheranism and Methodism, represents the purest tradition. But it is not denied that it may be amended by comparison with other types, and that in very important matters.

The superiority of this type is shown by two great affirmations which it makes. (1) The best way of life is a mingling of the active and the contemplative. It should be noted, however, that the mixed life was often limited, especially by Gregory and Bernard, to those who were set apart for the contemplative life, but who, out of love for their fellows and zeal for their salvation, devoted a good deal of time to evangelical work. It needed the strong witness of Luther and Wesley to extend the term to include those who lived in families amid the business and work and politics of the world, but who managed to find considerable time for prayer and Church service. (2) The best way of life is one which is possible Here and Now for All. There may be a still higher way of life hereafter ; but under the conditions of this mortal life there is a way which may be called perfect, which is open to all.

In regard to these affirmations the Eastern tradition has obscured, even in the West, the old sane and safe authentic tradition. Western Mysticism itself has been too much affected by Platonic and possibly Aristotelian teaching to retain the Gospel in all its purity ; but it is nearer the truth than the Eastern. The main purpose of Butler's book is to revert to it ; and to show that the technical use of the term ' contemplative,' as applied to certain orders, does not by any means exhaust the Catholic content of the word. The old Western usage, ' as defined by St. Gregory and endorsed by St. Bernard,' emphasizes not the absence of activity, but the presence of contemplation. ' According to this, the historical Western sense, it may be said that a contemplative life is one in which contemplative prayer is practised in an adequate measure.'[1] It is obvious that this is compatible with continuance in the ordinary avocations of life. Abbot Butler in a noble passage proceeds to show that the full religious life is the harmonious blending of many elements, of which the mystical is but one.

[1] Op. cit. p. 291.

'It is only by means of self-discipline in the spiritual formation of our own characters, and of the discipline of life in our relations with our fellow men; it is only by bearing ourselves bravely and overcoming in our appointed station in the great battle of life—it is only thus that those most intimate personal relations of our souls with God, which are the mystical element of religion, will attain to their highest and noblest and most fruitful consummation. Nor are these things the preserve of the intellectual and the educated, or of any spiritually leisured class; they are open to all—to the poor and the unlettered and the lowly workers, who spend their lives in alternation between the conscientious performance of their daily round of humble duties and the regular recourse to God in affective prayer and rudimentary contemplation—a union so commonly met with among the peasantry in Catholic districts. And so again we learn that Mysticism, like religion itself, is within the reach of all: " It is not too hard for thee, neither is it far off. It is not in heaven, that thou shouldst say, Who shall go up for us to heaven, and bring it unto us? . . . But it is very nigh unto thee, in thy mouth, and in thy heart, that thou mayest do it." ' [1]

I demur to too close an association of Mysticism with Perfection. The State of Perfection may include the practice of Mysticism, but not necessarily. Otherwise, the above quotation exactly describes the fundamental Methodist position, which sets forth Evangelical Perfection, not only as possible for those engaged in the world's business, but as the normal condition to which every Christian should attain. Such a position is not at variance with a full recognition of the validity and usefulness of ecclesiastical orders and grades. It is in accordance with a belief in perpetual spiritual growth, and in degrees of attainment in knowledge. Thus we may speak of perfect and imperfect contemplatives, but not as though the latter were outside the State of Perfection. All true contemplatives may be said to have entered into the State of Perfection in love; but that is consistent with the idea that within that state there is a progress in contemplative science.

[1] Op. cit. p. 292.

BIBLIOGRAPHY

PART I

Hastings : *Encyclopaedia of Religion and Ethics.* (*E. R. E.*)
Hastings : *Dictionary of the Bible.* (*H. D. B.*)
Hastings : *Dictionary of Christ and the Gospels.* (*H. D. C.*)
A. Harnack : *History of Dogma.* Trans. N. Buchanan (1905).
G. P. Fisher : *History of Christian Doctrine* (1916).
K. R. Hagenbach : *History of Christian Doctrines* (1883).
L. J. Tixeront : *History of Dogmas* (1916).
H. Martensen : *Christian Dogmatics.*
J. Caird : *Introduction to the Philosophy of Religion* (1901).
Hermann Lotze : *Outlines of the Philosophy of Religion* (1887).
A. Caldecott : *The Philosophy of Religion* (1901).
A. M. Fairbairn : *Philosophy of the Christian Religion* (1902).
G. Galloway : *The Philosophy of Religion* (1920).
James Ward : *The Realm of Ends, or Pluralism and Theism* (1912).
H. M. Gwatkin : *The Knowledge of God* (1906).
T. H. Green : *Prolegomena to Ethics* (1883).
Newman Smyth : *Christian Ethics* (1907).
C. E. Luthardt : *History of Christian Ethics* (1889).
W. T. Davison : *The Christian Conscience* (1888).
Theodor von Haering : *The Ethics of the Christian Life* (1909).
James Martineau : *Types of Ethical Theory* (1889).
E. H. Askwith : *The Christian Conception of Holiness* (1900).
Rudolf Otto : *The Idea of the Holy* (1925).
James Martineau : *The Seat of Authority in Religion.*
P. T. Forsyth : *The Principle of Authority in Relation to Certainty, Sanctity, and Society* (1912).

PART II

Brown-Driver-Briggs : *Oxford Hebrew Lexicon.*
Moulton and Geden : *Concordance to the Greek Testament.*
A. B. Davidson : *The Theology of the Old Testament* (1904).
E. Schultz : *Old Testament Theology* (1898).
F. R. Tennant : *The Origin and Propagation of Sin* (1902).
F. R. Tennant : *The Sources of the Doctrine of the Fall and Original Sin* (1903).
H. W. Robinson : *The Religious Ideas of the Old Testament* (1913).
A. Nairne : *The Faith of the Old Testament* (1920).
G. B. Stevens : *Theology of the New Testament* (1918).

H. R. Mackintosh : *The Person of Christ* (1913).
R. L. Ottley : *The Doctrine of the Incarnation* (1896).
A. M. Fairbairn : *Christ in Modern Theology* (1894).
W. B. Pope : *The Person of Christ* (1871).
A. Schweitzer : *The Quest of the Historical Jesus* (1911).
C. W. Emmet : *The Eschatological Question in the Gospels* (1910).
W. B. Selbie : *Aspects of Christ* (1909).
D. W. Forrest : *The Christ of History and Experience.*
W. Milligan : *The Ascension and Heavenly Priesthood of our Lord* (1898).
J. Stalker : *The Christology of Jesus* (1899).
J. Stalker : *Imago Christi* (1891).
L. Dougall and C. W. Emmet : *The Lord of Thought* (1922).
R. C. Moberly : *Atonement and Personality* (1911).
R. C. Moberly : *Ministerial Priesthood* (1919).
H. Rashdall : *The Idea of Atonement in Christian Theology* (1915).
G. B. Stevens : *The Christian Doctrine of Salvation* (1918).
J. Scott Lidgett : *The Spiritual Principle of the Atonement* (1897).
H. A. A. Kennedy : *St. Paul and the Mystery Religions* (1913).
H. B. Swete : *The Holy Catholic Church* (1916).

PART III

Zeller : *History of Greek Philosophy.*
E. Caird : *The Evolution of Theology in the Greek Philosophers* (1904).
Plato : *Works,* esp. *Myths,* ed. J. A. Stewart (1905).
Aristotle : *Works,* esp. *The Ethics,* ed. Sir A. Grant.
T. H. Billings : *The Platonism of Philo Judaeus.*
Plotinus. *Select Works,* trans. T. Taylor (1895).
Plotinus : *The Enneads.*
W. R. Inge : *The Philosophy of Plotinus* (1918).
C. Bigg : *Neo-Platonism* (1895).
T. Whittaker : *The Neo-Platonists, a Study in the History of Hellenism* (1918).
B. F. Westcott : *Religious Thought in the West* (1891).
C. Bigg : *The Origins of Christianity* (1909).
C. Bigg : *The Christian Platonists of Alexandria* (1913).
T. W. Rhys Davids : *Buddhism.*
J. Estlin Carpenter : *Buddhism and Christianity.*
St. J. Stock : *Stoicism.*
H. M. Gwatkin : *Early Church History* (1909).
F. J. Foakes-Jackson : *History of the Christian Church* (1909).
J. F. Bethune-Baker : *An Introduction to the Early History of Christian Doctrine* (1903).
A. Harnack : *Monasticism* (1913).
Clement of Alexandria : *Works,* esp. *Stromateis, Bk. VII.,* ed. F. J. A. Hort and J. B. Mayor (1902).
Origen and Ambrose in Ante- and Post-Nicene Library.
H. H. Scullard : *Early Christian Ethics in the West from Clement to Ambrose* (1907).

BIBLIOGRAPHY

Augustine : *Works*, esp. *Confessions* and *De Civitate Dei*.
W. Cunningham : *St. Austin* (1886).
Ad. Hatzfeld : *St. Augustine*.
Dionysius the Areopagite : *On the Divine Names and the Mystical Theology*, ed. C. E. Rolt (1920).

PART IV

H. B. Workman : *The Church of the West in the Middle Ages* (1898).
G. G. Coulton : *St. Bernard, His Predecessors and Successors* (1923).
St. Francis of Assisi : *Writings*, trans. by Constance, Countess de la Warr (1907).
Leo of Assisi : *Speculum Perfectionis* (1903).
Sacrum Commercium : Trans. Montgomery Carmichael.
St. Thomas Aquinas : *Summa Theologica*.
St. Thomas Aquinas : Translation by Dominican Fathers.
P. H. Wicksteed : *The Reaction between Dogma and Philosophy Illustrated from the Works of St. Thomas Aquinas* (1920).
F. von Hügel : *The Mystical Element of Religion as studied in St. Catherine of Genoa and her Friends* (1909).
St. Teresa : *The Interior Castle, or The Mansions* (1921).
The Way of Perfection (1919).
A. Rodriguez : *The Practice of Christian Perfection* (1886).
Walter Hilton : *The Scale or Ladder of Perfection* (1908).
Evelyn Underhill : *Mysticism* (1922).
W. R. Inge : *Christian Mysticism* (1912).
Rufus M. Jones : *Studies in Mystical Religion* (1909).
A. Ritschl : *The Christian Doctrine of Justification and Reconciliation* (1900).
A. Ritschl : *Christian Perfection.* Trans. in *Bibliotheca Sacra* (1878).
R. Mackintosh : *Albrecht Ritschl* (1915).
A. E. Garvie : *Ritschlian Theology* (1899).
John Wesley : *Works* (1829).
L. Tyerman : *Life of John Wesley* (1876).
L. Tyerman : *Life of George Whitefield* (1882).
L. Tyerman : *Life of John Fletcher* (1876).
J. S. Simon : *John Wesley and the Religious Societies* (1921).
J. S. Simon : *John Wesley and the Methodist Societies* (1923).
The New History of Methodism (1909).
H. B. Workman : *The Place of Methodism in the Catholic Church*.
J. W. Laycock : *Methodist Heroes in the Great Haworth Round* (1909).
J. H. Overton : *John Wesley* (1891).
John Fletcher : *Works*, esp. *Last Check to Antinomianism*, and *Entire Sanctification Attainable in this Life*.
R. Watson : *Theological Institutes* (1829).
W. B. Pope : *A Compendium of Christian Theology*.
C. G. Finney : *Lectures on Systematic Theology* (1923).
George Fox : *The Journal* (1901).
John Woolman : *The Journal*.

U

BIBLIOGRAPHY

R. Barclay : *An Apology for the True Christian Divinity.*
Elisha Bates : *The Doctrines of Friends* (1829).
H. C. Wood : *Quakerism and the Future of the Church.*
T. E. Harvey : *The Long Pilgrimage*
T. E. Harvey : *The Rise of Quakerism.*
T. B. Emmott : *The Story of Quakerism.*
Rufus M. Jones : *Later Periods of Quakerism* (1921).
Rufus M. Jones : *Quakerism : A Religion of Life.*
E. Grubb : *What is Quakerism ?*
E. Grubb : *The Historic and the Inward Christ* (1914).

PART V

P. T. Forsyth : *Christian Perfection.*
P. T. Forsyth : *Lectures on the Church and the Sacraments* (1917).
C. Ryder Smith : *The Bible Doctrine of Society* (1920).
G. H. A. Bell : *Documents on Christian Unity* (1924).
Oscar Hardman : *The Ideals of Asceticism* (1924).
J. B. Pratt : *The Religious Consciousness, a Psychological Study* (1921).
G. Steven : *The Psychology of the Christian Soul* (1911).
F. W. Barry : *Christianity and Psychology* (1923).
John Oman : *Grace and Personality* (1925).
R. H. Charles : *A Critical History of the Doctrine of the Future Life.* (1913).
J. H. Leckie : *The World to Come and Final Destiny.*
J. E. C. Welldon : *The Hope of Immortality* (1898).
H. N. Oxenham : *Catholic Eschatology and Universalism* (1876).
A. S. Pringle-Pattison : *The Idea of Immortality* (1922).
B. H. Streeter : *Immortality : an Essay in Discovery* (1920).
Dom Cuthbert Butler: *Western Mysticism : the Teaching of SS. Augustine, Gregory, and Bernard on Contemplation and the Contemplative Life* (1922).

INDEX

ABILITY, 225
Accidie, 187
Agnosticism, 164
Albertus Magnus, 188
Ambrose, 109, 140, 155ff.
Anchorite, 140
Anselm, 9, 66
Antinomianism, 136, 222, 225, 268
Aquinas, 104, 105, 172, 177, 187ff., 278
Arahant, 124
Aridity, 201
Aristotle, 102ff., 115, 188, 260
Arnold, Matthew, 81
Asceticism, 115, 121, 123, 126, 132, 138f., 275
Assurance, 7, 58, 213, 218, 242, 271
Attainment, 282
——Immediate, 166, 209, 219, 223, 242
——in this life, 124f., 162, 169, 222, 223, 242, 269
——Ways of, 8off., 104, 108, 111, 113, 173f.
Augsburg Confession, 204*n*.
Augustine, 20, 23*n*., 101, 118*n*., 127, 155, 162ff., 188*n*., 259, 263
Aurelius, Marcus, 107*n*., 109
Aureoles, 198

BARCLAY, 13, 25, 230, 234f., 239, 241f.
Bates, 237*n*., 241*n*.
Bellord, 196, 256
Benedictine Rule, 141
Benediction, 71
Bernard, 181ff.
Bigg, C., 17*n*., 111*n*., 152*n*.
Billings, 110*n*.
Blake, 57
Bohler, 208
Brainerd, 228, 259
Browning, 197, 274
Buddhism, 82, 121ff.
Bunyan, 259
Butler, 191*n*., App. p. 287

CAIRD, E., 97, 102*n*.
Caird, J., 4, 9, 83, 268
Calvin, 21, 37, 228
Campbell, Macleod, 84
Catherine of Genoa, 113, 147, 200
Catherine of Siena, 200f., 260
Celibacy, 157ff.

Charity, see Love
Charles, 68, 94
Christ, 15, chap. v.
——Blood of, 7, 70, 152, 214, 253
——the Historic and the Inward, 152, 238ff.
Chrysippus, 107, 109
Church, the, 22ff., 55, 63, chap. vii., 129, 133, 138, 149, 170f., 174, 176f., chap. xii., 183, 189, 205ff., 233, 262ff.
City of God, 170f., 263
Cleanthes, 107
Clement of Alexandria, 142ff., 221, 259
Clement of Rome, 128f., 256
Communication or Revelation, 62
Communion, 7, 16, 174, 183
Consummation, 59, 103f., 119, 148, 169, 178, 191, 271f.
Cooper, Jane, 211f.
Counsels, Evangelical, 156f., 160, 185
Cunningham, 168*n*.
Cyprian, 91, 134, 164

DALE, 91*n*.
Dante, 186
Definition of Thesis, 6
Descartes, 9
Detachment, 115, 186
Didache, 23, 132, 280
Diognetus, 23, 129
Dionysius, 172f., 188, 193, 287
Disciplina Arcani, see Reserve
Divergences, 18, chaps. xii-xiv.
Drummond, 111
Dynamic in Christ, 72

ECKHART, 200, 203
Edwards, 225
Emmet, 199
Emmott, 232
Encratites, 132ff.
End, 59, 69, 103
Enoch, 45
——Similitudes of, 51, 78
Environment, 51, 64, 77ff., 160ff.
Episcopal State, 195f.
Eschatology, 59, 69, 271ff.
Ethical Implications, 11
Eucken, 16, 17
Evangelical Implications, 14ff.
Expansion, 260f.

295

INDEX

FAIRBAIRN, 22
Faith, 14, 82f., 106f., 145, 164n., 211, 216f., 269ff.
Fall of Man, 43f., 151, 168f., 227, 238
Farquhar, 122
Finney, 225ff.
Fletcher, 221ff.
Flint, 121
Fomes Peccati, 12
Formula Concordiae, 67
Forrest, 67n.
Forsyth, 85, 203n., 269f.
Fox, 232ff., 245
Francis de Sales, 201
Francis of Assisi, 81, 183ff., 260
Free Church Council, 21
Freedom, 100, 146, 258
Friends of God, 231
Fullness, 56f.

GALLOWAY, 5, 11
Gardner, 65, 68, 143
Garvie, 204
Glory, the, 38, 48, 69, 74
Gnosticism, 113, 135ff., 144, 146, 152
Grace, 13, 166ff., 182, 226, 263, 280
Grant, Sir A., 105
Green, T. H., 63, 90, 283
Grimshaw, 213f., 256
Grubb, 239
Gwatkin, 133

HADES, Descent into, 68, 130
Hades, Ethicizing of, 68, 94, 273ff.
Haering, 218
Hagenbach, 127n., 171
Hall, 99, 137
Hardman, 275
Harnack, 24, 67, 111, 125, 127, 133, 139, 155, 164n., 167, 169, 170, 204, 217, 265
Hebrew Terms, 32ff.
Hegel, 9, 81
Hellenism, 31
Hermas, 23, 129
Hicks, 238
Hilton, p. ix
Holiness, 38ff.
Hope, 14, 269, 272
Hügel, 94, 113, 219, 231
Humanity, 43, 109, 237, 245, 275

IDEA, 98
Ignatius, 140
Image of God, 42, 73, 151
Immortality, 98f., 120
Inge, 235, 244, 272
Initiation, 61, 121, 137
Intercession, 71
Inward Light, 235ff.
Irenaeus, 69, 130, 136, 137
Irving, 65

JAMES, Saint, 80
John of the Cross, 200
Jones, Rufus M., 238, 240, 243, 245, 247, 270
Josephus, 49
Joy, 145, 259
Judaism, chap. iii.
Justin, 24, 73, 239

KENNEDY, 61, 79, 120
Kenosis, 65, 119, 261
Kingship, 49f., see Lordship
Knowledge, 85f., 123, 145, 164, 173f., 261

LAMBETH Appeal, 279
Law, 8of., 224, 226
Laycock, 6, 214ff.
League of Nations, 91, 276f.
Leckie, 51, 68
Leibniz, 8
Leo of Assisi, 184
Lidgett, 65
Logos, 48, 73, 74, 110f., 152
Logos Spermatikos, 24, 107, 239
Lordship, 261f.
Lotze, 9
Love or Charity, 3, 4, 14, 86ff., 121, 129, 182, 184, 209f., 213, 224, 255ff., 270, 278
Luthardt, 182, 183
Luther and Lutheranism, 26, 66–7, 208, 217, 269, 271, 275, 288

MACKINTOSH, H. R., 65, 67, 253, 254
Manichaeism, 125ff., 163
Marcion, 19, 138
Martineau, 18f., 25
Maturity, 60
Mean, the, 104
Mediator, 47ff.
Melchizedek, 70
Merits, 161, 164
Metaphysical Implications, 8
Methodism, chap. xiii., 226, 228, 240, 269, 288
Milligan, 70
Milton, 138, 146
Missionary zeal, 93, 186, 244, 284
Moberly, 13, 245
Monasticism, 123, 138ff., 263
Montanism, 73, 131, 132ff.
Morality, twofold, 99f., 108f., 126f., 132, 138, 156f., 163
Moravians, 207
Moulton, J. H., 83n.
Mystery Religions, 61, 119ff.
Mysticism, 10, 84, 170, 183, 199ff., 208, 212, 231, 287ff.

INDEX

NAYLER, 239
Neo-Platonism, 112ff., 164, 183
New Testament, chaps. iv-vii
Nirvana, 123, 125
Novatian Controversy, 134

OBEDIENCE, 66ff., 80, 183, 198, 224, 226, 228
Oberlin Theology, 225ff.
Old Testament, chap. iii.
One Act, 201, 231
Ontological Argument, 9
Orthodoxasts, 143
Origen, 15, 17, 21, 25, 68, 72, 91, 113, 149ff., 171, 266
Otto, R., 38
Overton, 207

PANTHEISM, 9, 201
Particularism, 40
Pascal, 6
Paul, Saint, 12, 16, 17, 23, 138, 159
Pelagianism,' 166f.
Pentecost, 223
Perfection, Adamic, 12, 40f., 77, 222
——Definition of, 6
——Hebrew Terms for, 32ff.
——Marks of, 257ff.
——Mirror of, 184, 186
——New Testament Terms for, chap. iv.
——Open to all, 194, 288
——State of, 7, 148, 158f., 193f., 258, 282
Perseverance, 228, 242
Personality, 11, 13
Pessimism, 4, 101, 123, 164, 260
Phaedo, 26, 99, 101, 102, 263
Philo, 48, 70, 110ff.
Pilgrimage, the Long, 237f.
Plato, 4, 26, 97ff., 114, 262
Platonists, Cambridge, 235
Platt, 86, 224, 255
Pleroma, 58, 135ff.
Plotinus, 15, 60, 112ff., 165
Plummer, 85
Pluralism, 137, 150, 172
Pneumatikoi, 135
Pope, W. B., 224
Posidonius, 120*n*.
Poverty, 185f.
Pratt, 234*n*., 259
Preparedness, 54f.
Priesthood, 49, 69ff., 195f., 263f.
Pringle-Pattison, 99, 110, 151, 270
Progress, 94, 108, 147, 148, 154, 267, 273
Prophet, 48, 65, 244
Propitiation, 70
Protagoras, 8

Purgatory, 94, 148, 153, 171, 177, 198f., 273-4
Purgatory at Death, 199, 219, 221, 222, 223f., 273
Purification, 114f., 120, 147, 153, 243

QUAKERISM, 25, chap. xiv.
Quest, Wide Extent of, 251f.
Quietism, 149, 201, 231, 243f.

RABINDRANATH Tagore, 82
Rapture, 191
Reality, 10, 201
Recapitulation, 130
Reformers, 66, 204
Religious Societies, 206f.
Religious State, 196ff.
Republic, the, 98, 99, 100, 101, 102
Reserve, 135, 142, 279-80
Rest, 5
Reunion of Christendom, p. viii., 18, 26, 277f.
Rhys Davids, 124
Righteousness, 36f.
Ritschl, 38, 204, 253
Rodriguez, 201, 261
Rogers, Mrs., 212f.
Rolt, 173*n*.
Roman Catholicism, chap. xii
Rule of Faith, 25, 132, 153*n*.
Ruskin, 80

SACRAMENT, 202f.
Sacrum Commercium, 186
Sanday and Headlam, 16, 59
Satan, 78, 130, 152
Schleiermacher, 65
Schweitzer, 62f., 67
Scripture, 19ff., 188, chap. xiii., 211, 217, 219, 222, 264f.
Scripture, Allegorical Interpretation of, 149f., 188, 266
Scripture, Historico-critical method, 21f., 217, 266
Scott-Holland, 92
Scullard, 132*n*., 156
Seed, the, 239, 243
Seekers, 231
Session, the, 69ff.
Sex, 246
Shakespeare, 52, 119, 168
Shekinah, 38, 65, 74
Sheol, 40ff.
Simon, J. S., 206f.
Sin, Original, 12f., 42, 64, 77f., 166ff., 175, 227f.
Single-mindedness, 46
Sinlessness, 15, 64, 219, 222, 242
Society, 275ff.

Soul, 100f., 103, 112, 116, 131, 136, 150, 154, 176
Sources, chap. ii.
Spinoza, 10
Spirit, the Holy, 24, 39, 72ff., 134, 144, 153, 226, 239, 253, 266ff.
Stalker, 265
Stewart, 100
Stillness, 243f.
Stoicism, 61, 82, 106ff., 155f., 239
Strauss, 62
Surrender of Self, 81, 182
Swedenborg, 21
Swete, 91, 94

TATIAN, 133
Taylor, T., 114
Teleological Argument, 19, 59, 103
Tennant, 12, 42, 44
Tennyson, 60, 78, 274
Teresa, 201f.
Tertullian, 15, 20, 120, 130f., 134, 164
Testaments of the Patriarchs, 47, 50
Theocracy, 49, see Kingship.
Thomas, Griffith, 70
Timaeus, 99, 120n.
Tixeront, 131
Trench, 281
Trent, Council of, 20, 94, 193
Trinity, 25, 173, 201f., 213, 216, 254

ULLMANN, 64, 66
Underhill, 201

Unification, 102, 162, 164, 285
Union with God, 84, 102, 117, 174f.
Utopia, 101

VALENTINUS, 58, 136f.
Victorinus, 136
Virginity, 157f.
Vision, Beatific, 117, 121, 174, 194, 262
Vows, 195, 197

WARD, J., 78, 271
Warren, 125
Watchers, the, 78
Watson, 223f.
Welldon, 273
Wesley, Charles, 208, 210
Wesley, John, 206ff., 218ff., 256, 271, 275, 282
Westcott, 70, 74, 111, 174
Whitefield, 210
Wholeness, 56
Whyte, A., 220n.
Wicksteed, 191, 197, 262
Wood, 233n.
Woolman, 223, 247
Wordsworth, 243n., 247
Workman, 141, 205

YAHWISM, 35ff., 110, 122
Yezer, 44

ZELLER,
Zeno, 107

www.ingramcontent.com/pod-product-compliance
Lightning Source LLC
Chambersburg PA
CBHW070233230426
43664CB00014B/2291